Reader Re

"At a time when our nation leads the w
tivists as well as politicians across the po
the first time whether the 'get tough' movement and the p......
tiveness have taken our nation down the wrong path, we would be wise to
pause and consider whether forgiveness might hold transformative power
and potential. We can theorize about what forgiveness really means, or we
can talk and listen to those we have viewed as unforgivable. *Where the River
Bends* does both, and thus offers depth of insight and perspective that is
rare yet essential if we are going to move to higher ground."

—Michelle Alexander, author of the best-selling *The New Jim Crow*

"In this book, Michael McRay shares the stories that should make the head-
lines, but usually don't. These are the stories of grace, mercy, and forgiveness—both the rewards and challenges. They are the stories of offenders
who made victims and were also victims themselves. These stories are about
folks who desire forgiveness but not forgetfulness, whose memories demonstrate the power and pain of mercy. On these pages, Michael McRay
proves that our wounds have the power to hold us hostage to the past or
to compel us to build a future where grace gets the last word. Here is a
book pregnant with the hope that comes through the power of forgiveness.
Don't just read this book—let it move you to become an agent of mercy in
a merciless world."

—Shane Claiborne, activist, abolitionist, and author of *Executing
Grace* and the best-selling *Irresistible Revolution*

"Michael McRay has written an extraordinary book. It tells the grand narrative of how justice, forgiveness from God, seeking and receiving forgiveness
from others, and struggling with forgiving the self come together like a turbulent river. The origin of this particular river is in McRay's understanding
of forgiveness, and McRay draws most heavily upon the superb theology
and psychology of theologian Miroslav Volf, and peacemakers John Paul
Lederach and Desmond Tutu. Then, fourteen prisoners' personal stories
form 'tributaries' that arise from the turbulent river. Those stories recount
crimes, address justice, and describe self-recrimination. It is forgiveness

that often bends the flow of narrative into the grand narrative that forgiveness of self and others changes lives. This book could actually change your life."

—Everett L. Worthington, Jr., author of *Moving Forward: Six Steps to Forgiving Yourself* and *Breaking Free from the Past*

"This book stands tall among the tomes on forgiveness. McRay takes us deep into the souls of prisoners, who explain the hard grubby work of releasing rage. Their stories make it clear: the recipe for forgiveness is not simple or easy. Yet the gritty work of letting go, opens the door to freedom even behind bars. Caution: reading these heart-wrenching stories may change your life."

—Donald B. Kraybill, co-author *Amish Grace*

WHERE THE RIVER BENDS

WHERE *the* RIVER BENDS

Considering Forgiveness
in the Lives of Prisoners

≈

Michael T. McRay

FOREWORD BY
Desmond M. Tutu

CASCADE *Books* · Eugene, Oregon

WHERE THE RIVER BENDS
Considering Forgiveness in the Lives of Prisoners

Cascade Books
An Imprint of Wipf and Stock Publishers
199 W. 8th Ave., Suite 3
Eugene, OR 97401

www.wipfandstock.com

ISBN 13: 978-1-4982-0191-9

Cataloging-in-Publication data:

McRay, Michael T.

Where the river bends : considering forgiveness in the lives of prisoners / Michael T. McRay.

xxvi + 188 p.; 23 cm—Includes bibliographical references.

ISBN 13: 978-1-4982-0191-9

1. Prisoners—Religious life. 2. Prison ministry. 3. Church work with prisoners. I. Title.

BV4465 .M5 2016

Manufactured in the USA.

To Richard Goode—
Words cannot express the depth of my gratitude for what you have
taught me with such
grace, wisdom, and boldness.
You are a prophet, a peacebuilder, and a friend.
I owe you more than I can ever repay.

To the men and women behind the walls—
You are seeds.

"Just as the course of every river changes with time, so does the flow of painful memory through our souls. If we allow them, the sands of grace accumulate day by day until slowly a *bend in the river* appears, and our hearts travel a new path across an old landscape to sink in to the rich soil of hope and renewal previously out of reach. That bend in the river that leads to life is forgiveness."

—JACOB L. DAVIS, TDOC #308056, EMPHASIS ADDED

"They tried to bury us, but they didn't know we were seeds."

—MEXICAN PROVERB

The names of all the individuals mentioned in the stories of chapters 2–15 have been changed. This is true with an exception: unless otherwise noted, the actual names of the prisoners are used, at their own request. They wanted the opportunity to present a counter narrative to the single stories told about them in the media. They wanted to redefine their names.

Table of Contents

TABLE OF CONTENTS

Foreword

WHEN WE EMBARKED ON the great journey of promoting truth and reconciliation in South Africa after the fall of apartheid in the early 1990s, I did not know what all we might discover. So much of the happenings of the oppressive apartheid regime had been covert. Families did not know where their loved ones had been taken; many did not even know for certain whether they were still alive. So much was secret. For this reason, we knew we needed to provide a public space for the telling of all our stories. We needed to know *what* happened, even if we could not always learn *why* it happened. Rumors and assumptions needed to die so that the truth could live.

The stories we heard were devastating. But even in the midst of confessions of murder and violence, we sometimes saw life emerge, not only for the victims and survivors who had suffered such profound losses, but also for those perpetrators whose guilt and shame had only been amplified by the secrets they had clutched so tightly. With the telling of their stories came liberation. I saw firsthand the power of confession, accountability, truth-telling, and forgiveness. Many who came before the Truth and Reconciliation Commission entered the bitterest of enemies; some—no, many—left reconciled, for we heal through the telling of our stories.

Stories help us make meaning of our often chaotic lives. Everyone's story is different, and everyone's story is important, even if only to that person. In my experience living and working in contexts of deep animosity and division, I am convinced that reconciliation is almost impossible without the respectful exchange of stories. If we are ever to build peace, we must listen to and *consider* the stories of others, perhaps particularly those whose stories we never wanted to listen to or never knew we needed to hear. When we encounter the stories of those whose stories we have not heard, our perspectives are challenged and sometimes even change. There must be great humility and risk if we are to open ourselves to seeing the world in a new way.

This book offers you the stories of numerous men and women to whom most of us would rather not listen. For this reason, this book is important, and I invite you into the humility necessary to read it. Prisoners are perhaps the most marginalized people in our Western societies. They are nonexistent to us during their incarceration, and pariah upon their return. Depriving them of their freedom does not seem to be enough for us; we often try to deprive them of their dignity and voices as well. Michael McRay has sought to help us in this regard. He has entered the prisons and received the stories and perspectives of fourteen imprisoned children of God. But they do not offer us their stories for the sake of justification. Instead, they speak for the sake of confession, accountability, truth-telling, and forgiveness.

Forgiveness holds remarkable power. In my life, I have seen forgiveness shorten the distance between enemies, or melt the rigid exteriors of the most hardened perpetrators. The stories in this collection demonstrate the power of forgiveness. The words of these incarcerated men and women reveal tragic loss and demonstrate our shared flawed humanity. We are all interconnected and interdependent. Forgiveness recognizes this and offers grace for the sake of our common brokenness.

In this book are the testimonies of human beings who have both victimized and been victims of terrible harm. Those who have found forgiveness show that the transformation that follows grows out of a newfound freedom. Forgiveness has the power to offer a form of freedom to prisoners, even while they remain confined behind walls. Some of the individuals in this book experience this freedom, even while they continue to long for their physical liberation. Unforgiveness chains us to our pasts, but forgiveness offers us a future.

This forgiveness is not easy, however, as the stories in this book show. These men and women have wrestled with forgiveness, much the way Jacob wrestled with God. Like Jacob, they may emerge limping, but walking nonetheless. The testimonies Michael brings to our attention offer us deeper insight into the profound difficulty of forgiving and being forgiven. These men and women speak of the long, daily journey of forgiving and re-forgiving, a process that likely never ends. They demonstrate remarkable strength, both in their confessions as well as their personal journeys. They certainly have not forgotten what happened, but instead seek to face their pasts with courage and forthrightness.

In the following pages, Michael and his brothers and sisters in prison speak of justice coupled with mercy, of the transformative power of stories, and of a forgiveness that is neither cheap nor quick. We cannot encounter these pages and remain unaffected. But what will happen to us if we listen to those we tend to ignore? This book is one way to find out. I encourage us all to listen.

Archbishop Emeritus Desmond M. Tutu
February 2015

Preface

FROM THE SOUTH-FACING WALLS at the Queen's University Library in Belfast, Northern Ireland, there is a beautiful view of the botanical gardens. In 2012–2013, while studying conflict transformation and reconciliation, I often wrote next to those wide windows, losing myself there while staring out at the greenery, as the steady rain soaked the ground and the melodies of Bon Iver provided the soundtrack to my musings. On the rare sunny day, I walked through the gardens during study breaks, perhaps reconstructing a class debate, fighting the urge to dance to the new Mumford and Sons album, or just thinking of home.

As much as I love travelling, the more I've wandered—having visited over thirty countries and as many US states—the more I've come to realize how deep my roots run in Tennessee. Members of my family have lived in Tennessee for generations, and it has been my home since I could crawl. To borrow John Paul Lederach's term, it is my "ancestral domain."[1] I do love travel, but I may love coming home more.

Studying in Belfast was no exception. In my life's journey, discontentment has been my constant carry-on. I have often wanted to be somewhere else. Encountering mindfulness and liturgical prayer has been salvific in that regard. But longing for home was not the only reason I eventually returned to Nashville to write my master's thesis. When my brother pursued his master's in conflict transformation at a well-respected US school, he noticed the same dynamic I saw abroad: that is, citizens of other countries sought peacebuilding skills so they could return home to help their communities, and US citizens tended to acquire these skills to help the rest of the world. Granted, this was a pattern, not a rule, but I was one of those who moved to Belfast marching steadily—though unknowingly—into the white-Western-savior complex. My passion was for peacebuilding in Israel-Palestine. I had

1. Lederach, *Moral Imagination*, 132.

studied the conflict's history in undergrad, volunteered in the West Bank in the summer of 2010, and interned with Christian Peacemaker Teams in early 2012, publishing my first book about that experience.[2] My plan was to write my thesis on that conflict and eventually return there to work.

One day, though, sitting in the Queen's library, staring at the blank Word document that would eventually display my research proposal, I wondered what "my" conflict was back home in Nashville. Since many of my classmates planned to return to home countries like Nigeria or India to build peace in their corners of the world, I wondered what issue I could engage back in Tennessee. And then it hit me: incarceration.

I first entered a prison in late 2009, when I began weekly visits to Riverbend Maximum Security Institution in Nashville as part of a contemplative prayer group. Before then, I never imagined I would share a table with someone guilty of murder or sit beside a man imprisoned for rape. Yet, in close proximity over the next few years, we cultivated some of the most meaningful relationships I have ever experienced. I had finally found my church. And as these relationships deepened, so too did my understanding of the problems with our criminal justice system—more specifically, our prison system. When I learned the US has 5 percent of the world's population but warehouses 25 percent of the world's prisoners, I knew something was wrong. When I learned the US incarcerates over two million of its citizens, I knew something was wrong. And when some of those two million are close friends, one cannot help but pursue avenues for constructive change. As I have come to learn, proximity affects ethics.[3]

Thus, though unsure of which particular focus to pursue, I decided to write my MPhil thesis on prison. A few weeks later, while researching

2. McRay, Letters from "Apartheid Street."

3. One of the costs of seeking change and advocating on behalf of men who became like brothers was that, several months into my work as a volunteer chaplain, and after completing my interviews, the administration barred me indefinitely from Riverbend. When the warden at Riverbend announced the implementation of a new "security" system that would significantly limit the livelihood and degrade the dignity of the men in minimum security, I organized as many volunteers as possible to inundate the Tennessee Department of Corrections (TDOC) with emails and phone calls expressing disapproval. After I received reprimanding calls from senior officials, the warden banned me for "subverting his authority," and the commissioner himself wrote in a memo that volunteers were expected "not to discuss [with an inmate] problems concerning the institution" and "not to challenge the policies of the institution or department." As of this writing, I have not been inside Riverbend since March 28, 2014, though I had regularly volunteered without incident for over four years prior. My first "offense" resulted in exile, a reality consistent with current standards of incarceration.

forgiveness for another paper, I noticed that the words *forgiveness* and *prisoners*, though clearly connected, have seldom shared the stage. Most writing on forgiveness is victim focused, addressing the possibilities and implications of forgiveness for those who suffer harm. Such writing, whether deliberately or not, often excludes the offenders' thoughts and experiences. Thus, as I discovered, little has been written about what currently incarcerated people think about forgiveness.[4] I knew this gap needed to be filled.

Prison is social exile, intended as punishment for those violating societal standards of acceptable behavior. The US system is built on retribution and revenge—i.e., unforgiveness. To me, it seems logical, even necessary, that researchers ask those living in this unforgiving system to share their perspectives regarding the possibility and importance of forgiveness. Not only have the majority of people in prison committed the crimes for which they were convicted—and many of those crimes involved harming other people—they also have been victims themselves. Paraphrasing Fr. Richard Rohr's expression, trauma that is not transformed is transferred—or, "hurt people hurt people." At least half the men with whom I spoke during my volunteer years at Riverbend and nearly all the women featured herein described childhood abuse. The victim/offender dichotomy is often misleading: victims can become offenders, and offenders were once victims themselves. We cannot function among other humans and not cause and receive pain. Our interdependence is a beautiful yet painful reality.

Thus, prison seems as relevant as any location for researching forgiveness, and the absence of such research suggested two possibilities: first, prison has succeeded in getting prisoners "out of sight and out of mind" so they are, at best, afterthoughts when it comes to researching forgiveness; or second, the magnitude and intimidation of the system paralyzes interested parties who do not know how to gain access. Regardless, I knew I had access to the prison, as well as the trust of insiders, and both were essential. I planned to return to Nashville in May 2013 to interview six men at Riverbend, incorporating their stories and perspectives into an overview of the conversations on forgiveness in the current literature. Four months later, I submitted my thesis, *Echoes from Exile*, and completed my degree.

---

4. In my reading, the three closest relating texts to what I originally sought to do with this project are Howard Zehr's *Doing Life*, Robin Casarjian's *Houses of Healing*, and Kirk Blackard's *Restoring Peace*.

That thesis has been revised and expanded here to include seven men and seven women imprisoned in Tennessee.[5] Yet, as I write this preface, I must ask myself, "How *dare* I write a book on forgiveness?" To some extent, this strikes me as a presumptuous writing project. Forgiveness is a radical, and often seemingly impossible, notion. That we humans can experience devastating harm and forgive is truly unbelievable, as when the Amish families of Nickel Mines offered immediate unconditional forgiveness to the disturbed neighbor who murdered five of their precious children.[6] I, however, have not personally experienced this degree of loss. I was not abused as a child; I have not been violently attacked; no one in my family has been murdered or raped. How can I write about forgiveness in circumstances that are so beyond my lived reality?

Yet, at the same time, forgiving is fundamental to the human experience, necessary for our relationships to survive and thrive. And even though I have not suffered the trauma of violence, I have certainly encountered the need to both give and receive forgiveness. I, like so many of us, am the recipient of unexpected and magnanimous forgiveness, both interpersonally and intrapersonally (in terms of self-forgiveness). I have also spent time with remarkable people who found that forgiveness was preferable to hatred—like Cynthia Vaughn, who visited Tennessee's death row and forgave her father who was convicted of murdering her mother; or Fr. Charlie Strobel, who publicly forgave the man responsible for murdering his elderly mother and leaving her body in the trunk of a car; or Hector Black, who embraced and forgave the man imprisoned for brutally murdering his daughter Patricia.[7] I have been privileged to meet and learn from people on both sides of the forgiveness process, and it is from these interactions,

5. The original master's project dealt exclusively with men for one reason only: I already possessed full access to the men's prison due to my status as a registered volunteer. Acquiring access to the Tennessee Prison for Women (TPW) and building trusting relationships there would have added too many complications in the limited time available for crafting the thesis. However, after my dismissal from Riverbend in April 2014, I spent several months visiting TPW regularly and cultivating good rapport.

6. Kraybill et al., *Amish Grace*.

7. Cynthia has asked me to assist with the writing of her memoir. Plans are underway for this project. Meanwhile, see Haggard, "Finding Forgiveness on Death Row." To hear Cynthia's first public telling of her story, see http://tenx9nashville.com/2015/03/25/cynthia-vaughn-confined/. For more on Fr. Strobel, see Patchett, "Worthless Servant." For more on Hector Black's story, you can listen to him tell it here: http://themoth.org/posts/storytellers/hector-black. A Google search on Strobel and Black reveals numerous avenues for further exploration.

as well as my academic training, that I presume to offer this book. I do not claim expertise; rather, I claim to have listened to those whose experiences warrant reflection, considering how their thoughts might weave into the existing conversations in the literature.

When I first began this project, I intended it to be an academic interaction with the perspectives of prisoners regarding forgiveness, and while that is still a feature of this work, the project gradually seemed to shift primary purposes. Upon completion, I realized its chief role had become providing a platform for the telling of stories most of us never hear. The majority of this book is the fourteen stories of men and women incarcerated in Tennessee prisons. While I adhere to the original format of the thesis—chart a map of the forgiveness terrain, present the stories of prisoners, and locate those stories in the map—I readily acknowledge that I have not mined these stories exhaustively. My purpose was to consider how their experiences resonated with the existing articulations of forgiveness. But these stories contain wisdom and insight stretching far beyond the realm of forgiveness. The book is not equipped or intended to examine these stories for all they are worth; the reader is tasked with receiving from the stories what the reader needs to receive. And there is much to receive.

Essentially, the book has two primary goals: first, to articulate a multi-stranded view of the forgiveness process that resonates with prisoners' experiences and the surveyed literature; and second, to present the stories of those whose stories are often unheard. Encountering the stories of the unheard has become a vocational commitment for me. From the time I was young, my parents taught me the importance of, in the words of German theologian Dietrich Bonhoeffer, seeing the world "from below, from the perspective of the outcast, the suspects, the maltreated, the powerless, the oppressed, the reviled—in short, from the perspective of those who suffer."[8] While studying at Lipscomb University, many of my classroom experiences reinforced this as Professors Richard Goode and Lee Camp opened my eyes and ears more fully to the unheard stories of the world's trampled and overlooked people. As a white, US-born, straight, cisgender, English-speaking, well-educated, and well-loved son of a doctor, I am as privileged as possible. I will likely always experience life from above. Thus, my view of the human experience will be incomplete without intentionally trying to see life from another vantage point, to see the familiar in an unfamiliar

8. Bonhoeffer, *Letters and Papers*, 17.

context thereupon challenging my view of the familiar and the normal.[9] I am committed to this pursuit and hope that presenting a platform for the telling of stories that people rarely hear, whether through my own narration or facilitating that of others, will continue to be my vocation.

I should clarify that my avoidance of the oft-used phrase "giving voice to the voiceless" is deliberate. As is clear below, prisoners are not voiceless; neither were the Palestinians of whom I wrote in my first book. Those with audiences do not need to "give voice to the voiceless." Rather, our first task is to listen to those voices ourselves, and then to invite others to *have ears to hear*. With my privilege comes audience, and thus I must use that privilege to present and amplify voices that so often are drowned out, muffled, ignored, or silenced. We cannot afford to continue excluding from the conversation table those whom we have heretofore discounted or rejected.

Perhaps if I could take away only one lesson from my study of history at Lipscomb, of reconciliation in Belfast, and my experiences engaging the Israeli-Palestinian conflict, it would be that no voice should be excluded from the table. To paraphrase John Paul Lederach's sentiment, peace comes through the building of improbable relationships. It is the people we least want at the table that generally are the most necessary. That means the British government finally had to sit down with the IRA. It means Hamas, the Palestinian Authority, and the Israeli government *all* need to have a conversation. It means, like Jesus, we must dine with the tax collectors, sinners, and prostitutes. It means we have to listen to prisoners. If we do not allow *even* those we claim as the "worst of the worst" to sit at the table and speak, then we do ourselves a disservice at best and enable our own self-destruction at worst.

"Granted," the reader may concede, "perhaps we do need to consider the thoughts of prisoners, but why tell fourteen stories? Why not just survey dozens, hundreds, or thousands of prisoners to gain a broader scope of prisoners' views?" Forgiveness addresses wrongdoing and harm, and these do not occur in vacuums. There is always a story connected. Victims often ask "why," needing to understand the reasons behind their trauma. Until

9. In literary terms, this is called *defamiliarization*: "tak[ing] the familiar territory, i.e., the repertoire, and plac[ing] it in a new or different context so that the familiar appears unfamiliar to the reader.... [The] process of defamiliarization seeks to depragmatize the norms, i.e., to take them out of their original context in which they had validity and a frame of reference, and to question the underlying assumptions of the norms." Resseguie, "Reader-Response Criticism and the Synoptic Gospels," 309.

this question is addressed, forgiveness may be impossible for most. To discuss forgiveness with these men and women, one must know the nature of the wrongdoing. To understand the wrongdoing, one must learn the story behind it. Thus, for this project, I was uninterested in polling prisoners and receiving abstract, unstoried statistics—though such data is certainly useful in research. Forgiveness is a deeply personal process, and stories reflect that.[10]

Indeed, presenting the stories of these men and women is itself a practice of forgiveness. In the context of harm and conflict, we humans tend to create "single stories" of the other, stories without nuance.[11] To us, the other becomes *evil, barbaric, demonic, a monster, a murderer*, etc. In our imaginations, we can create and rehearse simple narratives where the other is devoid of decency, complexity, even humanity. Our support of state execution, for instance, often stems from the belief that the condemned have passed the point of no return; they are irredeemable. Thus, central to forgiveness is storytelling and story-listening.

When the darkness of victimization descends, often the first step toward the light of freedom is telling the story of what happened.[12] Stories help give order and meaning to our lives. Matthew Hearn, my world literature professor in college, said our need to tell stories is what sets humans apart from other animals. Storytelling is as natural and essential as eating. It's how we put our lives together. The trauma of unexpected and unjustified harm can paralyze us; violence in all forms violates our belief in a safe and comprehensible world. But as we begin to tell the story of what happened, we begin to piece our shattered lives back together. Forgiveness is almost certainly impossible without first reconstructing the event(s) and our lives through story.

Storytelling, however, should not be confined only to the victim/survivor; the perpetrator must also tell his or her own story, addressing that *why* question. After telling the story of *what* happened and hearing the story of *why* it happened, both the victim/survivor and perpetrator may begin to recognize their shared humanity.[13] We may come to remember

10. For a compilation of numerous powerful stories of forgiveness, see Cantacuzino, *Forgiveness Project*, and visit the website: http://theforgivenessproject.com/.

11. McRay, *Letters from "Apartheid Street,"* 25–26, 108–16.

12. Tutu and Tutu, "Telling the Story," in *Book of Forgiving*, 67–89.

13. Howard Zehr identifies hearing the story, the *why*, of what happened as an essential need of justice. See Zehr, *Little Book*, 14–15.

that, as Desmond and Mpho Tutu write, "no one is born evil and . . . we are all more than the worst thing we have done in our lives."[14] Hearing the story of the one who has harmed us does not justify the harm; rather, it offers context. We can and should continue to condemn the violation while still allowing ourselves to reconsider the person. And in this reconsideration, we may realize that the other, like us, is complex and broken, that our humanity is bound up together. In short, without telling and hearing these stories, forgiveness will likely remain a pleasant fiction.

So I invite you into these pages. I hope they will contribute not only to the conversations on forgiveness, but also the encouragement of compassion. In our world, malice seems more common than grace. Best-selling author Thomas Cahill said in a 2013 conversation with Bill Moyers, "I have come to the conclusion that there are really only two movements in the world: one is kindness and the other is cruelty. . . . You can explain virtually everything by those two movements."[15] I want this book to be part of the former, reminding us that, as Archbishop Tutu has often claimed, we have no future without forgiveness.

Michael T. McRay
Nashville, Tennessee
April 2015

14. Tutu, *Book of Forgiving*, 125. I have heard friends in prison express this sentiment innumerable times: "We've been condemned for the worst thing we did on the worst day of our lives. Society will forever judge us by the worst decision we ever made." Though many habitual offenders cannot claim to be judged by the worst thing they did on the worst day of their lives, a great number certainly can.

15. For the video of this interview, see http://billmoyers.com/segment/thomas-cahill-on-the-peoples-pope/.

Acknowledgements

PROJECTS LIKE THIS ARE not accomplished alone, and so I am deeply grateful first and foremost to the men and women at Riverbend and the Tennessee Prison for Women for their courage and vulnerability in telling me these stories and allowing me to tell them to you.

As always, I am indebted to my family: to my parents, David and Joan, for their constant loving support—whether financially, emotionally, or otherwise—in all my pursuits; to my grandmother, Annette, for her keen eye and unmerciful red pen during the tedious proofreading days; and to my brother, John, who scattered seeds in our conversations that would later grow into ideas herein.

I thank David Tombs, my grad thesis supervisor, for his wisdom and guidance in my graduate education; Rev. Matt Frierdich and Dr. Sam Katz, for their editorial brilliance in helping refine my arguments; Naomi Tutu, for bringing this project to her father's attention; Archbishop Desmond Tutu, for his gracious contribution; and Everett Worthington Jr., Donald Kraybill, Michelle Alexander, and Shane Claiborne for their time and kind words of endorsement.

I am also grateful to Elli Whiteway, Laura Acuff, and my sister Anna, whose swift fingers were my salvation. Their aid transcribing the many pages of stories significantly sped up the progress of this book.

To my dearest friend, Jeannie Alexander, I extend my deep gratitude and love. She, along with Richard Goode—to whom this book is dedicated—gave me the priceless gift of connecting me with the men and women behind the walls. It was Jeannie who suggested I interview the men you meet in this book. It was Jeannie who asked me to become a volunteer chaplain and helped me see the need for prophetic imagination in prison. It was Jeannie who co-founded No Exceptions Prison Collective with me after I was banned and she resigned. It was Jeannie who furthered my understanding of the revolutionary act of loving someone in prison. And it was Jeannie who taught me that nothing holy is tame.

Finally, thank you to the good folk at Cascade Books and Wipf & Stock—particularly Rodney Clapp, James Stock, Heather Carraher, and Matthew Wimer—for bringing another of my books into print.

Abbreviations

RMSI – Riverbend Maximum Security Institution
TDOC – Tennessee Department of Corrections
TPW – Tennessee Prison for Women

1

UNDERSTANDING FORGIVENESS

An Exercise in Cartography

"A map is not the reality it interprets yet it can help a person to get their bearings, to understand where they are and what direction it would be helpful to go." [1]

THE SUMMER BEFORE HIGH school, I spent two weeks hiking the Wisconsin wilderness with my brother, John, and two best friends, Caleb and Daniel Meeks, as part of Honey Rock Camp's "High Road Experience." Dividing us into two groups of ten or so, two experienced group leaders led us on a trek toward the shores of Lake Superior. Each day, one of our team of high school boys would become the "day leader," sometimes guiding us on trails, sometimes bushwhacking through the woods. When my day came, I conferenced with the two group leaders, who produced the map that only the day leader was permitted to see. The rest followed blindly, trusting that the day leader knew where to lead. I remember feeling a wave of confidence and comfort as the group leaders pointed to various locations on the map, indicating our origin, progress, and destination. Having seen the map, I gave the instruction to pack up the camp and start the day's hike. As we climbed rocks, removed fallen trees, and navigated divergences in the path,

1. Little and Verwoerd, *Journey through Conflict Trail Guide*, 146.

I periodically checked the map to be sure I was still leading the group in the right direction. Once or twice, and much to my chagrin, I realized I made a mistake at a recent turn. Several minutes of backtracking put us back on the straight and narrow—or in this case, the curved and wide. Without the direction and context that map provided, we may never have arrived at Lake Superior.

In college, I sometimes grew weary of theories. I wanted quick, practical solutions to problems, not abstract theories. Though sympathetic, my mentor-professor Richard Goode would encourage me to try seeing theories as maps. He asserted that just as travel and map reading require a dialectical relationship, so too do theory and practice. Theories must consider the practicalities and lived experiences of those "on the ground," and practitioners can benefit from the context and frameworks theories provide. This metaphor has proved immensely helpful for me.

Maps and theories are important. They help orient us in unfamiliar, complex terrain. As the quote beginning this chapter states, "a map is not the reality it interprets," but it situates us in a larger context. It allows the traveler to zoom out and acquire perspective. Through maps, we can learn the relationships between places and topographies. We can chart the distances already traveled and those still to come. Thus, the cartographer's role is crucial: to give the wanderer context and direction. Engaging the stories to come, the reader may feel like a wanderer, perhaps trying to navigate through treacherous and unfamiliar landscapes. Just as I needed a map navigating the wilderness near Lake Michigan, so the reader may need a map to journey through these stories.

This first chapter is *my* map of the forgiveness terrain. I offer that emphasis because, as Marino Cantacuzino—founder and director of The Forgiveness Project—writes, "forgiveness is something viewed through a personal lens and every context and all content is therefore dissimilar. . . . [It is] intrinsically subjective. . . . [It] is fluid and active."[2] From this dissimilarity comes diverse richness but also misunderstanding. I hope this map will succeed in clarifying some of these misunderstandings. It is not definitive but rather interprets and presents others' experiences and integrates my own thoughts. To presume that I can offer the punctuation to the heated forgiveness debates would be foolish; I am just a commentator hoping to make a helpful contribution to the existing literature. This literature offers a wealth of insight into the intricacies of forgiveness through such various

2. Cantacuzino, *Forgiveness Project*, 2.

disciplines as psychology, ethics, theology, anthropology, sociology, and philosophy.[3] Some writers contribute via case studies, personal testimony, or multidisciplinary analysis; others utilize visual media such as documentaries, feature films, or art exhibits. I aim to make this project accessible to both the lay and academic reader by synthesizing and presenting wisdom drawn from selections of the above disciplines and media.[4]

Due to references to Christianity in the preface, I need to offer a disclaimer. Though placing theological significance on forgiveness due to my Christian faith, I do not proceed through theological arguments. Religious expectations of forgiveness can both aid and impede the path of forgiveness. Some find Jesus' words on forgiveness to be life-giving and encouraging; his teachings motivate and inspire. Others have experienced the often indiscriminate and careless promotion of forgiveness within churches as nothing short of traumatic. In too many churches, there are preachers but no pastors. Wounded parishioners hear pulpit pleas for forgiveness as part and parcel of Christian discipleship, but they experience little pastoral presence guiding them in that process. Forgiveness is demanded but not explained, proclaimed but not modeled. Perhaps feeling forgiveness is impossible for them; parishioners might experience guilt and shame at their supposed inadequacy as Christians. The wounds for which they seek healing become infected now with religious bacteria.

Thus, while I value deeply the example of Jesus regarding forgiveness, I echo the Tutus that "forgiveness does not require faith."[5] The world consists of billions of people who do not claim Christianity, and a great many who reject all notions of the divine. But forgiveness remains relevant in their lives. Thus, while still referencing Christian theologians below, I mapped the following process to be accessible to non-Christians. My degrees are not in theology; plenty of theologians far wiser than me have written well on the connections between forgiveness and Christianity.[6] This book has a different purpose. In the following pages, I will make academic arguments—interspersed with anecdotes—asserting forgiveness is necessary; cannot be

---

3. See Garrard and McNaughton's helpful overview "The Debate about Forgiveness," in *Forgiveness*, 1–19. Also see the numerous voices included in the second part of Wiesenthal, *Sunflower*, 101–274.

4. All such selections and recommendations are included in the bibliography.

5. Tutu and Tutu, *Book of Forgiving*, 57.

6. For example, see Tutu, *No Future Without Forgiveness*; Volf, *Free of Charge* and *Exclusion and Embrace*; and Jones, *Embodying Forgiveness*.

equated with forgetting, excusing, condoning, or reconciling; and is best understood as a multi-stranded process.

The Necessity of Forgiveness

Renowned philosopher Hannah Arendt argues that life guarantees two "predicaments": "irreversibility" and "unpredictability." Humans cannot change the mistakes of the past; neither can we control the events of the future. She argues therefore that human relationships require *forgiveness* to address irreversibility and the *making and keeping of promises* to address unpredictability. As Richard Holloway notes, "a single act of passion or thoughtlessness can destroy someone's future happiness." Therefore, forgiveness is essential in human interactions so that connections are not always irrevocably destroyed by impulsivity. In other words, forgiveness answers the *event*.[7]

The term *event*, used often herein, does not mean a simple moment or occurrence in life, something planned for and expected, like a wedding or a birthday. Rather, the *event* described herein, engaged within the context of harm, is chaotic and unexpected. Once it occurs, it is lasting reality; before it occurs, one can neither control it nor truly prepare for it. Philosopher-theologian John Caputo writes in *The Weakness of God* that "events happen to us; they overtake us . . . [and] although we are called upon to respond . . . an event is not our doing but is done to us." It becomes something we "must deal with, like it or not." The event often is sudden and shocking, catapulting the sufferer from a familiar reality into a new one. What life once was, it is no longer. In Arendt's terms, the event is "unpredictable" and "irreversible." Thus, forgiveness is necessary because the events of life exist beyond the ability to control.[8]

7. Arendt, *Human Condition*, 236–47; Holloway, *On Forgiveness*, 63. Archbishop Desmond Tutu asserts, as is evident in his book title, that there is no future without forgiveness. Because of unbelievable acts of forgiveness, South Africa's horizon contains the possibility for peace rather than a seemingly inevitable bloodbath. See Tutu, *No Future Without Forgiveness*, esp. 206–30.

8. Caputo, *Weakness of God*, 4. He writes that the "event requires a horizon of expectation or anticipation, not in such a way that it must abide within it, but in order precisely to shatter and overflow it." In the introduction to his book, Caputo analyzes with precision and insight the nature of *event* and its relationship to *name*. Events are uncontainable, Caputo argues. Names try to contain events, but events cannot be fully contained in a name. Names cannot then be "taken with literal force" because names never equal the event simmering within. Take, for example, the name *rape*. That nominal

Regarding Arendt, commentators rightly and frequently affirm her work, but Arendt also puts forward two contentious claims: i.e., people cannot forgive themselves, and "crime and willed evil" are unforgivable in human interactions. She suggests that forgiveness depends on "plurality, on the presence and acting of others," and thus "no one can forgive himself."[9] Though her formula (forgiveness requires plurality) is correct, her conclusion (self-forgiveness is impossible) is not, as the following stories and analysis in chapter sixteen will demonstrate. Additionally, Arendt confines forgiveness to the sphere of mundane trespasses that are "everyday occurrence(s)."[10] Claiming that only God can forgive "crime and willed evil," Arendt posits that everyday trespasses need forgiveness and dismissal "for life to go on by constantly releasing men from what they have done *unknowingly*."[11] Several times, she references "unknowing" offenses, emphasizing that "willed" and "radical evil" exist beyond the capacity of human forgiveness. Given her ethnic, cultural, and temporal proximity to the events of the Holocaust—writing as a Jewish philosopher in the 1950s—one can understand her refusal to place deliberate evil within the realm of forgivability. Though understandable, her assertions are mistaken, as people do genuinely forgive themselves, and even such willed evil as the crimes of the Holocaust have been forgiven by some.[12] As the following chapters will show, many men and women in prison have responsibly forgiven themselves for harms committed, and in some circumstances, have received forgiveness from those harmed by their actions, even such actions as murder.

---

description cannot contain the magnitude of the corresponding trauma, the deep and intimate personal violation that the event of rape is for an individual. Names, therefore, reduce events to the confines of the names themselves. See ibid., 1–12.

9. Arendt, *Human Condition*, 237.

10. Ibid., 240.

11. Ibid., emphasis added. Arendt makes this theological claim based upon her understanding of the religious teaching of Jesus, who she argues was the "discoverer of the role of forgiveness in the realm of human affairs." Ibid., 238. I would agree with L. Gregory Jones, however, that Arendt's interpretation of the gospel's understanding of forgiveness is "problematic." Jones, *Embodying Forgiveness*, 90n29.

12. For example, consider the film *Forgiving Dr. Mengele*, which documents the journey of forgiveness by Eva Kor, a woman who suffered under the medical experiments of the notorious Nazi Dr. Mengele; or consider Gobodo-Madikizela's *A Human Being Died that Night*, exploring forgiveness regarding the apartheid perpetrator Eugene de Kock, known as "Prime Evil."

Regarding this notion of unforgivability, those instances of "willed evil" may in fact be the very places where forgiveness is essential. For some actions—like genocide or ethnic cleansing—the "strict justice" of *lex talionis* ("an eye for an eye") is both impossible and undesirable.[13] Few, if any, would advocate that, following the Rwandan genocide, the surviving Tutsi population should attempt the genocide of the Hutus. Likewise, I have yet to meet anyone who would advocate that those who have raped should thereupon suffer rape themselves. Some violations are so terrible that equal reciprocity cannot, or at least should not, be sought.

Philosopher Jacques Derrida addresses this when he writes, "there is only forgiveness, if there is any, where there is the unforgivable."[14] For Derrida, the "unforgivable" are those actions that are unjustifiable, inexcusable, inexplicable, and inexpiable—i.e., that constitute "willed," or perhaps "radical," evil. Thus, forgiveness is entirely necessary in macro cases like South African apartheid, the Rwandan genocide, the Israeli-Palestinian conflict, or the Northern Irish Troubles precisely because "strict justice" cannot be achieved, nor perhaps should it. There can be no "getting even." Derrida would undoubtedly disagree with Arendt's relegation of forgiveness to mundane trespasses, as he argues that forgiveness is only relevant in the context of that which is unforgettable and unimaginable. Regarding these types of actions, Holloway writes, "There are some deeds that are so monstrous they will drive us mad if we do not forgive them, because no proportional reparation is possible, no just accounting, nothing that makes any sense."[15] Whereas forgiveness, as it relates to letting go of resentment, certainly applies to the mundane trespasses that people unknowingly commit, it must not be confined there. For it to have weight and substance, it must also have something to say to those acts of *willed* violence, in whatever form, from which many of us might wonder if we could ever recover. Without forgiveness for "willed evil" and for self, individuals would forever be chained to events of an irreversible past.[16]

13. See Volf, "Forgiveness, Reconciliation, and Justice," in Helmick and Petersen, eds., *Forgiveness and Reconciliation*, 39.

14. Derrida, *On Cosmopolitanism and Forgiveness*, 33.

15. Holloway, *On Forgiveness*, 86.

16. See Smedes, "Forgiving Monsters," in *Forgive and Forget*, 78–81.

What Forgiveness Is Not

Especially in the context of prison, and thus concerning offenses serious enough to have warranted social exile, it is important to separate forgiveness from common misunderstandings that are perilous to healthy forgiveness praxis: namely, forgetting, excusing, condoning, and reconciling. Numerous scholars have made similar addresses, adding and subtracting various distinctions.[17] The Tutus, for example, also assert that forgiveness is not weak, easy, or a subversion of justice.[18] That forgiveness is difficult and requires strength should be evident from the below exploration, and the connection between forgiveness and justice will be addressed in the section "Forgiveness as Release." Here, I will discuss the notions of forgetting, excusing, condoning, and reconciling.

Forgetting

Too often, forgiveness is promoted with such phrases as, "Just forgive and forget." One could appropriately protest, especially regarding severe cases of harm, that it is entirely important that forgiveness not be equated with forgetting; we must remember so that the wrong never happens again.[19]

To be fair, the phrase "forgive and forget" often targets the types of wrongdoing that Arendt called "everyday mundane trespasses." Regarding such insignificant offenses, forgetting may indeed be possible, and perhaps even likely. Unless additionally qualified, *forgetting* herein refers to the actual extinction of a memory, which is likely true of certain events from one's childhood. Even with persistent prompting, one may never recall them. Regarding deep violations and major trauma, however, such forgetting is

17. See McCullough et al., eds., *Forgiveness*, 8; Enright and North, eds., *Exploring Forgiveness*, 48; Worthington Jr., *Just Forgiveness*, 74; Smedes, "Some Nice Things Forgiveness Is Not," in *Forgive and Forget*, 38–49; Murphy, *Getting Even*, 13–16; Hemenway, *Forget Them Not*, 77–81.

18. Tutu and Tutu, *Book of Forgiving*, 31–39.

19. However, as Jones observes, we would all likely acknowledge that remembering for the sake of using it against the wrongdoer in the future does not constitute forgiveness. See Jones and Musekura, *Forgiving As We've Been Forgiven*, 87. See also Schimmel, *Wounds Not Healed by Time*, 48; Smedes, *Forgive and Forget*, 38–40; Kurtz and Ketcham, *Spirituality of Imperfection*, 223–24; Blackard, *Restoring Peace*, 137. For those interested, Volf's *The End of Memory* offers a thorough, albeit theological, exploration of the connection between suffering, memory, and forgiveness.

almost certainly impossible.[20] Even if forgetting were possible, one could rightly argue it would be immoral, at least in terms of collective memory. Speaking of the Holocaust, Baudrillard writes, "[f]orgetting the extermination is part of the extermination itself."[21] To forget is to risk repetition, for salvation is in memory. On a wall at Auschwitz death camp in Poland, I first read the words of George Santayana: "Those who cannot remember the past are condemned to repeat it." If forgiving and forgetting are synonymous, then many victims/survivors have no chance of forgiving, for most will, and should, always have the capacity to remember.

Forgetfulness makes forgiveness unnecessary. Once an event occurs, its existence continues, often indelibly, in the memories of those involved. Without the memory, then essentially the offense disappears. Thus, if one forgets an offense, nothing remains to forgive, for psychologically the offense has ceased to be. Forgiveness, then, is actually only relevant regarding harms one cannot, or will not, forget.[22] It requires memory, followed by grace.[23] Therefore, forgiveness must be seen as kinetic, fluid, renewable; it rarely, if ever, is a one-time proclamation or extension. It is not pronounced in a moment, and then left untouched. Each time the violation

20. As Shriver notes, "modern psychiatry has made us aware . . . [that] traumatic pain and guilt plant a time bomb in the depths of the human psyche and in political history." See Shriver, "A Bridge Across Abysses of Revenge," in Helmick and Petersen, eds., *Forgiveness and Reconciliation*, 155.

21. Quoted in Minow, *Between Vengeance and Forgiveness*, 118.

22. Garrard and McNaughton write that if forgiveness is to make sense, it must entail awareness of the wrongdoing and a memory of it. Garrard and McNaughton, *Forgiveness*, 89. Using the example of Mirabeau, Friedrich Nietzsche argued in *On the Genealogy of Morals* that forgetting replaces forgiving: "(. . . Mirabeau, who had no recall for the insult and slights directed at him and who would not forgive, simply because he—forgot)." Nietzsche, *Genealogy of Morals,* 24. Regarding memory and trauma, Ariel Dorfman states well the challenge: "How do we keep the past alive without becoming its prisoner? How do we forget it without risking its repetition in the future?" Quoted in Minow, *Between Vengeance and Forgiveness*, 119. Donald Shriver Jr. writes: "Pain can sear the human memory in two crippling ways: with forgetfulness of the past or imprisonment in it. . . . The mind that fixes on pain risks getting trapped in it. Too horrible to remember, too horrible to forget: down either path lies little health for the human sufferers of great evil." See Shriver, *Ethic for Enemies*, 119.

23. See Tutu, *No Future Without Forgiveness*, 219; Lederach, "Five Qualities of Practice in Support of Reconciliation Processes" in Helmick and Petersen, eds., *Forgiveness and Reconciliation*, 201. As Shriver writes, "'Remember and repent' and 'remember and forgive' are better formulas" for restoring health after injury. Shriver Jr., "A Bridge Across Abysses of Revenge" in Helmick and Petersen, eds., *Forgiveness and Reconciliation*, 157.

is re-membered—literally restructured and reformulated in the brain[24]—forgiveness is required again. In this way, forgiveness deals with the past, present, and future simultaneously. The wrongdoing happened in the past and, in the presence of memory, is happening now, and will continue to happen so long as the memory remains. Thus, forgiveness is not and cannot be entirely past oriented but rather addresses the "temporal simultaneity" of trauma and pain, existing in the "eternal now."[25]

Therefore, the relationship of forgiveness to memory is not one of forgetfulness or the erasure of memory. It is not the repression of memory, when we "forget" because we cannot tolerate remembrance. It is not denial, pretending a wrong and its subsequent harm did not occur. If forgiveness has *any* relation to forgetting, it is found in the fading of the memory's *immediate recall*. This type of forgetting, or "not-coming-to-mind" as Mirsolav Volf terms it, entails a full acknowledgement and condemnation by both parties of the harm caused and comes only after a complete and truthful memory has been constructed and thoroughly reviewed.[26] It can never be coerced and should not be demanded. Instead, it simply "happens," since dutifully trying not to think of something only keeps that thing at the forefront of one's mind. "Not-coming-to-mind" is an organic process where the *constancy* of the memory's *immediate recall* becomes inconsistent, and potentially nonexistent. When one encounters one's wrongdoer, the *first* thought to enter the mind is not the memory of the harm that person caused. The memory itself is not gone; in fact, one maintains a clear memory of the hurt, and forgiveness is re-required each time the memory reemerges. Instead, the memory's *immediacy* is lessened, and it no longer controls oneself or the relationship with the wrongdoer.

Nearly everyone has surely experienced this type of forgetting. Perhaps we were injured by a sibling's vicious word, or the pain of an assumed friend's treacherous rumors, or the trauma of learning of a partner's infidelity. For various lengths of time following the initial infliction of damage, each encounter with our harmer is cloaked in painful memory. The moment we hear our sibling's name, or pass our friend on campus, or receive a text from our partner, we immediately think of the wound he or she inflicted; it stays always at the forefront of our minds. Yet, with forgiveness, the

24. Abumrad and Krulwich, "Memory and Forgetting."

25. Lederach and Lederach, *When Blood and Bones Cry Out*, 134–41. The temporal orientation of forgiveness is addressed again in "A Multi-Stranded Process" below.

26. Volf, *End of Memory*, 145–46.

immediacy fades so that we can encounter that person without having the painful memory spring to mind. Whether or not we actually come to like that person again, the reflexive pain felt at seeing him or her has dissipated, and our interactions are no longer dominated by that instinctive memory. However, if someone asks us if we remember when our partner cheated on us, or when our friend told lies about us to others, we likely could recall the pain again. But through forgiveness, the memory of that pain no longer consumes our perception nor controls our interactions with that person.

Excusing and Condoning

I have grouped these two because they similarly address the notion of blame. Excusing refuses to blame by virtue of no one being at *fault* for the wrong that occurred, perhaps due to circumstances beyond one's control; condoning refuses to blame by virtue of naming the event as a *good*. In other words, excusing is dismissing; condoning is justifying. In either case, forgiveness is unnecessary. As Volf argues, blame is inherent to forgiveness, for to forgive is to name and claim a wrongdoing. Innocence does not require forgiveness, and thus to offer forgiveness is intrinsically to blame someone for a wrong.[27] This is why if I say to my partner "I forgive you," she will likely ask, if unaware of an offense, "What did I do?" because in offering forgiveness I have communicated that I have been harmed.

Thus, forgiveness entails judging an act to be wrong; offering forgiveness is confrontation. It involves looking a wrongdoing directly in the face, naming it, and feeling justified anger toward it. Only then can forgiveness occur. Forgiveness does not excuse; it does not justify. It hears, sees, and condemns a wrong, then moves beyond. To confuse forgiveness with either excusing or condoning, one may feel insurmountable guilt at attempting forgiveness, seeing the harm as inexcusable. If that is correct, then that is the very space where forgiveness is relevant and necessary. It does not ignore, avoid, or deny. Rather, forgiveness is the intersection of judgment and grace.[28]

27. Volf, *Free of Charge*, 166–69.

28. Jones uses similar language when he speaks of forgiveness as a "judgment of grace." See Jones, *Embodying Forgiveness*, 146.

Reconciliation

The dialectic between forgiveness and reconciliation is not the focus of this work, but the two terms are frequent companions and too often conflated. The two processes interweave and intersect, as will be evident in later sections, but they differ primarily regarding the nature of the relationship. Forgiveness primarily deals with the internal, while reconciliation addresses the external. As Jean Vanier writes, "reconciliation is a bilateral affair."[29] While one can forgive and then sever the relationship, wanting nothing more to do with the other, reconciliation is the process of finding a way to *be* together, to exist in some form of relationship. The two are connected but distinct.

Many hesitate, or even vehemently reject, speaking of forgiveness as any part of reconciliation. Such a claim, some argue, promotes impossible expectations for most people.[30] Susan Dwyer writes frankly:

> It seems to me that any conception of reconciliation—at either the micro- or macro-level—that makes reconciliation dependent on forgiveness, or that emphasizes interpersonal harmony and positive fellow-feeling, will fail to be a realistic model of reconciliation for most creatures like us. If we care about reconciliation, let us advocate it in terms that make it credible to the relevant parties.[31]

Dwyer clearly assumes that forgiveness is a more difficult task than reconciliation, and she may be right. Additionally, she is determined to withhold from reconciliation any notion of "interpersonal harmony and positive fellow-feeling." Given such macro cases as genocide, enslavement, human trafficking, or protracted social conflict, and micro cases like serial adultery, domestic abuse, or murder, one can easily understand why Dwyer recoils at such seeming niceties regarding reconciliation.

This is the danger, though, of unnecessary simplifications of complex notions. *Confining* reconciliation to the development of "interpersonal harmony and positive fellow-feeling" would indeed set it out of reach for numerous wounded people, and thus I argue that, like forgiveness, reconciliation is best understood as multi-stranded: minimal, moderate, and

---

29. Vanier, *Becoming Human*, 155.

30. This is a frequent criticism of the forgiveness emphasis in South Africa's TRC. See Bloomfield, *On Good Terms*, 23–25.

31. Dwyer, "Reconciliation for Realists," in Prager and Govier, eds., *Dilemmas of Reconciliation*, 108.

maximal. In minimal reconciliation, both parties tolerate coexisting without violence. The moderate level consists of affected parties interacting and working together regarding mutually beneficial pursuits. And the maximal level entails mutual appreciation, a sense of togetherness, and the joy of positive relationship.[32] In other words, reconciliation can be understood as follows: *reconciliation as nonviolent coexistence, reconciliation as mutually beneficial cooperation,* and *reconciliation as beloved community.*[33] The full potential of forgiveness is not necessary in each. Thus, to define reconciliation by its first strand, and most attainable, would indeed remove the need for forgiveness, save for mercy. One need not necessarily overcome ill will and certainly need not extend goodwill in order to coexist without violence. Likewise, antagonistic peoples can come together nonviolently for mutually beneficial purposes without giving up resentments and animosities.[34] If the aspiration is the achievement of beloved community, however, all below strands of forgiveness are required. Dwyer is right to observe the unfairness of limiting reconciliation to this notion of beloved community. Yet, it is likewise unfair to *exclude* it from an understanding of reconciliation, for some have experienced this.[35]

Though forgiveness and reconciliation are not synonymous, they are clearly interconnected. Etymologically, *reconciliation* comes from the Latin words *re* (again), *com* (together), and *calare* (to call). Thus, reconciliation signifies this notion of "calling together again," rooting it in a context of encounter and interaction.[36] It means reuniting to some degree that which

32. This language comes from a master's class lecture by David Tombs. See Tombs, "Meaning of Reconciliation."

33. The term *beloved community* was popularized by Dr. Martin Luther King Jr. in the 1950s and 60s. For more on this notion, see Charles Marsh and John Perkins's very helpful book *Welcoming Justice.* Though confessedly theological, the book provides practical information on pursuing reconciliation that can relate to the non-Christian and non-theological reader.

34. Belfast is a prime example of this. Many of those deeply affected by the Troubles have not forgiven those who wronged them and their loved ones. Yet, for the most part, they exist in the same city without violence, and the violence that does occur is far less in scale than during the Troubles. The people are generally able to cooperate socially and professionally, though forgiveness is by no means pervasive. Some, though, have embraced beloved community with individuals on the other side, and in such cases, forgiveness is present. Yet, even where it is not, the people of Belfast and broader Northern Ireland experience some degree of reconciliation.

35. See, for example, "Linda Biehl and Easy Nofemela," in Cantacuzino, *Forgiveness Project,* 132–35.

36. Redekop, *From Violence to Blessing,* 285.

has been divided, or bringing together that which never was together. This requires proximity, "a social space . . . that holds relationships wherein direct conversation and exchange take place."[37] Forgiveness can help create this proximity, as the extension and acceptance of grace can shorten the distance resulting from harm and subsequent animosity. Through the processes of encounter and interaction, individuals may come to acknowledge, and potentially embrace, their interdependence. Indeed, if people do not believe they belong together, or at least will remain together, then no impetus exists to reconcile.[38] Thus, I would define full reconciliation as the renewable journey of nurturing relational resonance and building trust through encounter and collaboration, wherein people engage division through storytelling and truth telling, transcend animosity through empathy and grace, embrace interdependence, and extend goodwill. The practice of forgiveness points toward this possibility and is included in the process, but it need not always lead there.[39]

In other words, forgiveness is *naturally oriented toward* reconciliation, but reconciliation is not an inevitable consequence of forgiveness. Because forgiveness is not synonymous with naivety, one can acknowledge a pattern of behavior that is likely to continue and thus forgo attempts to reconcile the relationship, while still choosing to forgive the other regarding his or her continued destructive behavior. Patterns of behavior such as addiction or domestic violence are quintessential examples. A spouse may forgive her chronically abusive, alcoholic partner, but legitimately deny that person a place in her home. Someone may surrender all ill will toward a significant other whose sex addiction has led to multiple affairs without choosing to maintain or reenter intimate relationship. Thus, though forgiveness does

---

37. Lederach and Lederach, *When Blood and Bones Cry Out*, 206.

38. Byron Bland writes, "Reconciliation involves a profound rediscovery that those who have been deeply divided in the past do indeed belong together in the future." Quoted in Tombs and Liechty, eds., *Explorations in Reconciliation*, 67.

39. Drawing from language of the Psalms, John Paul Lederach speaks of reconciliation as the meeting point of truth and mercy, justice and peace, a "process of encounter and . . . [a] social space." Lederach, *Building Peace*, 29, 27–31; Lederach, *Reconcile*, 83–92. In *When Blood and Bones Cry Out*, John Paul and Angela Lederach call upon an aural metaphor for reconciliation, writing that it "emerges as the mix of voices finds its natural frequency." They continue: "Reconciliation as sound suggests the need for constant nurturing, circling engagement, mixing and remixing of voices and the repeated deepening of meaningful conversation." See Lederach and Lederach, *When Blood and Bones Cry Out*, 205–6.

not necessitate the realization of reconciliation, it is certainly naturally oriented toward it.

A Multi-Stranded Process

To argue that forgiveness is necessary and clarify its misunderstandings does not fully demonstrate its qualities. Qualitative questions frequent the literature: Is forgiveness inward or outward? Is it for the forgiver or forgiven? Does it address the past or the future? Is it an event or a process? Should it follow or precede offender contrition? While valid, such questions can tempt one toward unnecessary reductionism.

Consider, for example, the debate over whether forgiveness is a choice or a discovery. Some argue that people must choose to forgive, while others say people tend to discover unexpectedly, as if through an epiphany, that they have forgiven.[40] Some, for instance, choose forgiveness simply out of fatigue, as animosity toward others or oneself can be exhausting. Anyone who has suffered a wrong and felt the subsequent anger and resentment knows that such emotions can greatly increase stress, lead to depression, produce temporary periods of disassociation (depending on the severity and permanence of the harm), and numerous other negative health effects. Thus, as in the stories of Jamie Rouse and Tonya Carleton below, forgiveness might be chosen because the individual lacks the sufficient energy for maintaining vindictiveness.[41] In reality, both choice and discovery may well be true. In most cases, the one who suffers harm must *choose* the journey toward forgiveness by taking concrete steps toward its fruition, but the *result* of this journey may come when least expected.[42] In other words, forgiveness is both a choice and a realization; one often leads to the other.

To illustrate, Cynthia Vaughn was seven when her mother Connie was murdered in Memphis, Tennessee in 1984. Within twenty-four hours, she lost both her mom and dad, as he was arrested the next day and later sentenced to death for Connie's murder, a crime for which he has consistently

40. Enright, *Forgiveness is a Choice*; Kurtz and Ketcham, *Spirituality of Imperfection*, 216–17. Kurtz and Ketcham cite research by Seattle University which asserted that forgiveness "cannot be 'willed,' [and] becomes more impossible the harder one tries to will it."

41. Sternberg, "Stress and the Balance Within,"; McCullough, "Getting Revenge and Forgiveness."

42. For more on how one pursues the path of forgiveness, see Tutu and Tutu, *Book of Forgiving*; and Vanier, *Becoming Human*, 152–54.

claimed innocence. Along with her brother, Cynthia grew up in her aunt's house, where she suffered physical, emotional, psychological, and religious abuse. But Cynthia blamed all of it on her father Don, who awaited execution on Tennessee's "death row." She told me, "If he hadn't killed Mama, none of that would have happened." Over the next twenty-eight years, Cynthia's hatred for Don metastasized, and she became well-known on pro-death-penalty online forums for wanting the "freak to fry." In June 2012, she drove to Riverbend Maximum Security Institution in Nashville to confront Don for the first time since his arrest in December 1984. After spewing her venom at him for over an hour, Cynthia paused from exhaustion and says she heard a voice in her head telling her, "That's enough. It's over. Let it go." She turned to Don and said, "I don't care whether you killed my mom or not. I can't go another day hating you. It's killing *me*. So I forgive you." Cynthia describes this moment like an epiphany—"it came out of nowhere"—but this discovery was followed by a deliberate choice to pursue this journey and eventually rebuild her relationship with Don, whom she now hopes the governor will pardon and release. For Cynthia, the discovery led to the choice. "I forgive you" was not the final word but the beginning of something new.

This is also debated in the literature: Is forgiveness past- or future-oriented? The experience of forgiveness is so often situationally dependent; people experience forgiveness differently. Thus, for some, like Cynthia, the proclamation of forgiveness was future-oriented. The same is true for the Amish of Nickel Mines. Immediately after Charles Roberts IV shot and killed five Amish schoolgirls in October 2006, the bereaved families walked to his widow's home and offered forgiveness, eventually inviting the Roberts family to the girls' funerals, giving the family a portion of the numerous incoming international donations, and even attending the funeral of the man who killed their daughters. When the Amish said, "We forgive you," the hard work of forgiveness was not complete; rather it was just beginning. They saw that two paths lay before them: vengeance and hatred, or forgiveness and reconciliation. Their declaration of forgiveness was a declaration of which path they would pursue.[43]

Others, though, offer forgiveness as an acknowledgement of the long journey they have just come through. At the end of the 2013 Oscar-nominated film *Philomena*, Philomena encounters Sister Hildegarde, a nun who,

---

43. As Cantacuzino writes, forgiveness is a "direction rather than a destination." Cantacuzino, *Forgiveness Project*, 6.

e film, represents the epitome of ecclesial corruption. When Philomena got pregnant as a teenager, she was sent to a Catholic convent where her child, like the children of other young girls in similar situations, was given away to foreign parents—without Philomena's prior consent. After fifty years of searching for her son, she learns his whereabouts and travels to the US, only to discover he has died and was buried back at the convent where the nuns first separated them. When she returns to the convent to visit his grave, Martin Sixsmith—the journalist who has been accompanying her—confronts an elusive, bitter, wheelchair-bound Sister Hildegarde. Philomena enters during the confrontation and, much to Martin's dismay, forgives the remorseless old woman. "What? Just like that?" Martin exclaims angrily. "No, not 'just like that,'" Philomena replies quickly with tears in her eyes. "That's hard. That's hard for me." For her, the words "I forgive you" were the punctuation to the story she had been writing for decades. It spoke to the end result of years filled with anger, loss, hate, confusion, and longing. Her journey was not "just like that." Thus, forgiveness can be both a declaration of where one is going—as with the Amish and Cynthia—as well as an acknowledgement of where one has been—as with Philomena.

In the end, the complexity of forgiveness can be embraced by seeing forgiveness as a paradox, "hold[ing] together seemingly contradictory truths in order to locate a greater truth."[44] Here I resonate with Marina Cantacuzino's words:

> the more I delve into this expansive and complicated topic, the more entangled I seem to become. Not because I am ambivalent about the benefits of forgiveness but because I am reluctant to pin it down. Something that is so multifaceted and has such profound consequences for the human condition should not be consigned to clichés or glib phrases.[45]

Thus, I promote a multi-stranded view of forgiveness, wherein complex multiplicity is welcome and unhelpful reductionism avoided. Acknowledging different strands of forgiveness can help ease the tension inherent in the reductionist definitions of "clichés and glib phrases." To borrow Lederach's phrase, it allows one to engage complexity as a "friend rather than a foe."[46]

---

44. Lederach, *Moral Imagination*, 36. Gilbert Keith Chesterton wrote that paradox is "Truth standing on her head to attract attention." Quoted in Kurtz and Ketcham, *Spirituality of Imperfection*, 19.

45. Cantacuzino, *Forgiveness Project*, 2–3.

46. Lederach, *Little Book*, 53.

For this work, I identify five strands, expanding from the work of Joseph Liechty: *forgiveness as release, forgiveness as transcendence, forgiveness as goodwill, forgiveness as absolution*, and *forgiveness as reinterpretation*.[47] The strands, though presented here linearly, do not necessarily progress unimpeded. Forgiveness is rarely a clean-cut, orderly, systematic process. In reality, these strands may interweave, sometimes realized chronologically, other times engaged simultaneously. Thus, one of forgiveness's paradoxes is that it can occur and be understood both in terms of linear progression—i.e., one strand leading to another—but also as a vibrating circle, the resonance of which deepens with repetitive movements. To a certain extent, a linear understanding is supported through experience and logic, as one could argue that each strand seems to need the previous. At the same time, forgiveness does not end once the line is traversed. Forgiveness is ongoing, re-given with each re-membering, as will be addressed in "Forgiveness as Reinterpretation." The linearity of forgiveness also does not imply that, as one moves along the proverbial line, all that lies behind the current point is a matter of the past. In other words, when one finds it possible to extend goodwill to one's wrongdoer, this does not mean one will never feel animosity again or desire to "get even." Rather, though forgiveness may be seen as a continuum, the line of progression is continually looping, doubling back, spiraling up and down, forward and backward. Thus, a linear paradigm provides only partial insight.

When John Paul and Angela Lederach speak of healing in *When Blood and Bones Cry Out*, they use the metaphor of a Tibetan singing bowl. As the wood cylinder—or some other instrument for producing vibrations—rolls around the rim of the bowl, sound emerges. With increased circling, the sound deepens and broadens, filling in reverberation. Repetition produces depth and resonance, much like praying the liturgy or saying "I love you"—sometimes, the more times we do something, the more meaningful it becomes.[48] Using this metaphor for forgiveness suggests that "going in circles," or re-experiencing earlier strands, does not indicate regression or failure, but rather is a natural and important way to acquire stability and depth. Both these paradigms offer helpful insight into the complexity of

---

47. Liechty identifies only three strands of forgiveness, which he calls *forgiveness as letting go, forgiveness as "love-given-before,"* and *forgiveness as absolution*. See Liechty, "Putting Forgiveness in its Place: The Dynamics of Reconciliation" in Tombs and Liechty, eds., *Explorations in Reconciliation*, 62–66.

48. Lederach and Lederach, "The Tibetan Singing Bowl," in *When Blood and Bones Cry Out*, 89–110.

forgiveness. They are held together in a creative, paradoxical tension. While recognizing this tension, I am presenting these strands separately and linearly primarily for the sake of clarity and detailed analysis. When the reader encounters language of "completion" herein, do not read this as suggesting that forgiveness's practices "short" of all five strands are insufficient. Rather, this language, though problematic, simply notes that the forgiveness process *can* go further, though it is not required. In other words, this language is not used to establish a rubric for judgment, but rather as recognition of potential.

It is worth noting at the outset, however, the potential futility inherent in an academic analysis of an experience that for most is neither academic nor analytical. When forgiving, people do not often meticulously examine the process, asking themselves, "What strand am I working through now?" Forgiveness is something that is often simply done, experienced, discovered. It rarely happens with rational execution of a plan. In fact, people often do not understand what exactly they are doing; they just know something has changed. This becomes evident when seeking definitions of forgiveness. Often, people cannot formulate a tight, well-structured definition because they do not know how to speak about it. Forgiveness for many is something that is felt rather than analyzed. As Kraybill, Nolt, and Weaver-Zercher write, "Forgiveness is a concept that everyone understands—until they're asked to define it."[49]

Before moving forward, I need to make a note on language. Language is important, powerful, and political. It matters how we name people; the names we assign others inform our relationship to them. Names like *criminals, terrorists, untouchables, unbelievers,* etc. give the ones being named an "otherness" that can justify our distance and judgment. These labels allow for violence—physical, structural, and cultural—caused by condemnation, apathy, and superiority. Yet, we still need a way to talk about those involved in acts of violation and pain, especially in a book on forgiveness. Choosing these identifiers is tricky, though: assigning terms like *offender* and *victim* to one party and not another can risk attaching a permanent identity to someone. Neither victims nor offenders desire confinement in such labels. There is a growing search for alternative identifiers regarding violations: e.g., harmed and harmers, violators and violated, harm giver and harm receiver, perpetrator and survivor, wrongdoer and wrong sufferer, etc. In the following pages, I will use many of these terms interchangeably, though

49. Kraybill et al., *Amish Grace*, 126.

none completely suffice. In the individual case of rape, for instance, there is a clear distinction between the one who violated and the one who suffered the violation. If we zoom out, though, we might see that the one who committed the rape may also have been violated by someone else. Again, trauma that is not transformed is transferred. As Tonya says in one of the stories below, "I'm in prison today because I grew up as a broken individual who was traumatized emotionally beginning at a young age and never healed from it." While one may be an offender in one case, one may be a victim in another, and thus I ask that the reader see these identifiers as clarifications, not condemnations.

Regarding incarcerated people, I most often have chosen to use the terms *prisoners* and *insiders* rather than *inmates, offenders, felons, convicts,* or *criminals* because, in my experience, *prisoner* and *insider* are the preferences of most people in prison. Some do not like the term *prisoner* because they do not want the negative connotation of that label to define their identity; *insider* sounds more temporary and less condemning. Others strongly prefer *prisoner,* saying it most accurately relates the visceral nature of their confinement. Since no term exists that can satisfy everyone, I will use different identifiers in recognition of the diversity of preference.

Consider now the first strand of forgiveness: release.

Forgiveness as Release

Forgiveness as release entails releasing claims for revenge or proportional punitive reciprocity—that is, "getting even." Arendt rightly notes that contained within "every action" is a "chain reaction" that tends to escalate in the spiral of vengeance. Thus, she concludes that forgiveness and vengeance are antithetical: forgiveness liberates one from the "original trespassing" and vengeance binds one to it.[50] For example, one cannot *forgive* a murder and actively seek vengeance or advocate the death penalty. In *forgiveness,* one must let go of pursuits of equal or greater reciprocity, whether vigilante or criminal justice.[51]

50. Arendt, *Human Condition*, 240.

51. See Tutu, *No Future Without Forgiveness*, 219. The difficulty of this should not be trivialized. Neuroscience demonstrates that the desire for revenge is a craving, such as craving water or food. In the midst of personal trauma, one may be *famished* for vengeance, and the brain can interpret the sensation felt after revenge as pleasure. The choice to let go of this is significant, as it means denying oneself a psychological pleasure deemed to be well deserved. See McCullough, *Beyond Revenge*, 143–46; McCullough,

This begs the following question: Are notions of forgiveness and justice incompatible? This question is worthwhile, especially given the prison context of this exploration. The answer naturally depends on the type of justice. Many Western readers will likely think of justice in terms of retribution, the *modus operandi* of the current judicial system. Retribution is interested in punishment, inflicted through pain, aimed at creating suffering. Retribution and forgiveness, therefore, are incompatible.[52]

But what about distinguishing between retribution and punishment? One could argue that parental punishment of a disobedient child is born not out of retribution and a desire to inflict pain, but out of love and desire to mold and instruct. Thus, retribution and punishment are not synonymous. What then of the relationship between forgiveness and punishment? Some claim that one *can* forgive and still seek punishment, but *only* as a deterrent for others or in hopes of offender rehabilitation. Philosopher Charles Griswold notes that "one could forgive one's offender while also insisting that judicially determined punishment be carried out."[53] Legal scholar Martha Minow writes:

> In theory, forgiveness does not and should not take the place of justice or punishment. Forgiveness marks a change in how the offended *feels* about the person who committed the injury, not a change in the actions to be taken by a justice system.[54]

Volf echoes the above caveat about punishment, asserting that while forgiveness and retribution are fundamentally incompatible—for to forgive means "*not to press charges* against the wrongdoer," giving up "the demand for retribution"—forgiveness does not rule out "discipline" for the sake of "reform or restraint," as with parenting.[55] In other words, one cannot

---

"Getting Revenge and Forgiveness."

52. Regarding the prevalence of Western justice definitions centering on the notion of retribution, David Cayley brilliantly states that "rational argument cannot prevail against the conviction that imprisonment [and retribution] is an effective means of crime control. The paradigm itself determines what counts as rationality. Belief in the efficacy of imprisonment is self-validating." Cayley, *Expanding Prison*, 89. Thus, Westerners tend to accept unquestioningly the connection between justice and retribution because Westerners do not see retribution through the lens of justice, but rather see justice through the lens of retribution. The need, then, is to change lenses. For more on this, see Zehr, *Changing Lenses*.

53. Griswold, *Forgiveness*, 39.

54. Minow, *Between Vengeance and Forgiveness*, 15, emphasis added.

55. Volf, *Free of Charge*, 169–71, emphasis original.

forgive and seek punishment for the sake of suffering itself. Thus, central to the connection between forgiveness and punishment is retributive motive.

Philosophy and law professor Jeffrie Murphy suggests that, at least in the case of legal punishment, societies punish for two reasons: deterrence and retribution. Deterrence is future-oriented, offering the perpetrator and all observers an incentive not to repeat a similar offense. Retribution, on the other hand, is past oriented, seeking to levy a *deserved suffering*.[56] Considering this, I would assert that forgiveness and punishment are entirely incompatible insofar as punishment is retributive, desired out of a vengeful craving for reciprocal suffering, a need to "pay back" or "get even."[57] Only insofar as the notion of punishment *can* relate to social safety, accountability, and appropriate aspirations for the transformation of the wrongdoer, does one need not see forgiveness and punishment as mutually exclusive.[58]

Visiting the maximum security side of Riverbend, one quickly realizes numerous men have deep propensities toward violence and should perhaps never reenter general society. One man who self-identified as a serial rapist sorrowfully said to me a couple of years ago, "It is a good thing I am in here. If I were released, I know I'd rape again. I can't help it." Though such individuals are likely incapable of living healthily among the general population, they can still be forgiven. Forgiveness and social separation can certainly coexist; forgiveness and retribution cannot.[59]

56. Murphy defines this deserved suffering as "a level of suffering properly proportional to the wrongfulness of his [or her] criminal conduct." Murphy, *Getting Even*, 42. See also Benn's essay "Punishment" in Murphy, ed., *Punishment and Rehabilitation*, 8–19. Cayley analyzes four common justifications for legal punishment (i.e., imprisonment): deterrence, incapacitation of criminals, vindication and just deserts, and rehabilitation. Following the excellent work of Thomas Mathiesen's *Prison on Trial*, Cayley debunks each of these claims, demonstrating that imprisonment—as it exists here in the United States—fully fails at all such endeavors. See Cayley, "Something Must Be Done: Rationales for Imprisonment" in *Expanding Prison*, 89–99.

57. Murphy suggests that while one can forgive and still seek punishment for the offender, it would be "inconsistent" to claim forgiveness and "still advocate punishment" for the satisfaction of "personal vindictive feelings." Murphy, *Getting Even*, 14.

58. Cayley is quite right to claim that "punishment can function as correction only where there is a committed and consequential relationship." Arguably, little to nothing currently exists under the initiation of the prison industrial complex that can claim to be rehabilitative. Rather it "abandons the offender to a dog-eat-dog world in which he is apt to form new criminal associations, become further habituated to violence . . . and therefore become even less fit to live in society. . . ." Cayley, *Expanding Prison*, 97.

59. Noting the banishment sanctions of the Blackfoot Indians of North America, Holloway writes that the community imposed exile "on members who refused to comply

Yet, while social exile—surely a potential apparatus of punishment—may at least be temporarily necessary to protect greater society and facilitate personal transformation, I would argue that if rehabilitation is indeed the desired goal, then retributive punishment is counterproductive.[60] James Gilligan concludes, after extensive experience directing psychiatric services in Massachusetts prisons:

> The basic psychological motive, or cause, of violent behavior is the wish to ward off or eliminate the feeling of shame and humiliation . . . and replace it with its opposite, the feeling of pride.[61]

Shame and unwilled inferiority can compel people to violence, and thus a prison system that punishes some through solitary confinement via consistent twenty-three-hour lockdown, serves primarily to shame and degrade its residents rather than facilitate their rehabilitation.[62] Men at Riverbend referred to solitary as 23/1: twenty-three hours locked down with one hour of rec time per day for the full extent of one's confinement. Caged in a small, concrete, often white-washed cell alone in 23/1 can break the minds and humanity of even the most resolute and decent person.[63] I met men in soli-

---

with the group ethic. There was a sophisticated recognition among them that *persistent* offenders against the harmony of the community had, in effect, separated themselves from the life of the group, so banishment was an explicit recognition of the real situation, without resorting to any method of retributive punishment." Holloway, *On Forgiveness*, 73, emphasis added. Helpful here is the qualifier "persistent." Many prisoners are "one-timers," often committing a single act of passion, desperation, or foolishness. These individuals are unlikely to reoffend. Award-winning journalist Nancy Mullane, in researching for her 2012 book *Life After Murder*, "was able to determine that 988 convicted murderers were released from prisons in California over a 20 year period. Out of those 988, she said 1 percent were arrested for new crimes . . . [and] *none* of the 988 were rearrested for murder." See Slifer, "Once a Criminal," emphasis added.

60. See Gilligan, *Preventing Violence*; Menninger, *Crime of Punishment*; Murphy, ed., *Punishment and Rehabilitation*, 169–231. Even if deterrence is the desired goal, the current system of incarceration is surely failing given the high rates of recidivism. See Shipp, "What Has Happened Since 1973?" in Campbell and Goode, eds., *And the Criminals With Him*, 35.

61. Gilligan, *Preventing Violence*, 29.

62. As Francis Allen writes, "there is a strong tendency for the rehabilitative ideal [that prisons often promote] to serve purposes that are essentially incapacitative rather than therapeutic in character." Quoted in Murphy, ed., *Punishment and Rehabilitation*, 185. As Zehr points out, "retributive theory believes that pain will vindicate, but in practice that is often counterproductive for both victim and offender." Zehr, *Little Book*, 59.

63. See "My Experience in Solitary Confinement," written by an anonymous Tennessee prisoner at http://prodigalsons1.blogspot.com/2014/12/my-experience-of-solitary-

tary confinement at Riverbend who were confined there for years, one for more than a decade. This environment leads to increased levels of violence and mental deterioration.[64]

Thus, Volf rightly claims that those who forgive will promote an alternative justice paradigm, one "tempered with compassion," to use the phrase of Antoinette Hill, a woman imprisoned at TPW.[65] As Carolyn Yoder has concluded, after witnessing bitterness and hatred envelop and destroy individuals trapped in the "cycles of victimhood and violence," forgiveness—while by no means implying relinquishing justice claims—is necessary so as to release "the cycles of revenge and retribution to pursue a justice in a way that is restorative to victims and aggressors alike."[66] In other words, while retribution and forgiveness are mutually exclusive, justice and forgiveness are not. This justice, though, must be viewed through an alternative paradigm, such as restorative justice.

Restorative Justice

If justice is understood as *lex talionis*—an eye for an eye—all one could realistically achieve in most cases is partial or insufficient justice, which—theologian Miroslav Volf rightly points out—is therefore partly unjust.[67] As noted earlier, "getting even" is often impossible and undesirable, and thus another set of justice lenses is required. The very notion of justice itself must be reimagined. In my previous book, I wrote:

---

confinement.html.

64. Consider the case of Clayton Fountain, who entered the prison system due to murder and, as the system sought to punish him, became increasingly violent. Thus, the system increased its punishment in response to Fountain's increased aggression, which in turn intensified his violence. The spiral continued until Fountain came to be regarded as the most dangerous man in federal prison. For the amazing story of Fountain's violence, transformation, and eventual aspirations toward monastic living while in solitary confinement, see Jones, *Different Kind of Cell*. For another firsthand insight into the torture of solitary confinement, see Cabral, "How Solitary Confinement in Pelican Bay Almost Drove Me Mad." For three related personal stories of mine, see "A Human Being (Almost) Died that Night," "Scars," and "Razors" in the appendix.

65. Volf, *Free of Charge*, 171.

66. Yoder, *Little Book*, 61.

67. Volf, "Forgiveness, Reconciliation, and Justice," in Helmick and Petersen, eds., *Forgiveness and Reconciliation*, 39.

> Here in the West . . . we assume that justice entails a fitting (or proportional) punishment for a certain crime. Looking through our default retributive lenses, we see what we believe justice *is* without asking the important preliminary question, "Where should justice lead us?" . . . Injustice divides people from each other, creating rifts in the fabric of society. . . . It seems to me that the ultimate hope of justice should be to serve as a stepping stone on the path to healing [those rifts], whether personally, communally, or societally.[68]

Thinking of justice not as an end, but as a means toward holistic peace, lends itself toward the framework offered by restorative justice.

Restorative justice is an increasingly popular lens for viewing alternatives to systems and structures of retribution. Consider this articulation, which Jeannie Alexander and I coauthored as one of the core values of No Exceptions Prison Collective (NEPC) in 2014:

> The contemporary criminal justice system conceptualizes "crime" as the breaking of the state's laws and thus views the offender as accountable to the state for due consequences. It assumes justice is synonymous with distributing punishment, which is categorized by pain; vengeance; and exile for an arbitrarily assigned, mandatory number of years. Restorative justice holds that the primary offense of the "crime" entails a violation of human relationships, harm caused to another person, not to a state. . . . When we divorce harm from individuals and communities and perpetuate the illusion that non-human, political constructs are the victims, then we . . . cannot heal the real physical bodies and minds of a community. We become deaf to the complexity of narratives, and we take shortcuts to justice, which results in no justice, no healing, and no possibility for redemption for either victims or offenders. Restorative justice, therefore, entails addressing the harms done and the needs of all involved, naming the obligations of the offenders, providing a space to include the voices of all who have a stake in the offense (that is, victims/survivors, the offenders, and their communities), and putting forth an effort—to whatever extent possible—to make things right. Restorative justice embraces a holistic approach to dealing with the aftermath of crime, valuing collaboration, healing, safety, and social transformation. Restorative justice understands that crime itself is not as much a problem as a perceived solution to a problem. In other words, many who commit crimes do so because, at the time, the act may seem to remedy present problems. Thus, in recognizing that crime does

68. McRay, *Letters from "Apartheid Street,"* 117.

not occur in a vacuum, restorative justice seeks to address the underlying issues of offenses, such as social inequalities, trauma, shame, mental illness, etc. Restorative justice posits that trauma which is not transformed is transferred: "Hurt people hurt people." Essentially, restorative justice offers a new set of lenses for thinking about crime and punishment, ones that see the need for the transformation of individuals, relationships, and societies; ones that take into account people's stories; and ones that believe justice should lead us closer to social healing and reconciliation, and not away from them.[69]

Restorative justice lends itself more to the possibility of forgiveness and reconciliation than does the adversarial system of retributive justice. In his brilliant essay "Redemptive Imagination," Jacob Davis discusses the critical connection between reconciliation and restorative justice: "Reconciliation, instead of a self-destructive obsession with retribution, is a vital interest for us all. Rather than insisting that no crime go unpunished, we must insist that no hurt caused by crime must go unhealed." Restorative justice and forgiveness are interested in healing harms, rather than inflicting new ones.[70]

However, as Howard Zehr—often referenced as the grandfather of restorative justice theory in the West—is quick to point out, restorative justice is not "primarily" about forgiveness and reconciliation. It provides a "context" for the realization of both forgiveness and reconciliation, but such pursuits must be the choice of participants.[71] Zehr also writes that

69. No Exceptions Prison Collective, "Core Values."

70. Davis, "Redemptive Imagination," 461. Jacob Davis is one of the prisoners whose story is told herein. (See chapter fifteen.) Jacob was arrested his senior year of high school and never got to take advantage of the full scholarship awaiting him at college. Fifteen years later, he finally had the opportunity for formal college study through the Lipscomb Initiative for Education (LIFE) program that offers insiders the opportunity to pursue Lipscomb University degrees. For his first class, one that I was privileged to teach, Jacob wrote a paper called "Oblivious Justice" arguing that one of the major issues with the current justice system is its failure to care for the needs of local communities. The paper was exceptional, and I sent it to Wendell Berry, a well-known writer Jacob often referenced. Mr. Berry responded with a letter for Jacob saying it was "more literate, intelligent, and thoughtful than nearly all the papers I have read by college students." Jacob expanded that paper and changed the title, and we were able to get it published in the *Contemporary Justice Review* as "Redemptive Imagination." His first college paper became an academic journal article.

71. Zehr, *Little Book*, 8. See also Shriver Jr., "Is Justice Served by Forgiveness," in Biggar, ed., *Burying the Past*, 35.

restorative and retributive justice are not *theoretically* antithetical, as both promote vindication through some degree of reciprocity, but they differ in perspectives on what will "effectively right the balance."[72] Retributive justice claims punishment and pain will even the score; restorative justice claims acknowledgement and restitution offer the best chance of making things as right as possible. As Archbishop Tutu wrote in an endorsement of Lipscomb University's new Restorative Criminal Justice program, "Restorative justice believes in healing relationships. It values people over punishment, reconciliation over revenge, accountability over abandonment."[73]

Forgiveness and Mercy

When discussing forgiveness in the context of justice, a discussion of mercy should arise. Thus, it is worthwhile to consider briefly the relationship and distinction between forgiveness and mercy. Insofar as the wronged individual has the ability to exact revenge or some manner of reciprocity but abstains from such actions, then one could perhaps call this first strand *forgiveness as mercy*. Yet, as evident in such usage, the two terms are not fully synonymous.

Mercy cannot exist without a standard of deserving proportionality, however defined, by which to measure it; thus, its meaning is in relation to just deserts. To grant mercy to someone is to give that individual the *gift* of receiving less than he or she deserves, according to one's standard of just desert.[74] Solomon Schimmel contrasts mercy and forgiveness by claiming that mercy is an action toward an offender over whom one has authority, "especially the authority to punish." Forgiveness, on the other hand, can exist "irrespective" of the power dynamic between victim and offender.[75] A state, for instance, can grant mercy to one who commits murder because the state has assumed the authority to administer punishment for murders within its boundaries. Yet, at least within an understanding of forgiveness as discussed herein, a state cannot *forgive* someone for murder because the

72. Zehr, *Little Book*, 58.

73. For more on restorative justice, see Zehr, *Changing Lenses*; Woolford, *Politics of Restorative Justice*; Campbell and Goode, eds., *And the Criminals With Him*; Toews, *Little Book*; Cayley, *Expanding Prison*; Magnani and Wray, *Beyond Prisons*; Tulluis, "Can Forgiveness Play a Role in Criminal Justice?"

74. Murphy, "Forgiveness and Resentment," in Murphy and Hampton, eds., *Forgiveness and Mercy*, 20–22.

75. Schimmel, *Wounds Not Healed*, 52.

murder was against an individual and not the governing body. The state has no need to overcome resentment (the next strand); its proclaimed task is to decide and exact punishment. Thus, one could say that forgiveness *begins* with mercy, with relinquishing any power of retribution one has over another or by forgoing the pursuit to acquire such, but the two terms are not interchangeable. One might say, alluding to Cornel West's sentiment on justice, mercy is what forgiveness looks like in public.[76]

Forgiveness as Transcendence

Forgiveness as transcendence references feelings of hatred and all its subsets.[77] Most writers and scholars agree that forgiveness involves the victim transcending, overcoming, or releasing feelings of resentment and animosity toward his or her offender.[78] The term *transcendence* is important, as it suggests emergence, having meaning only in relation to that from which one emerges. Thus, associating the term with feelings of hatred and its subsets indicates that the existence, or legitimacy, of such feelings is central to the meaning of forgiveness.[79] Arendt relegated forgiveness' relevance to the realm of "mundane trespasses," but I wish to retrieve forgiveness from such compartmentalization and recognize it beyond minor encroachments. I would argue that forgiveness is for those violations for which one must overcome expected and legitimate feelings of hatred and its subsets. Indeed, mundane offenses committed unknowingly, without deliberate malice (i.e., accidents), often can be more easily forgiven for precisely this reason: the

76. Mercy in the political realm is often called "political forgiveness." For more, see Digeser, *Political Forgiveness*; "Political Forgiveness: Acts and Agents," in Bole et al., *Forgiveness in International Politics*, 61–86.

77. Liechty (in *Explorations in Reconciliation*) includes the release of hatred in his first strand, but I find it helpful to separate the first two releases, as mercy can be granted without overcoming resentment. Separating them allows for more nuanced analysis as well as a respect of each release's significance.

78. See Garrard and McNaughton, *Forgiveness*, 90; Murphy, "Forgiveness and Resentment," in Murphy and Hampton, eds., *Forgiveness and Mercy*, 20; Worthington, Sandage, and Berry, "Group Interventions to Promote Forgiveness," in McCullough et al., eds., *Forgiveness*, 229; Enright, *Forgiveness Is a Choice*, 25; McCullough, *Beyond Revenge*, 114–115; Shriver Jr., *Ethic for Enemies*, 6ff; TRC of South Africa, *Final Report*, Ch. 5, para. 48; Volf, *Free of Charge*, 168; Arnold, *Why Forgive?*, 2; Gobodo-Madikizela, *Human Being Died*, 97; Brudholm, *Resentment's Virtue*.

79. See Smedes, "We Hurt," in *Forgive and Forget*, 3–19.

individual meant no harm.[80] These accidental trespasses can usually simply be ignored, overlooked, or dismissed, often with quick phrases like "It's fine, it's okay, don't worry about it"; the term *forgiveness*, though, may be too substantial for the insignificance of such mundane encroachments.

Some advocates favor a model focusing almost exclusively on the benefits for those forgiving, seeing forgiveness as unquestionably positive as it offers freedom from both bitterness and imprisonment to the past.[81] Murphy, however, cautions against a "hasty and uncritical" embrace of forgiveness, asserting that though forgiveness is often virtuous, it may sometimes indicate a lack of self-respect, making vindictiveness the more responsible path.[82] In *Getting Even*, he suggests the notion of vindictiveness may serve a positive purpose in human interactions, arguing that various "vindictive passions," notably resentment, are connected to self-respect and self-defense, which are "good things."[83] In her work with the South African Truth and Reconciliation Commission, Gobodo-Madikizela came to believe that setting "hatred and resentment [as] a necessary prior condition for an expression of forgiveness" judges victims "too harshly" and "fails to recognize the legacy of oppressive systems and just how much damage they leave behind in the lives of those who have suffered years of abuse." She suggests that "people who have been marginalized by an oppressive system [or person] may know nothing other than to shrink in the presence of those who embody power." Some may have so internalized a position of inferiority or powerlessness that, when wronged, they do not even *experience* emotions of hatred and resentment, much less respond outwardly with vindictiveness. Indeed, in such cases, the more appropriate initial task may be to *cultivate* "vindictive passions" rather than work to overcome them.[84]

80. I do not reference in this sentence casualties caused by accidents like drunk or careless driving. Though the violence of such acts usually occurs unintentionally and without malice, death or serious injury caused by reckless, irresponsible behavior can be extremely difficult to forgive.

81. For more, see Garrard and McNaughton, *Forgiveness*, 11, 28–31. I will return to the notion of forgiveness as liberation in "Forgiveness as Absolution."

82. Murphy and Hampton, eds., *Forgiveness and Mercy*, 17; Murphy, "Two Cheers for Vindictiveness," in *Getting Even*, 17–25. This is echoed in Garrard and McNaughton, *Forgiveness*, 100. Murphy suggests this is the case primarily when forgiveness is promoted as "cheap grace," i.e., not requiring repentance.

83. Murphy, *Getting Even*, 18.

84. Gobodo-Madikizela, *Human Being Died*, 100–101. Though forgiveness is chiefly a good, when it comes as a result of internalized perpetual victimization, its harm may outweigh its good.

In Murphy's assessment, feeling resentful when undeservedly wronged demonstrates that one has an appropriate respect for one's worth and dignity. It communicates, both to oneself and the other, that boundaries have been violated, saying, "I am worth more than your actions and words suggest." Referencing the "powerful sermon" of Bishop Butler titled "Upon Resentment," Murphy notes that resentment's hazard comes not in its existence, but rather when it dominates and consumes an individual to the extent that "one can never overcome it and acts irresponsibly on the basis of it."[85] Thus, these first two strands of forgiveness reference this refusal to be *perpetually* inundated by legitimate feelings of vindictiveness, aware that clinging to resentment can prove toxic.

In *The Big Book of Alcoholics Anonymous*, the writers state: "Resentment is the 'number one' offender. It destroys more alcoholics than anything else. From it stem all forms of spiritual disease."[86] According to the Twelve Step tradition, resentment contributes to the emergence and progression of addictions. Holding on to bitterness is like picking at an old scab to cause someone else pain, or as the adage goes, it's like drinking poison and hoping the other person will die. Many in AA believe resentment kept them drinking; *resentment* was destroying them. People in recovery programs often work to release resentments promptly, recognizing that an addiction to resentment can be as real as addictions to alcohol, narcotics, sex, etc. Forgiveness in these circles is promoted not as a preferable pursuit, but rather as an *essential* one—for while immediate resentment when wronged can indeed indicate healthy self-respect, lingering resentment can corrode and corrupt. Indeed, vindictiveness itself can become an addiction. In this regard, forgiveness is truly life-giving.

Forgiveness and Empathy

Stating that *forgiveness as transcendence* means transcending these "vindictive passions" does not explain how one does this, however. Though the how-to of forgiveness is not the focus of this book, one possibility central to forgiveness is acknowledging one's own shortcomings and intentionally

---

85. Murphy, *Getting Even*, 19. For a clear example of this, read the story of Don Robeson, whose anger and vindictiveness consumed him and plagued his family, after he was fired from his prestigious job for reporting financial improprieties. See Whitney, *Forgiveness*, 51–58.

86. *Alcoholics Anonymous*, 64.

trying to see the positive in the other.[87] In the Gospel of Matthew, Jesus asked, "Why do you look at the speck of sawdust in your brother's eye and pay no attention to the plank in your own eye?"[88] Forgiveness is facilitated by recognizing the faults of self and the good of the other, to look for our common humanity.[89] In an interview by Krista Tippett, Jean Vanier said:

> We don't know what to do with our own pain, so what to do with the pain of others? We don't know what to do with our own weakness except hide it, pretend it doesn't exist, so how can we welcome fully the weakness of the other if we haven't welcomed our own weakness?[90]

Thus, one can realize *forgiveness as transcendence* by coming to embrace the weaknesses within oneself, acknowledging the strengths in the other, and thereby coming to see his or her humanity. This notion of humanity is essential to forgiving. As the late Lewis Smedes notes, only someone entirely human can forgive and be forgiven. When we allow ourselves to see people as monsters, then we have in fact allowed them to exist beyond the realm of forgiveness, for we have excused their actions. Smedes writes: "A monster is excused from judgment by the fact that he or she is beyond humanity. This is the paradox of making any human being *absolutely* evil."[91] Perhaps most central, then, to transcending animosity is cultivating empathy, seeing the world as the other might see it and understanding that actions do not occur in vacuums.[92] Smedes referred to this as the acquisition of "magic eyes," beginning to reinterpret the other and the other's story outside the context of our animosity and woundedness.[93] While empathy does not necessitate excusing, which would make forgiveness irrelevant, it may prompt understanding, allowing the wounded to "stand in their [wounder's] shoes" and

87. For more on how to forgive, see Tutu and Tutu, *Book of Forgiving*.

88. Matt 7:3 NIV.

89. Tutu and Tutu, *Book of Forgiving*, 22–23, 125–127; Vanier, *Becoming Human*, 153; McRay, *Letters from "Apartheid Street,"* 81.

90. Vanier, "Wisdom of Tenderness." This notion of learning to embrace our own weaknesses is central to self-forgiveness, which will be addressed in chapter sixteen. For more on Vanier's understanding of weakness, see Hauerwas and Vanier, *Living Gently in a Violent World*, esp. 63–69.

91. Smedes, *Forgive and Forget*, 80, emphasis original.

92. McRay, *Letters from "Apartheid Street,"* 114–115.

93. Smedes, *Forgive and Forget*, xviii. I will explore this notion of reinterpretation as the fifth strand of forgiveness.

appreciate the circumstances that may have influenced his or her ac..
In *The Book of Forgiving*, Desmond and Mpho Tutu write that "we find it easier to practise forgiveness when we can recognise that the roles could have been reversed," that even in some of the most horrific instances of violence, given the same triggers and conditions, we might have behaved similarly.[95]

In another interview by Krista Tippett, Israeli spokesperson of The Parents Circle-Families Forum Robi Damelin spoke of the death of her son David, an Israeli soldier who was killed by a Palestinian sniper in the West Bank. She acknowledged that upon hearing of her son's murder, she immediately understood that the man who killed him did not kill "David," so to speak, but rather killed a symbol of the oppressive occupying force. She stated that the Palestinian could not have killed David had he really known David. Her ability to put herself in the place of her son's killer, acknowledge his situation under oppression, and understand his desire to resist greatly enabled her journey of forgiveness, though it certainly did not alleviate the pain of utter loss.[96]

Empathy is a humanizing exercise where one comes to acknowledge the complexity of the other and his or her context. When harmed, we often create single stories of each other wherein the other is devoid of all complexity. But humans are neither wholly good or wholly bad: "each of us stands at one moment as the one who has been hurt, and at the next moment as the one who is inflicting the hurt."[97] To forgive, we must work

94. Tutu, *No Future Without Forgiveness*, 219. For more on this, see Halpern and Weinstein's very helpful article on the role of empathy in reconciliation, "Rehumanizing the Other," 561–83.

95. Tutu and Tutu, *Book of Forgiving*, 22. Often, people—including Archbishop Tutu—use the phrase "There, but for the grace of God, go I" when referencing the possibility of such role reversal. With the utmost respect to the archbishop, I admit I find this phrase problematic. I cannot begin to count the number of times well-meaning Christians said this to men at Riverbend, often during chapel services. The *intent* of the message was positive: it could be any of us in here. But the *implication* of the message was troublesome, even offensive to the men: the grace of God kept me out of here, but it did not save you. Men would often vent, "If God could show you the grace to keep you of prison, why couldn't God show me the same? Am I less deserving of God's grace? Does God love me less?" Thus, though certainly meant as an expression of empathy and kindness, the phrase tends to disturb those it is meant to encourage.

96. See Damelin, "No More Taking Sides." For more on Parents Circle-Families Forum, see the film *Encounter Point* and visit their website: http://www.theparentscircle.com/.

97. Tutu and Tutu, *Book of Forgiving*, 5.

hard to see all the qualities of the other, both the ones we prefer and the ones we do not.[98]

In Whitney's *Forgiveness*, Deb Lyman writes of forgiving her adulterous husband:

> Dave had to come off the pedestal. I had to see how he has all these different qualities, both light and dark, and that a relationship can't work if we idealize only one and don't see the bigger picture. It was critical to have empathy for his weaknesses and vulnerabilities so I could see him as a whole person, complete with both flaws and goodness; I had to have some empathy for what it was like to walk in his shoes before I could forgive him.[99]

Forgiveness as transcendence is the indispensable core of the whole process. Without it, there is no forgiveness. What is forgiveness if not essentially overcoming hatred and its relatives? The first strand could be categorized as mercy, and thus, though important, can be distinguished from the *intra*personal workings of forgiveness itself. Each of the following strands increases in rarity and difficulty. Though certainly relevant to a full understanding of forgiveness, even in their absence, most people would feel that forgiveness can still occur. Not so with *forgiveness as transcendence*: without the overcoming of ill will, forgiveness is nothing.

Forgiveness as Goodwill

In the first two strands, one has released claims for vengeance and let go of ill will. While some analyses on forgiveness stop here, I, along with Liechty and others, suggest that the full potential of forgiveness includes more.[100] Liechty names his second strand "love-given-before." This notion, however, does not carry any sentimental references, but rather speaks of "willing, seeking and extending oneself for the good of another."[101] One moves from

---

98. See McRay, *Letters from "Apartheid Street,"* 114–15.

99. Whitney, *Forgiveness*, 35.

100. See Hampton, "Forgiveness, Resentment and Hatred," in Murphy and Hampton, eds., *Forgiveness and Mercy*, 87; Garrard and McNaughton, *Forgiveness*, 90; Fitzgibbons, "Anger and the Healing Power of Forgiveness," in Enright and North, eds., *Exploring Forgiveness*, 65ff; Smedes, *Forgive and Forget*, 29.

101. Liechty, in Tombs and Liechty, *Explorations in Reconciliation*, 62.

wishing vengeance and experiencing hateful emotions to beginning to wish the other well, which the Tutus name as the mark of true forgiveness.[102]

After overcoming animosity toward the offender, one may then come to *desire* her or his well-being. This is an important and tremendously difficult transition, moving *from* negative *through* neutral *toward* positive emotions. After releasing feelings of animosity, one likely does not immediately develop a positive disposition toward the other. It does not happen overnight. Rather, one may begin to *hope* for such, and if it comes, it likely comes unexpectedly.

It is important to emphasize here that arriving at a place of positive wishes toward one's offender does not mean that one statically and permanently remains in such a state. This would not account for the ebb and flow of human relationships, the potential for revictimization (especially in the absence of offender acknowledgement and thereupon contrition), or latent resentments that could emerge later. Thus, though one may have made the transition from ill will to goodwill, one may circle back again and again. The desire for the well-being of the other must often be rekindled time and again.

Forgiveness as transcendence, then, means one ceases to wish ill for the offender, while *forgiveness as goodwill* entails the development of positive perspective regarding the other. *Forgiveness as transcendence* lets go of *active malevolent* wishes; *forgiveness as goodwill* pursues *active benevolent* wishes. It is not apathy or indifference concerning the other's future, nor necessarily an active search to enrich the other's life. Rather, it is cultivating well-wishes within the self.

A well-known Cherokee anecdote illustrates this: When a young boy asks his grandfather what to do about the anger he feels toward someone who wronged him, his grandfather replies that each person has two wolves living within, one that is evil—full of anger, hatred, disregard, self-centeredness, arrogance, malice, etc.—and one that is good—full of love, compassion, sincerity, kindness, loyalty, humility, etc. These wolves are constantly battling, the grandfather tells the young boy. When the boy asks which wolf wins, the grandfather wisely replies, "The one you feed." Thus, one must feed and nurture goodwill through thoughts and acts that facilitate its growth.

Finally, upon cultivating the desire for the other's well-being, one *extends* oneself in goodwill. This is the watershed moment of forgiveness:

102. Tutu and Tutu, *Book of Forgiving*, 128.

moving *outside* of self and into the realm of the other. Forgiveness becomes a social interaction, pregnant with reconciliatory potential. To this point, all strands of forgiveness—*forgiveness as release, transcendence*, and the first aspect of *forgiveness as goodwill* (*desiring* goodwill)—can, and often do, exist without verbal or behavioral expression to the offender. Indeed, for individuals who have suffered deep trauma, these efforts are truly magnanimous. Yet, while they may not require interpersonal expression, this final aspect of *forgiveness as goodwill* does.[103]

After extending goodwill, or even after transcending ill will, the forgiver may decide to release, or sever, the relationship and move on, having nothing else to do with the one who harmed him or her.[104] While forgiveness may lead to reconciliation, as explained above, it does not require it. As will be discussed below, sometimes the best, or only, choice is to release the relationship. Not all relationships can be reconciled. To forgive and then release the relationship, forgoing reconciliation pursuits, is to choose not to expect from the offender what he or she might rightfully owe—i.e., amends, reparations, remorse, etc. They are released, though not prohibited, from the responsibility to atone for their actions. Though they might (and should) still seek atonement, it is not required, since any maintenance or pursuit of relationship has ended. If, however, the forgiver hopes to renew or build an ongoing relationship with the one who caused the harm, the next strand becomes necessary.[105]

103. Volf rightly observes that wrongdoing and injustice are social affairs, and thus, for him, forgiveness is "insufficient" if confined only to "someone's mind and heart. . . . A person whom I've wronged doesn't just forgive; she forgives *me*. Wrongdoers, and not just those who are wronged, are always involved in forgiveness." Volf, *Free of Charge*, 181, emphasis original. If by his last sentence, Volf is suggesting that *any* exercise in forgiveness is insufficient without outward expression, he is too simplistic, if not harsh. A monolithic notion of forgiveness may indeed require personal interaction as a component, but acknowledging forgiveness's multi-stranded nature liberates forgiveness from needless rigidity.

104. As the Tutus write: "You might think you are not in a relationship with the stranger who assaulted you or the person in prison who killed your loved one, or the cheating spouse you divorced so many years ago, but a relationship is created and maintained by the very act of harm that stands between you." Tutu and Tutu, *Book of Forgiving*, 145.

105. For more on renewing or releasing a relationship, see ibid., 143–55.

Forgiveness as Absolution

In his final strand, Liechty discusses *forgiveness as absolution*. This strand essentially erases any relevance of the wrongdoing within the context of an *ongoing relationship* between the forgiver and forgiven. Life proceeds—to the fullest extent possible—as if the harm never existed; in Volf's terms, we release them from the reality of "once an offender, always an offender."[106] It is akin to claiming the wrong is "as if not."[107] Thus, absolution is rarely realized, especially in the context of deep trauma, either being psychologically impossible or unnecessary, as it should assume two realities: the practice of *forgiveness as goodwill* and the acceptance of forgiveness by the wrongdoer.

The extension of goodwill in the previous strand creates the potential for relationship that can lead to absolution. For absolution to genuinely and sustainably occur, though, the forgiven must accept the forgiveness extended and make amends. Absolution accompanies contrition. Thus, absolution is a social exercise, done for the sake of the wrongdoer and the relationship between the conflicting parties. As far as the forgiver is concerned, she or he has already overcome ill will and extended goodwill. The forgiver does not need absolution; the offender does. Thus, from the other- or relationship-oriented purpose of absolution, it follows that *forgiveness as absolution* exists only in the context of reconciliatory pursuits, and thus requires repentance. In short, *forgiveness as absolution* is conditional.

Conditional vs. Unconditional Forgiveness

Much tension surrounds arguments for and against unconditional forgiveness—i.e., not requiring offender repentance. In what follows, repentance can be understood as an intentional effort by an individual to change his or her thoughts and actions, a process germinating from and including acknowledgment, remorse, genuine apology,[108] willingness to make repa-

---

106. Volf, *Free of Charge*, 175.

107. Palestinian priest Naim Ateek writes that this is "genuine forgiveness," when the "slate has been wiped clean . . . [and] the debt has been cancelled." Ateek, *Palestinian Christian Cry for Reconciliation*, 185. He would claim that such a gift must always be unconditional, for thus it comes from God and thus it must be distributed among humanity.

108. For a helpful explanation of "genuine apology," see Gobodo-Madikizela, *Human Being Died*, 98; Tutu and Tutu, *Book of Forgiving*, 178–80. For a thorough examination of the controversies surrounding apology and reparation—covering such case studies as slavery, South Africa, and the Nazi Holocaust—see Brooks, ed., *When Sorry Isn't Enough*.

rations, and a conviction not to repeat the wrong. Repentance entails the turning from the current path onto a new one, one that is believed to be safer and healthier for both self and others.

The initial strands of forgiveness require nothing from the offender; their existence entirely depends on the willingness and capabilities of the one hurt. Not so with *forgiveness as absolution*, however. Here, the wrong-doer must also participate in the dynamics of forgiveness by acknowledging the harm and injustice committed, expressing remorse, demonstrating this remorse through pledges and acts of repentance, and making—or at least being willing to make—reparations. When this occurs, *forgiveness as absolution* becomes possible. Without offender contrition, however, this strand falls appropriately under Dietrich Bonhoeffer's notion of "cheap grace . . . [that is] the preaching of forgiveness without requiring repentance . . . [or] absolution without personal confession."[109] Such grace grants solace without expecting constructive behavioral modifications.

The danger of such unqualified pardons is recognized by many scholars.[110] Others, though, promote a forgiveness that requires nothing from the offender.[111] Here again, confining forgiveness to a monolithic concept

109. Bonhoeffer, *Cost of Discipleship*, 43–45. Though he explores this term in a theological context, it can be sufficiently transferred to interhuman affairs. For a helpful analysis of this aspect of Bonhoeffer's writing, see Jones, *Embodying Forgiveness*, 9–23.

110. For example, see Schimmel, *Wounds Not Healed by Time*, 7; Murphy, *Getting Even*, 36; Griswold, *Forgiveness*, 62–72.

111. In the context of political forgiveness, the South African Truth and Reconciliation Commission did not set remorse and repentance as conditions for receiving amnesty, though full public confession was certainly required. See Tutu, *No Future Without Forgiveness*, 48. Enright claims that repentance is not a prerequisite to forgiveness, but does write that forgiveness may be offered "in the hopes that the offender will offer an apology after receiving forgiveness." See Enright, *Forgiveness Is a Choice*, 190. Garrard and McNaughton suggest that unconditional forgiveness is an act of "human solidarity" with people at their worst. Garrard and McNaughton, *Forgiveness*, 110ff; Garrard and McNaughton, "Conditional Unconditional Forgiveness," in Fricke, ed., *Ethics of Forgiveness*, 97–106. This notion of human solidarity is similar to the South African notion of *ubuntu* referenced in Tutu, *No Future Without Forgiveness*, 34–35; Tutu and Tutu, *Book of Forgiving*, 125–27. See also Derrida, *On Cosmopolitanism and Forgiveness*, 34ff. Often promotions of unconditional forgiveness contain a Christian underpinning, claiming that God's forgiveness for humanity is a free gift "conditioned by absolutely nothing on our part," and human forgiveness should mirror this reality. See Volf, *Free of Charge*, 179; Ateek, *Palestinian Christian Cry for Reconciliation*, 186. Frequently, biblical texts referenced in support of such a view include Jesus' request from the cross, "Forgive them for they know not what they do," the parable of the Prodigal Son, and the Lord's Prayer. For more on this, see Kraybill et al., *Amish Grace*, 88–98; Murphy, *Getting Even*, 34–36;

forces an unnecessary acceptance of an either/or approach to conditional versus unconditional forgiveness. The multi-stranded understanding I am exploring, however, does not require that the process of forgiveness be relegated to either category. I would argue that both conditional and unconditional approaches to forgiveness are valid. Some definitions of forgiveness understand forgiveness to include interactions that may lead toward reconciliation and therefore appropriately advocate a conditional form of forgiveness, for reconciliation is impossible without the one who committed the harm taking responsibility for his or her actions.[112] Other definitions comprise only the first two or three strands and thus promote forgiveness as unconditional.

FORGIVENESS AND LIBERATION

In the initial three strands—*forgiveness as release, transcendence,* and *goodwill*—forgiveness should in fact be understood as an unconditional albeit risky pursuit. With Yoder, I promote this unconditional forgiveness, if only for victim empowerment and liberation: "If we link our conditions for forgiving to the response of those who hurt us, we stay forever in their power."[113] Desmond and Mpho Tutu echo this:

> The problem is that the strings we attach to the gift of forgiveness become the chains that bind us to the person that harmed us. Those are chains to which the perpetrator holds the key. . . . We continue to be that person's victim.[114]

Requiring conditional forgiveness in the first three strands essentially locks victims to the identity of "victim," remaining emotionally and psychologically hostage to those who have harmed them. Thus, *if only* so victims/survivors can take their healing into their own hands, the initial strands of forgiveness must be unconditional, beginning on their terms and at their pace.[115]

Holloway, *On Forgiveness*, 69–70, 79–80; Vanier, *Becoming Human*, 154; Garrard and McNaughton, *Forgiveness*, 14.

112. Tutu and Tutu, *Book of Forgiving*, 173.

113. Yoder, *Little Book of Trauma Healing*, 62.

114. Tutu and Tutu, *Book of Forgiving*, 20–21. See also Blackard, *Restoring Peace*, 138.

115. This is the argument Auschwitz survivor Eva Kor gives for forgiving Dr. Mengele and all Nazis: To require the prerequisite of remorse or repentance potentially makes victims *remain* victims forever. See *Forgiving Dr. Mengele*.

Certainly regarding the first three strands, forgiveness has social, emotional, and psychological benefits, rejecting the spiral of violence and offering freedom from resentment. Vanier writes that "the Greek word for forgiveness is *asphesis*, which means to liberate. . . . It is used when the prison door is opened and the prisoner can go free," and indeed, forgiveness is, in many ways, about liberation. The Tutus, for example, write of Ben, who struggled for years to forgive his abusive father—a man who beat and tortured him—until "eventually I realised that I was carrying him with me everywhere I went." When Ben finally forgave, his father did not transform into a kinder person. Ben learned that expecting this from his father was making Ben "a victim to him all over again." As Ben concluded, "Forgiveness did not save him or let him off the hook. It saved me."[116]

Holloway argues that forgiveness allows both harmer and harmed to reclaim a future denied them by the violation, asserting that an "inability to forgive may have the tragic effect of binding [the victims] to the past and condemning them to a life-sentence of bitterness."[117] For those in Alcoholics Anonymous:

> It is plain that a life which includes deep resentment leads only to futility and unhappiness. To the precise extent that we permit these, do we squander the hours that might have been worth while [sic].[118]

Not only is living in unforgiveness robbing oneself of potential happiness, it is a form of mental and emotional imprisonment. Many of the people in the stories to come have experienced both literal and metaphorical imprisonment. Forgiveness has offered them at least one form of freedom, allowing the future to be "unshackled from [the] past."[119]

Cynthia Vaughn experienced this liberation after unexpectedly forgiving her adoptive father Don at Riverbend's "death row" in June 2012. When she spoke her forgiveness across the glass partition, it "felt like twenty-eight years of baggage just went flying off."

> I did not understand what it meant at that time, but saying those words opened this gate to a whole new world for me. I had been

---

116. Vanier, *Becoming Human*, 134; quoted in Tutu and Tutu, *Book of Forgiving*, 131–32.

117. Holloway, *On Forgiveness*, 15–37, 55.

118. *Alcoholics Anonymous*, 66.

119. Tutu and Tutu, *Book of Forgiving*, 21.

stuck inside this little fence of, "Oh, my mom's a murder victim, and I had a bad childhood, and I hate everybody, and everybody's mean to me, and I hate him." [But] when I said that [I forgave him], it felt like the gate opened up and this whole world, this whole life was out there for me.[120]

Forgiveness freed Cynthia from a life of reflexive judgments to a life of empathy and understanding, allowing her to offer help to those in need instead of dismissing them as not "her problem." Cynthia even experienced forgiveness liberating her senses. When she left her meeting with Don, she exited alongside the chaplain and felt "overwhelmed" by the sounds of birds singing outside, something she had not heard when entering the prison unit just ninety minutes earlier. When she exclaimed to the chaplain in disbelief at the loudness of their chirping, the chaplain responded, "Maybe now you are just hearing them for the first time." This liberation cannot be attached to expectations from one's offender; it is the gift forgivers give themselves.

FORGIVENESS AND REPENTANCE

Moving toward absolving wrongs in an ongoing relationship, however, forgiveness becomes conditional.[121] Nigel Biggar promotes "two moments" of forgiveness, which he names as "compassion" and "absolution." The first, relating to the first three strands discussed herein, is unconditional; the second, relating to the final two strands, is conditional. In this second moment, the victim addresses the perpetrator by saying that their future "will

---

120. Cynthia Vaughn, personal interview.

121. If fully absolving a wrong was unconditional—again, in the context of continuing relationships—*forgiveness as absolution* may risk more harm than good, as it may give the unrepentant offender the sense of untouchability, wielding damaging power without consequences. As Pumla Gobodo-Madikizela writes: "It may be that perpetrators, by receiving the forgiveness they want, also regain some of the control they are used to, particularly control over the victim. In other words, forgiveness may indirectly bestow power back on the perpetrator instead of empowering the victim and restoring some of the power she or he lost during the moment of trauma. It is possible that the encounter favors the perpetrator, who, because the victim is still struggling with asserting herself or himself and her or his rights, has the advantage as a person used to being in control and so is able to define the agenda even while asking forgiveness. The forgiveness then reawakens the victim's feelings of powerlessness instead of becoming a vehicle for shifting the power dynamic." Gobodo-Madikizela, *Human Being Died*, 100.

no longer be haunted" by the past event(s).[122] Thus, with this expression of forgiveness, the forgiver draws the forgiven into the conversation. The forgiver has offered forgiveness to the other, who must now decide whether to accept it as a gift, an invitation to repentance.[123] Accepting forgiveness should then be coupled with the commitment for renewal of action and intention. Volf argues that forgiveness and repentance are intricately connected in that repentance is a *consequence*, rather than condition, of forgiveness.[124] Though the wrongdoer may not have repented before, the extension of forgiveness (primarily *as goodwill*) to him or her—the gift of unconditional forgiveness—may provide the impetus for change.[125] As Holloway writes, "There is a kind of forgiveness that is so absolute and unconditional that it can create repentance [or softness] in the heart that has been hardened against change," as in the cases of Gary Ridgway and Jean Valjean.[126]

Gary Ridgway, known as Washington state's "Green River Killer" in the 1980s and '90s, was convicted of forty-nine murders and confessed to twice as many. In Helen Whitney's 2011 documentary *Forgiveness*, the opening scenes depict, among other images, Ridgway's trial. Witness after witness came forward with questions of dismay, confusion, anger, and vitriol. The accused sat still, face hardened and unsympathetic. But then a man with a thick white beard took the stand and gently extended forgiveness. Ridgway broke down weeping. One cannot be certain whether this extension of forgiveness sparked *repentance* in Ridgway, but it certainly broke through this rigid exterior and touched some human place within.

Perhaps the most well-known literary example of this is Jean Valjean in Victor Hugo's *Les Misérables*.[127] Valjean spends nineteen years doing

122. Biggar, "Forgiving Enemies in Ireland." For a helpful response to Biggar's essay, see Tombs, "The Offer of Forgiveness."

123. Holloway writes: "You cannot receive or make active use of forgiveness until you acknowledge that you need it. . . . I, as the victim, may already have forgiven you and moved on, but unless you can admit to the trespass the value of my forgiveness will lie there like an uncashed cheque." Holloway, *On Forgiveness*, 60–61.

124. Volf, *Free of Charge*, 183.

125. For two short parables illustrating this, see Rollins, "The Father's Approval" and "The Unrepentant Son," in *Orthodox Heretic*, 131–37, 144–51.

126. Holloway, *On Forgiveness*, 61–62.

127. As I am a lover of the musical, all *Les Misérables* references come from lyrics and adapted story line of the score written by Claude-Michel Schönberg, Alan Boubil, Jean-Marc Natel, and Herbert Kretzmer.

hard labor for theft and attempted escape. Upon his release, he stumbles into a harsh world of marginalization and want. After Valjean steals silver from a hospitable bishop, police drag him back to return the silver and face punishment, telling the bishop that Valjean claimed the silver was a gift. Rather than deride Valjean, the bishop claims Valjean is telling the truth, and adds that Valjean left "so early" he forgot the finest pieces, which the bishop then offers. The undeserved grace from the bishop causes Valjean deep remorse, compelling him to change. Throughout the rest of the story, the full effect of received forgiveness is evident as Valjean reroutes the direction of his life, becoming a respected man, who eventually raises an orphaned child and finally extends mercy and forgiveness to Javert, the inspector who has haunted and hunted him for decades.

As John Reed notes, "The forgiven must act likewise and be forgiving."[128] In Valjean's story, forgiveness exists in its purest and fullest form: an unearned gift that, once acknowledged and accepted, paved the way for repentance and generated a life of grace and forgivingness. Therefore, full forgiveness—i.e., given and received—multiplies. Forgiveness in this way may lead to repentance rather than vice versa, for if this unconditional gift is truly accepted, remorse and repentance will follow. Joanna North writes:

> While I reject the view that forgiveness requires repentance on the part of the wrongdoer, I certainly believe that the wrongdoer's *acceptance* of forgiveness . . . must involve his being sorry . . . and determining to reform.[129]

In other words, repentance need not always be a prerequisite *for* but can be a possible fruit *of* extending forgiveness.

Amidst the continuation of relationship, though, repentance is essential. This requires first that the harmer acknowledge the injustice. Volf goes so far as to argue that the only unforgivable harm is one unacknowledged and therefore not leading to repentance.[130] He argues rightly, as addressed earlier, that to forgive is to fully condemn an action. Likewise, "to repent is

---

128. Quoted in Minow, *Between Vengeance and Forgiveness*, 18. See also Jesus' parable of the Merciful Servant in Matthew 18:21–35.

129. North, "The 'Ideal' of Forgiveness," in Enright and North, eds., *Exploring Forgiveness*, 29, emphasis original.

130. The Tutus name acknowledgement of harm as the first necessary step toward receiving forgiveness. See Tutu and Tutu, *Book of Forgiving*, 171–75.

to accept the condemnation. Not to repent is to reject [it]."[131] Repentance, then, is an act that unites wrongdoer and wrong sufferer in "repudiating the degrading and insulting message" communicated in the harmful act.[132] In this union, reconciliation becomes possible and absolution far more likely.

Thus, because absolution is conditioned upon repentance and falls under the umbrella of reconciliatory pursuits, *forgiveness as absolution*, unlike the other strands, can be seen as an exchange. Some, like Hampton and Caputo, might protest naming any exercise of forgiveness as an exchange, arguing that forgiveness contingent on repentance is simply fair, just, and reasonable treatment in light of the wrongdoer's "change of heart."[133] If "forgiveness is to be a gift instead of an economic exchange," Caputo writes, it must be for the "sinner who is still sinning":

> We all agree that forgiveness is for sinners, but when we speak of forgiving sinners, we usually mean those who are not sinners anymore, former and reformed sinners, or sinners who at least *intend* to sin no more. But if by sinners you mean people who *are* sinners and are *still sinning*, with little or no intention of ceasing their sin, then it appears unreasonable or mad to forgive them, because they do not deserve it and common sense tells us we might not be doing them any favors in forgiving them when they have no intention of reform . . . [but] it is the sinner *qua* sinner, the sinner who is still sinning, whom we must forgive, who, in a certain sense, is the *only* one we *can* "forgive" if forgiveness is a gift and not an economic exchange.[134]

Caputo is quite right that if forgiveness is a gift, it must indeed be *given* and not traded. Thus, the first three strands of forgiveness must be considered unconditional, as they concern the wrong-sufferer's personal healing, empowerment, and gift to the wrongdoer (the latter regarding *forgiveness as goodwill*). *Forgiveness as absolution*, however, is the major transition toward reconciliation, offered in the context of creating or re-cultivating a relationship. It is the most radical form of forgiveness available—claiming the wrong is "as if not"—and therefore, out of respect for the interests of both

131. Volf, *Free of Charge*, 183. Volf says that for those who reject it, forgiveness may be "construed as a false accusation . . . despised . . . [or] deemed unbearable."

132. Murphy, *Getting Even*, 35.

133. Hampton, in Murphy and Hampton, eds., *Forgiveness and Mercy*, 41–42. And thus, in Hampton's mind, it is not really forgiveness.

134. Caputo, *Weakness of God*, 212.

forgiver and forgiven, needs a measure of significant amends to be made. In this manner, *forgiveness as absolution* is a moral exchange.[135]

On Courage and Virtue

Volf too would likely challenge whether this strand, if it is to be conditional, should be considered forgiveness at all. In his excellent essay "Forgiveness, Reconciliation and Justice," he argues that if one withholds forgiveness until wrongs have been fully redressed, then one does not thereupon act virtuously by forgiving, but rather would "*wrong* the original wrongdoer" if one did not forgive. He writes:

> [Forgiveness after reparation or repentance] means no more than the refusal to allow an adequately redressed wrongdoing to continue to qualify negatively one's relationship with the wrongdoer.[136]

In this way, *forgiveness as absolution* could be seen less as a virtuous or courageous undertaking—as might be said particularly of *forgiveness as goodwill*—and more as a morally appropriate response to contrition. While it is true that *forgiveness as absolution* could be suitably described as a morally appropriate response to an "adequately redressed wrong," I would assert that it is still an act of both great courage and notable virtue.

Since I have argued that *forgiveness as absolution* emerges within a process of some form of reconciliation, it must also exist within a context of trust-building.[137] Though the offender may have acknowledged the wrong-

135. Liechty writes that *forgiveness as absolution* is essentially recognizing that contrition and the preceding initiatory strands of forgiveness have already occurred. He rightly stresses that discussions of forgiveness become more problematic than already necessary when the multiple strands of forgiveness are conflated into a single definitive concept. Too often, this conflation tends toward *forgiveness as absolution*, thereupon setting forgiveness out of reach for most anyone who has suffered deep violations, especially when forgiveness is promoted as an unconditional gift. The multi-stranded approach described herein, and also by Liechty, maintains forgiveness's specialized and profound nature—particularly with regards to the full spectrum—but it also presents aspects of forgiveness that are tangible for even those who have suffered the worst trauma. Liechty, in Tombs and Liechty, eds., *Explorations in Reconciliation*, 63–64.

136. Volf, "Forgiveness, Reconciliation, and Justice," in Helmick and Petersen, eds., *Forgiveness and Reconciliation*, 40–41.

137. For more on the relation between trust and reconciliation, see Govier and Verwoerd, "Trust and the Problem of National Reconciliation." Though clearly their essay considers reconciliation on a macrocosmic scale, the relationship between trust and reconciliation described therein can be applied well to the interpersonal dimension.

doing, expressed remorse, and committed to repent, one may wonder whether the contrition is in fact genuine or perhaps a form of manipulation. In this regard, absolution is courageous as it chooses to trust that the forgiven's change is pure. Forgiveness, like reconciliation, is always risky; it is a leap of faith.[138] *Forgiveness as absolution* is also virtuous in that some violations of particular depth—e.g., the murder or rape of a loved one, rape or violence oneself suffered, or betrayal—are incapable of full restoration or reparation. Despite even the most arduous attempts to make things right, the loved one cannot be revived, the sexual violation erased, or the betrayal sanitized. Thus, absolution, even in the presence of amends, can be considered virtuous, as it acknowledges the permanence of the relational imbalance caused by the violation, but then erases its relevance to the relationship's progress. In short, though one may appropriately consider *forgiveness as absolution* to be exchanged for offender contrition, one should also consider it an act of courage and virtue.

Forgiveness as Reinterpretation

The fifth strand, *forgiveness as reinterpretation*, refers to the relationship between forgiveness, memory, and perception. As addressed at the chapter's opening, though forgiveness does not erase pain or the memories of harm and loss, over time it may soften the impact those events continue to have on one's emotional, spiritual, and physical well-being. Not remembering an offense could be "inappropriate and dangerous . . . [as] memory is a shield that protects from future harm." Through forgiveness, though, the memories "will simply fail to surface in one's consciousness." This is perhaps the natural consequence of *forgiveness as absolution*.[139] As one decides to let the wrongdoing no longer dictate the nature of the relationship, the decision becomes less an intentional choice and more a natural reality, as the memory—and thus the wrongdoing's continued existence—becomes less immediate and consuming.[140] The pain has not vanished; rather, it may

138. See Tutu and Tutu, *Book of Forgiving*, 37.

139. Volf, *Free of Charge*, 176; Volf, *End of Memory*, 145. Volf writes, "Though non-remembrance of wrongs suffered is a gift, it presupposes both that the one who suffered wrong has forgiven and that the wrongdoer has repented, received forgiveness, and mended his ways." Ibid., 143.

140. See Volf, *Free of Charge*, 173–77.

remain forever—particularly regarding deep violations—but these are all now reinterpreted, and forgiveness is given again.[141]

Forgiveness need not permanently expel all anger either. When the memory of the event is recalled, one may feel anger again. In defending the emotion of anger as the "executive power of human decency," Smedes argues that if anger does not accompany the suffering of a wrongdoing, then "you lose part of your humanity." What changes is that one "lose[s] the passion of malice. Malice goes while anger lingers on." Palestinian doctor Izzeldin Abuelaish argues similarly, speaking of when his daughters were killed by an Israeli mortar in Gaza:

> It is important to feel anger in the wake of events like this; anger that signals that you do not accept what has happened, that spurs you to make a difference. But you have to choose not to spiral into hate. All the desire for revenge and hatred does is drive away wisdom, increase sorrow, and prolong strife.[142]

Anger need not be destructive. That emotion provides us with vital information about ourselves: some boundary has been violated, some line crossed. Anger at injustice is necessary. A Franciscan prayer I learned as a teenager puts it this way: "Bless us with anger at injustice, oppression, and exploitation of people, so that we may work for justice, freedom and peace." If channeled constructively, anger can be transformative.[143]

When the wrongdoing occurs, it leaves a scar, sometimes visible and sometimes invisible. With the mark is a stinging pain, perhaps speakable, perhaps so visceral it cannot be expressed with words.[144] The pain produces bitterness, anger, hatred, and confusion. For a time, the memory rules the mind, potentially consuming both consciousness and unconsciousness. With memory, pain; and with pain, vindictiveness. *Forgiveness as reinterpretation* describes a change in the way one views, verbalizes, engages,

141. In the film *Forgiving Dr. Mengele*, Eva Kor says, "Forgiveness . . . means that whatever was done to me, it's no longer causing me such pain that I cannot be the person I want to be." Note that she qualifies the pain with "such." The pain is not necessarily extinct, but rather is not inhibiting personal growth and recovery.

142. Smedes, *Forgive and Forget*, 108–9; Abuelaish, *I Shall Not Hate*, 196.

143. See McRay, *Letters from "Apartheid Street,"* 109.

144. John Paul and Angela Lederach speak of violations that exist at the bone level, the impact of which cannot be clearly articulated because it did not occur at the level of rationality and cognitive comprehension. These violations must be articulated through some other medium than normal speech. See Lederach and Lederach, *When Blood and Bones Cry Out*, esp. 180–84.

and perhaps even feels the pain of the event: one re-members the memory, putting it together differently than before. As the event is reframed, the pain may become less debilitating, and the offender reinterpreted.[145] With marital infidelity, for example, the betrayed spouse—through a long and difficult process—may come to forgive the other, eventually being able to absolve the wrong. The betrayed spouse may then fall asleep and awake next to his or her betrayer without constantly, or even often, thinking of the betrayal. Through forgiveness the wronged partner may be able to see the betrayer with Smedes's "magic eyes," reinterpreting him or her as a broken person in need of love rather than a heartless and unfeeling traitor. In short, *forgiveness as reinterpretation* is about telling a new story.[146]

Here, the metaphor of a palimpsest proves insightful.[147] A palimpsest is a parchment where the text has been removed—perhaps scraped or washed off—so that one can inscribe new text. Yet, though the text has been removed, the *indentation* remains. The pressure of the writing instrument left an indelible mark. The original text can be erased and new text written, but the imprint of the original remains and cannot be eliminated. This is *forgiveness as reinterpretation*. The indentation of the memory itself and the corresponding pain remain, but the resulting story is reimagined. *Forgiveness as reinterpretation* writes a new story over the imprint of the old.[148]

After Jean Valjean accepted the grace and forgiveness offered by the bishop, he decides to leave behind the old self-narrative and script something new: "I'll escape now from that world/ From the world of Jean Valjean/ Jean Valjean is nothing now/ Another story must begin." The same has happened for Cynthia Vaughn. After she forgave Don that June day on Riverbend's "death row," she began writing a new story about herself:

145. See Smedes, *Forgive and Forget*, xviii. For a difficult, compelling story of forgiveness in such a context, see Whitney, "Deb Lyman and David Long," in *Forgiveness*, 25–35.

146. Desmond and Mpho Tutu use this same expression, writing that as we recognize and accept the common humanity and vulnerability we share with our perpetrators, which they argue is the bedrock of forgiveness, "we can write a new story . . . [in which] we are able to learn and grow from what has happened to us." Tutu and Tutu, *Book of Forgiving*, 53.

147. This metaphor emerged from a personal conversation with my brother Jonathan McRay, who introduced it for consideration.

148. Lederach and Lederach write: "The retrospective telling and retelling of the event or events, a creative act that simultaneously links perception, memory and inventiveness—for none of us can re-create past events without some dose of storytelling creativity—provides opportunity to reframe, that is to rename the experience." Lederach and Lederach, *When Blood and Bones Cry Out*, 124.

Before that day, I cried each night I was alone without my kids. I wanted my mother. I wanted [Don] to die. I wanted it all to go away. But now? I share chicken tenders and fries with the best roommate on earth. We laugh and watch movies. We talk about our boyfriends and our lives and how ironic it is that we live together. I love her. I go on vacations with friends from church. I never did that before because I didn't have many friends, and they *certainly* weren't from church! I laugh on the phone with this crazy friend of mine who always makes me giggle. . . . My favorite part of my life? I actually am *there* when my kids are at my house. My oldest daughter comes to me with her teenager issues and I can actually help. My son asks me about the mind of his sixteen-year-old girlfriend and her latest emotional drama—and I help. My oldest daughter plays DJ as I cook and my little one giggles making Vine videos. At night, she and I snuggle; we giggle even more. I love my life now.[149]

Cynthia's primary identity is no longer "murder victim's daughter." She no longer tells herself what she cannot do, excusing herself by virtue of her trauma. She no longer tells herself and others the story of victimhood and injustice, even though those remain true aspects of her experience. Instead, she is rewriting her story to one in which she is not a character to be pitied but rather to be celebrated; one in which she does not remain a victim but becomes a victor; one in which she has something to offer, not just something to take; and one in which she will not allow her children to lose *their* mother even though she lost hers. Forgiveness allowed her to write new words over the indentation of the old.

Taking Stock

Before continuing, retracing the map may prove helpful. In *forgiveness as release*, the wrong-sufferer lets go of legitimate claims and desires for "getting even"; *forgiveness as transcendence* involves overcoming ill will toward the offender, and *forgiveness as goodwill* entails desiring, cultivating, and extending benevolence toward the other; in *forgiveness as absolution*, the forgiver pronounces that the violation is "as if not" in the context of an ongoing relationship, whereby one may discover the wrongdoing's immediacy and consuming nature begin to fade after fully engaging the harm

149. Taken from her live telling of this story at Tenx9 Nashville on March 23, 2015: http://tenx9nashville.com/2015/03/25/cynthia-vaughn-confined/.

and cultivating its memory. *Forgiveness as reinterpretation*, then, reframes the event, the person who committed it, the pain caused by it, and one's own identity, refusing that those involved stay permanently confined to the roles originally cast.

In short, *forgiveness as reinterpretation* encompasses a full understanding of the multi-stranded nature of forgiveness. It, in a sense, summarizes all other strands. Forgiveness is the attempt to reinterpret the past, the present, and the future—to reimagine ourselves, the other, and our stories. Forgiveness prevents the story written by pain and violation from becoming the final words; instead, it re-visions life and its characters in the context of a new story. Granting mercy, pursuing empathy, overcoming hatred, extending goodwill, and absolving are all essential to this reinterpretation: they each orient toward and are encompassed by it.

It is regarding this difficult journey that the following stories of prisoners speak. The men and women presented below long to break out of the character roles they chose and that were chosen for them years ago, the ones society has determined they will forever play. They yearn for a forgiveness accompanied by renewed and redemptive imagination. Essentially, they seek the ultimate goal of forgiveness: to give victims and perpetrators the opportunity to reinterpret the irreversibility and unpredictability of life, and thereby reimagine their futures—separate or together—outside the imprisonment of perpetual victimization or condemnation.

On These Prison Narratives

IN THE FOLLOWING CHAPTERS, I present the stories and perspectives of seven men at RMSI and seven women at the TPW in Nashville, Tennessee.[1] Between May 2013 and December 2014, I spoke with each individual about the project, explaining in detail what I was doing and why I was doing it. Since I was not permitted to bring in a recording device, I gathered these stories either through written correspondence or careful note-taking. In the cases of note-taking, I read aloud the notes at the end of our conversation, checking for accuracy and giving an opportunity for alterations. Upon completion of the following stories, I distributed each back to the respective individual for final approval. Some made revisions; some did not, but nothing is printed in these stories without the written consent of that person. They have each read carefully and approved the final versions.

These stories are solely the accounts given by the individuals at RMSI and TPW. The events recorded here are as these fourteen women and men remember and wish to tell them. I did not cross-reference the stories with the victims or family members. Thus, only the prisoners' names are truthful, unless otherwise indicated; all others have been changed—even in quotations—since I did not receive permission to use their real names. In these stories, I aimed to keep my voice minimal, simply offering transitions and editing. My task in this section was to report the stories without analysis or interpretation.

Because forgiveness requires humanizing one's perceptions of the other, the stories below are detailed, an approach aimed at communicating the messiness of human life. The descriptiveness of the stories intends to cause the reader some discomfort as the instinctive anger felt when first encountering the offenses confronts the obvious complexity of these broken

1. Of these seven men, only one remains at Riverbend. Five were transferred to various TDOC facilities across the state and one was released.

pasts. This discomfort is commonly felt when people try to reinterpret the other. But telling the stories of what has happened, though difficult and uncomfortable—for both the teller and hearer—can be healing. Many of these men and women expressed their gratitude for the opportunity to tell their stories, saying that speaking of and writing their stories gave meaning, clarity, and understanding to their experiences. Some said thinking carefully about forgiveness in the context of their lives helped them see how much they need to receive forgiveness and how much they need to give it. One of women decided to reconnect with family she had not spoken to in more than a decade.

In short, these stories reflect experiences of deep pain and the journeys to reconstruct themselves and the world around them.

2

TONYA CARLETON

Age: 38
Current Time Imprisoned: 12 years

"You asked 'why' not 'what' questions. There is always more to being incarcerated than the 'what happened.' The process began years before."

TONYA MOVES WITH AN energy and smile that seems out of place for the narrative she tells. With each new sentence of her story, my bewilderment grew as to how someone finds such apparent peace after a life filled with poignant pain and terrible loss. For Tonya, though, this is the power of forgiveness.[1]

> I was raised in a highly dysfunctional home with a twin brother who was sick a lot and two younger sisters. Our parents' own struggles and addictions in their lives led to physical and emotional abuse. I grew up not knowing how to love or be loved—that's not to say I wasn't loved; they just did not know how to show it. Unfortunately, as a kid I did not understand that, so I became emotionally distant from my parents. What I did receive from them is the idea that it was up to me to take care of and protect my siblings to no end,

1. "Tonya Carleton" is a pseudonym chosen by the subject.

taught to me as I overcompensated for the neglect in our lives. I learned to hate my parents, but not because of what they did to me but rather because of what they did to my [siblings]. For every tear they cried, I hated my parents even more. For every hurt they experienced, I wanted my parents to hurt even more. I hated them for the situations they placed us in. When I was between the ages of eight and eleven, I spent an hour propositioning myself to a man who was preying on my sisters. I was raped that night. I do not ever remember blaming him. Instead, I blamed my [parents]. Again, it was up to me to take care of my sisters because they had better things to do. My hatred for them grew [as] my anger turned into rage. For as long as I could remember, I was fighting at school, often because someone was doing something to my sisters that I didn't believe was appropriate.

At seventeen, Tonya's sixteen-year-old sister Amanda "became involved" with a boy Tonya's age. To Tonya, both then and now, he was a "complete jerk." The night her sister got pregnant, Tonya could not celebrate. Instead, she ambushed Amanda's boyfriend. Over the next nine years, this became routine.

Every occasion I found him away from the children, I would attack him. I even hit him with my car the day my sister was giving birth to his son. For those nine years, he came and went in her life at his leisure. He stayed long enough to tear apart her home and then was on his way again, [even] leaving them homeless at one point. He seemed to love to beat on her, burn her, and abuse her in every way imaginable. And I loved hating him for it.

His abuse was not just for her, though; the children suffered too. More than once, Tonya found her sister's children "bathed, fed, and locked in a bedroom for the night, long before dark" so he could not hurt them when he came home.

She tried to leave several times, but he would find her, and she would have to go back. The police were called numerous times by my mom, their children, or the neighbors. Unfortunately, [the police] found it unreasonable to break up such a "happy home." As strong as my hatred for him was, I was just as angry at the system—the lack of protection, care, and the inexcusable [display] of "justice." The last time the police were called on them for fighting, I was there, and their eight-year-old made the call. [My sister's boyfriend] was attempting to leave; she was holding their son from the waist down, and he was pulling the top half. His number one threat was always taking the boy. When the policed arrived, he got on his knees, begging my sister to let him stay, laced with love-you's and apologies . . . I wanted to kick him in the face. She defended him to the police and asked him to stay. Despite what they witnessed, the police walked away: dumb, ignorant, lazy, blind, or just not caring—who knew but them? I approached two of them, yelling and demanding to know what it would take to get them to do something. They had no answer, no comfort for what the children were feeling. They had nothing whatsoever to offer any of us. The following week I watched my sister as she hugged and kissed each of her children for the last time.

One night, Amanda, her boyfriend, and their kids unexpectedly came by Tonya's house. Amanda's "blotchy" face and red eyes revealed her emotional anguish. Marks covered her neck. Soon after arrival, Amanda picked up Tonya's youngest and left for the next room, pretending she needed to change the child's diaper.

> She yelled that she could not find a diaper. When I went in, she was crying. She made me promise not to let the kids leave with them. She gave me all the money she had; he had taken everything else. I didn't ask her what happened; I did not have to. I did not ask her not to go with him. . . . There were no questions for me to ask, no advice for me to give, and no solution. There never was. I told [Amanda's boyfriend] I would keep the kids for them . . . since they had to go to the next town over . . . [and] I agreed to meet them when they got back.

After they left, Tonya drove to her mother's house to process her anxiety, but her mom was already in bed. "As always, she was fully dressed," Tonya remembered, "with her phone and keys in her pocket 'waiting to hear bad news about your sister.' I watched her sleep like that for years."

Later that night, everyone met at Amanda's house for a fireworks show. "There was this quiet understanding between me, him, and my sister," she explained. When the time came to leave, Tonya gathered the kids to say goodbye to their mother.

> I watched her pick up each and every one of those children. Hugging and kissing them goodbye, whispering sweet I-love-you's! It seemed to go in slow motion. She tried to hug me, but physical affection [has never been] a familiar part of my life . . . I jokingly pushed her away and teased her a bit. She told me she loved me, but I could not say it back. I did not know how.

Early the next morning—or rather closer to the night before—my niece was playing video games to fight her sleep. She began to talk about little things she found funny, things that only she would find funny this time of morning. She told me she had a doctor's appointment Monday, and this led to her asking a few questions about her visit. The questions developed into more of a comparison of what the doctor was going to do and what her father had done. . . . He had sexually abused her. I am not [actually] sure if she understood exactly what happened. I sat with her until she fell asleep.

Something snapped inside Tonya. The dam holding back the rivers of hatred inside her broke, and a flood of rage poured out. "I had one goal," she recounted. "I wanted nothing more than to make him hurt. [So] I took my hunting knife and ran to my sister's. I went into the house. I went straight to their room. I lifted his head and cut his throat."

They began to wrestle and control of the knife alternated between Tonya and Amanda's boyfriend. Amanda tried to break up the fight, but Tonya pushed her away.

I then saw the look on her face. I saw blood on her, and something happened in me. It was as if that was the first time I had seen her [that night]. Up until that point, it never crossed my mind that she was there.

My sister died in the hospital bed next to mine while asking for her babies. She died because of me, because of my rage. She died by the very hands that were supposed to protect her.

I could hear my mom and other sister wailing out from another room. Hours later, they were allowed to come in with my brother [in] exchange for my statement to the TBI [Tennessee Bureau of Investigation] for what I had done. I gave them what they wanted, minus my niece's story. I remember grabbing my mom and sister, telling them all "I'm so sorry!" over and over again. It was all I could say. They left without touching me or saying anything to comfort me in any way.

Almost a year later, I was sentenced to forty years to be served at the Tennessee Prison for Women: twenty years for Second Degree Murder, and twenty years for First Degree Attempted Murder (he lived). I did not even think about her being there. I was so blinded by my hatred toward him and all he symbolized in our lives. I killed her. Though I did not do it intentionally, I killed her. I [actually] may not have even done it at all; he could have—we will never know. Still, because of me, she is dead, and I am in prison.

Tonya explained that harm caused to another person disrupts relationships, and forgiveness is the process of making possible the "opportunity" to mend those relationships. But this mending is not just interpersonal: "This restoration in relationship will also be present in my relationship with myself through self-forgiveness and with God as I receive his forgiveness." She believes receiving forgiveness from her family would produce a "deeper level" of connection as they repair the relationship, and as that connection deepens, so too would her "sense of freedom from the punishing blame that I inflict on myself." But Tonya sees little benefit in receiving forgiveness from Amanda's boyfriend. "There is nothing to mend between us," she acknowledged. "There is nothing for either of us to offer the other in any way. I have no expectations, care, or concerns with regard to him forgiving me."

Despite the fact that Tonya did not intend to harm her sister that night, she recognizes that no one in her family "could have walked away . . . untouched" by Amanda's tragic death.

> I have shared with them all, including the children, that it is very much okay to be mad at me, and it's also okay to tell me so. I expressed to them my own self-anger [and] that yelling and screaming at me was also acceptable. I knew this process would lead them to a place of freedom, [even] if only a small bit, from their pain and anger. My oldest daughter is the only one who has taken me up on this offer. She was blunt, to the point of me "screwing up her life." [She would say,] "My mother is in prison; my aunt is dead; and I don't have a father." I was able to validate how she felt, apologize for my choices, and ask for forgiveness. It was healing and freeing to us both, and our relationship was restored a bit more.

Tonya then spoke at length about her own process of self-forgiveness and the resulting transformation and healing.

> [Both interpersonal] forgiveness and self-forgiveness have a foundational similarity in meaning [as they both] provide an emotional freedom from the bondage of anger, bitterness, and retribution. In addition to this, self-forgiveness has a complexity beyond forgiving others and receiving forgiveness from others. For me, this process includes surrendering, accepting, and having accountability.
>
> [Regarding surrender, I had to relinquish] a hope of what could be, of what should be had I not gone into that house . . . declaring that there is nothing I can do to change anything, succumbing to my emotions by allowing myself to really feel what was and is underneath the façade of who I believed I was as a failure

to my entire family, a monster in disguise. I had to surrender to a loss so devastating to us all, the loss of my sister and me, that it will forever be a part of our lives.

[Concerning acceptance, I must regard] my emotions as being valid and true, accepting that my current practice of self-inflicting torment was and is a danger to myself and my relationships. [And accountability involves] not only taking responsibility for what I did years ago, but also answering for what happened and how that affects tomorrow, not only for me but [for] my family. I am responsible for how I react with my emotions.

Self-forgiveness is a continual process simply because [our] minds and hearts fail to release it all. The memories are still there, the reminders of what was and what could be are constant. Self-forgiveness, for me, has become a daily walk [of] choosing not to do harm to myself emotionally or physically. I am not allowed to torment myself with an all-consuming hate and shame . . . I'm not allowed to wish for circumstances outside my control. Ultimately, self-forgiveness means I'm given an opportunity to take my sister's death, my life in prison, and all that transpires from these circumstances and [try] to achieve purpose in my life and others' so that it brings honor to us all.

Tonya continued to speak to the "daily decision" to forgive herself, having realized that self-forgiveness does not erase everything, "as if the anger, guilt, and shame just go away." Tonya said the reminders will always be there.

I'm reminded of the pain and struggle I cause my family every single day I wake up in prison. With every thought of them, every phone call, and every visit, the pain is there. It doesn't just go away . . . . So, it only makes sense that I'll continue to have moments of experiencing anger and self-guilt and will have to process through these emotions while again making the choice to walk in forgiveness. I can say that the shame and self-hatred no longer reside in me . . . [but] I'm not sure it's possible not to feel guilty considering the pain my family and I experience. . . . I think some would say I've not really forgiven if I have to continuously forgive. I completely disagree. My forgiveness did not equate to "my sister was killed, I went to prison, I forgave myself, and everyone lived happily ever after."

Tonya's process of self-forgiveness has been long and arduous, working to counter years of self-inflicted emotional torment. Often, she longed for death, but guilt restrained her.

I honestly believed death was too easy an avenue for me. My constant regrets of words unspoken and hugs unshared increased my guilt and shame. [My sister] died not knowing how much I loved her, [n]ever hearing me say those words, hugging her, or telling her how valuable she truly is. . . . I knew I deserved to live in [the] pain and misery of what I had done for the rest of eternity while I made sure I knew just what a piece of crap I really was. Every thought of my sister was an opportunity to beat myself down a little more. Every thought of my nieces and nephews was an opportunity to curse myself for breathing. Every thought of my mom, dad, brother, and especially my younger sister allowed me an opportunity to cut myself deeper. Every thought of my daughters was a constant reminder of my failure as a mother. . . . I believed they would all be better off without me. Sounds suicidal, but again, [suicide] was the easy way out; I was undeserving of death.

Instead, my anger and hate were aimed at all around me here. I would hit anything, sometimes anybody, within reach—for little reason. I would have verbal outrages toward people I didn't even know. I stayed in trouble: fighting; threatening, intimidating, and disrespecting staff; getting tattoos; sexual promiscuity; getting high (though before prison I had never been high). I had a complete disregard for myself and this place. I couldn't find any solace in the people here.

Tonya's only sense of comfort came from interactions with her family, but her unhealed trauma and anger began to push them away, one by one. According to Tonya, the family felt she quit on them. "But I didn't quit them," she clarified. "I quit me." Tonya's dad has not yet visited her, and her mother came because she "had to." The children, however, never let go. "When I think about it, they are stronger and more resilient than us all."

Tonya reconnected with Christianity and entered a program called Theotherapy, searching for direction and purpose. But Tonya's faith did not offer immediate salvation from her demons. "There was no euphoric process of finding God (as if God was the one lost), receiving forgiveness, forgiving others, forgiving myself, and then life was great. That might look good for the parole board . . . . [In actuality] that road tormented me even more." God just became another recipient of her anger, and she continued to punish herself until she was "suffocating [in an] all-consuming torment."

There is a saying of truth in Theotherapy that, "When the pain of staying the same becomes greater than the pain of change, you will begin the process of change." I believe that's what brought me to the door of wanting to forgive myself. I was beyond tired. I was beyond sick of living the way I was living. I knew I had more to offer my family, especially my daughters. Something completely shattered inside me . . . I was not living. I wasn't loving myself.

Over her years of Theotherapy, Tonya learned to grieve her many losses, coming to understand that the problem with anger was not the fact of its existence but rather the nature of its expression. She began to recognize what she could control and what she had to surrender. This grieving process, in Tonya's estimation, has made self-forgiveness possible.

There was one question that brought me to acceptance and accountability. [The facilitator] asked, "If your sister could say one thing to you, what do you think she would say?" I laughed. I actually laughed as I imagined her calling me a "stupid fool" for acting the way I've been acting and [how I've been] treating myself. I then cried as I thought of her forgiving me and telling me she loved me. I think that was an "ah ha!" moment. I began to forgive myself—[even] if only a little. I have continued this process for the past five years and expect it to be a daily walk. Some days are much easier than others, but I can say my relationships are at their peak . . . [and] I make it a point to love myself even on those bad days. [And] God and I worked out our love/hate and are on track.

I asked Tonya whether her family had expressly forgiven her and whether that forgiveness was necessary for her to forgive herself.

I do not believe self-forgiveness is dependent upon the receipt of forgiveness from my family. However, I think it would become easier for me to forgive myself if I knew I was forgiven. I have come to the realization that some may never come to a place of forgiving me or may never display or express that forgiveness to me. So for me to wait on that forgiveness to take place could have meant a lifetime of living in [the self-inflicted] pain and hate [I experienced] before I began my forgiveness journey. It's important for me to remember that my self-forgiveness is a choice I have made for my own good; otherwise it would be easy for me to return to my previous state of self-hatred. Without sounding self-centered, my forgiveness is for me; it's about my healing, though there will always be a hope of my family coming to that same place of freedom as they forgive me and [we restore] our relationships. I had to move forward in my forgiveness journey without receiving forgiveness from anyone. I've yet to know if I've been forgiven by any of my family except for my oldest daughter. Prior to [your] questions, I've not ever considered what their forgiveness would change in my life [though] I've often thought of what their forgiveness would bring to them. I do believe that our relationships' healing and growth are dependent on forgiveness. Without it, there is always some raw emotion separating us.

Tonya's journey through forgiveness has not only meant receiving forgiveness from others and forgiving herself; she has also had to forgive others: her parents, abusers, even Amanda "for her role in staying in the abusive relationship." Forgiving Amanda's boyfriend proved the most difficult.

I spent endless hours focusing my hate on him. I was so angry that he lived and my sister died. I believe it was completely unfair. I hated him even more because of that. It literally made me sick and violent [and] I would hit anyone or anything. I eventually came to a place of knowing this wasn't just going to go away and knew I had to forgive him. I went through the grieving process for all he has taken from my family. Eventually, and it took a long time, I chose to forgive him.... I had to come to a place of understanding, acceptance, and surrender [for] what I had done to him. I had to forgive myself and ask God to forgive me for the harm I inflicted on him. It was in that moment, when I actually hit my knees begging God for forgiveness, that I knew I had completely forgiven him.

This process is one that clarified that self-forgiveness and forgiveness extended to others is truly for me. I still have nothing to offer him, nor does he have anything to offer me in the respect of a relationship—not even cordiality.... He has done horrible, horrible things in my family's lives. [But] forgiveness freed me from that pain and hate that I held for him. I no longer want him to pay for what he did, at least not by my hands. I have given all desire for retribution over to God to handle. I'm completely free of him.

In conclusion, I wondered about the relevance of forgiveness regarding systems: Did Tonya feel the need to forgive the prison system, the justice system? Did incarceration hinder the forgiveness process or facilitate it? Tonya admitted that she still has "some work to do" to forgive the systems that have failed her and her family since her youth. She is immersed in such a system now, and its failures are new every morning. In Tonya's mind, incarceration has not helped her.

Prison—the physical building and all it represents: separation, warehousing, loss of family, friends, community, etc.—does nothing to encourage or support avenues of healing, forgiveness, or rehabilitation. [Yes] the system [sometimes] allows programs to be present within this prison, but volunteers [actually] make that happen. I don't believe it is allowed in order for the well-being of us "inmates," from the system's standpoint.

[Incarceration was not] the driving force of any beliefs or ideas I have about the possibility of forgiveness. It just so happens that I am incarcerated as this process takes place. I believe I would have eventually reached the need of forgiveness in my life and I would probably be further along in this journey if I was not in prison.

Prison is a continual emotional punishment and a constant reminder of my choices and the effect those choices have on my life and the lives of my family. This hinders the self-forgiveness process. I believe incarceration prevents me from being able to move forward. Instead, I have to make that forgiveness journey every day—sometimes more often—depending on [how much I] focus on the destruction to my relationships this institution encourages. Incarceration also makes it difficult for me to forgive the "systems" that failed me as a child, the "system" that failed to protect my sister, and the "system" that holds me captive. I find it extremely hard to forgive in this aspect while witnessing the on- slaught of injustices every day in here.

I do have one belief that incarceration has led me to in regards to the importance of forgiveness. Every day I witness pain, hurt, and injustices in the lives of the women here. Not only the injus- tices they face due to their incarceration, but also from offenses in their pasts. I hear their stories over and over again while facili- tating Theotherapy groups. I see their anger, their victimization, and their masks in their daily behaviors. I also know that had they reached a place of forgiveness for those that have harmed them or forgiven themselves for their choices and mistakes, many of their [judicial] convictions would not exist today.

I know that my life would have turned out a lot different if I had walked in forgiveness toward the man who raped me, for my mom and dad for the abuse I experienced as result of their negligence, and for myself for my own poor choices. I do not be- lieve I would be in prison today if I had healed from my childhood emotional trauma. I would not have been bound so tightly to my negative emotions nor would I have displayed such destructive behaviors in my life. I didn't come to prison because one day I got mad and tried to hurt someone and my sister was killed in the pro- cess. I'm in prison today because I grew up as a broken individual who was traumatized emotionally beginning at a young age and never healed from it. I was fueled by hate beginning at a young age and carried it through to adulthood.

The health Tonya experiences now, the peace she feels within herself, exists entirely in spite of the prison. For Tonya, the prison wants to hold her back, but she is determined to move forward. "I have chosen a journey of forgiveness and healing that will continue for the rest of my life," she closed. "It seems a long time, but when I consider the place that I was and where I am now, I know that it is a journey of progress."

Tonya's sentence expires in 2040. In July 2026, she can try for parole.

3

TONY VICK

Age: 53
Current Time Imprisoned: 18 years

"I knew I was gay since I was twelve. But the church said homosexuality was unforgivable."

TONY GREW UP IN a Christian family who seemed to have it all together externally: attending weekly church services, practicing charity and kindness toward those in need, etc.[1] Tony was "a good Christian boy," but Tony was also gay, and that presented a deep dilemma in the theological world of his upbringing. With a pastor constantly preaching condemnation of "those that did not believe like we did," Tony felt that going to church would surely destroy him. Homosexuality was considered one of the greatest "deathly pandemics" facing the world. He knew he was "infected," so to speak, but firmly believed God would "heal" him, praying ceaselessly for such a "miracle."

---

1. The following details of Tony's story come not only from my personal interview with him, but also from a series of unpublished autobiographical reflections on his life titled "Coming In and Coming Out".

At sixteen, Tony opened up to a pastor in a nearby community, confessing his attraction to other boys. After immediately asking whether Tony had been abused or had acted on his feelings, the pastor told him this same-sex attraction came from Satan, and if Tony indulged it, he would burn in hell's eternal fires. "He told me, 'Act straight and God will heal you,'" Tony said in his quick-paced but gentle Southern drawl. "But God didn't. I often wondered if it was because I didn't have enough faith."

Believing he could perhaps act his way into heterosexuality—thus supposedly pleasing God and avoiding eternal torment—Tony convincingly impersonated a straight man, compromising his identity for everyone, and eventually married Debra. For eight years, they lived together in Franklin, Tennessee—even having a son, Daniel—until Tony could not live his lie another day. He drowned Debra in the hot tub. But her death appeared accidental to detectives, and so Tony was not arrested.

"I thought God was giving me another chance at being straight." So Tony remarried, this time to Kelly, in continued hopes of "curing" himself of his identity "curse." But the cure never came, and so he killed Kelly too. After a year on the run, he was arrested and has now served eighteen years of his two concurrent life sentences, one for Kelly's death and one given retroactively for killing Debra.

When I sat with Tony, he spoke highly of Debra and Kelly, expressing deep remorse for killing "these wonderful women God placed on this earth." When I asked why he chose murder instead of divorce, he said he knew the truth about his homosexuality would bring them tremendous shame and grief. Looking me directly in the eyes, he said carefully:

> It was easier for me to kill my wives than to be honest and have them see me in the light of God's unforgiveness. Everything about me couldn't be forgiven: I was gay. I thought, "What in the hell does it matter what I do then?" I was taught in church that God forgave murder and other sins like that. But not being gay.

Tony said he knew Debra and Kelly would be in heaven. They were "good Christian women," and because of that, he could not bear for them to know his secret. "Untruth is what will kill people," he continued. "We can deal with truth when we get it out there, but lies are lethal."

Tony never made an attempt in our conversation to excuse his actions or pass off responsibility. He did not blame his family, environment, church, or theology: "My own cowardliness, selfishness, and greed enabled to me to do things I never thought possible."

I asked Tony how he would define forgiveness. He replied:

> Forgiveness is absolving transgressions. You have no further ill
> will toward the other person. I think forgiveness should be uncon-
> ditional. But it's not about forgetting. You can't forget.

Tony went on to tell me that he always gave forgiveness quite easily because
he desperately wanted it for himself. I asked him to describe his personal
process of self-forgiveness.

> For me to forgive myself, I had to accept who I was. I realized
> I didn't need forgiveness for being homosexual. I no longer feel
> judged by God. God made me this way. . . . Coming to terms with
> my context in prison was also a big step in forgiving myself.

In his early days of incarceration, Tony prayed constantly for God's forgiveness. The guilt was so overwhelming he felt even a single smile was
undeserved.

"I would have killed myself if it wasn't for my theology of hell. Hell was
very real to me, and it was *forever*. Forever." Through prayer, acceptance
of the permanent reality and legitimacy of his identity as a gay man, and
the discovery of a deep and genuine love, Tony said he has come to forgive
himself.

I asked if he felt it appropriate to ask for forgiveness from his victims'
families and if he had received any extension of forgiveness from them.

> I do believe requesting forgiveness is important. A few years after
> the event, I wrote a letter to the parents of my second wife, Kelly,
> expressing my remorse and asking for forgiveness. Sometime later
> I got a card in the mail. Nothing was written inside, but on the front
> of the card was the word *forgiven* . . . I felt good for them. I had
> already forgiven myself, so not much changed for me. But I *was*
> able to sleep better at night knowing they were in a better place.

I pushed back slightly at this point, introducing the varying perspectives regarding self-forgiveness without interpersonal forgiveness. Tony responded
with sensitivity but assuredness, "We can't rely on interpersonal forgiveness
to get right with God and ourselves. It's psychologically destructive. We
may have to wait forever in such cases." Twenty years after murdering his
son's mother, Tony has yet to be offered forgiveness by Daniel.

> It doesn't bother me too much that my son hasn't forgiven me. His
> forgiveness wouldn't change my life. But it would change his, and
> so I do wish he would for his own sake. . . . I still weep and feel

remorse when I think about what I've put those families through. That's good for me to feel. The sorrow is actually easier to deal with being here in prison. I know I deserve to be here. But I do have to remind myself that I'm forgiven by God and I've forgiven myself.

In closing the conversation, I asked Tony about the reality of living unforgiven by society.

Yeah, we are unforgivable to society. Society's perspective of unforgiveness makes it impossible for it to change this system. I do think prison as societal separation is necessary. There needs to be a place where some of us who are dangerous to society can go. But prison should be focused on reintegration.

He connected the pervasive unforgiveness of society to the high rate of recidivism. Referencing the section on most application forms inquiring into personal criminal history, Tony said:

There's always the box. That can really fuck up someone's psychology. And why limit such questions to prison? What degree of past behavior should become permanent accountability? Why wouldn't you talk to teachers to find out, "Did this person cheat? Were they tardy much?" When is the curiosity of the *probability* of someone succeeding advantageous to you? And why is this one-sided for felons?

He ended our time together by speaking of how his perspective has changed since arriving in prison.

Before I came here, I participated in society's unforgiveness. I would have advocated for the death penalty or life imprisonment for murderers. They had no value to me. But that's changed. When I got here, I realized that these are normal people with value. I started hearing stories and realized it's not as easy as we all like to think. There are more veins than just one. The men in here are not the product of the worst thing they ever did. . . . You know, we all try to take care of things we think are valuable. We recycle paper and plastic because we think they still have value. Yet we don't recycle human life—blood, flesh, and spirit. But we all have value.

4

CRYSTAL STURGILL

Age: 36
Current Time Imprisoned: 17 years

"The debt I owe cannot be paid by my eternal incarceration."

CRYSTAL DID NOT OFFER many details about her early childhood. When I asked her about her story, she began at the end of high school.[1]

> 1996 and 1997 were the most tumultuous years of my life. I was a senior in high school. I should have been feeling like I was invincible, [like] the world was my oyster; instead, I felt like the world was a cruel joke. At the age of seventeen, I had been abused verbally, physically, and sexually since I was four. My sister was turning thirteen in December of '96. This gave me more anxiety than words can describe. I was so worried she would be the next target of the monster in our home.

Overwhelmed with fear, Crystal "began self-medicating," turning to "pills, booze, weed," and other substances to numb the pain and escape the pressure. A new relationship brought a temporary reprieve from the sexual

---

1. For more on Crystal's story, see James, "Life Sentence."

abuse but no relief from her anxiety. "I didn't know what to do and I had no one to turn to," she told me. "After years of praying with no answer—first for deliverance and finally for death—God was at best an afterthought." Finally, in December of 1996, Crystal decided to act.

> The web of lies that supported my fragile existence came tearing down. I finally told someone how scared I was to go home, how afraid I was for my sister. I decided to kill myself, leaving behind a note telling how horrible my life was. I figured an eternity in hell was better than the hell I lived with now. The police came to my school. From somewhere deep within, I found myself pouring out the painful secrets of my abuse. I thought at last it would be over. My abuser confessed and was arrested. Life should have gotten better. Instead, I was going full-kilter off a cliff.
>
> My mother abandoned me [and] I went to live with my aunt. When I think about how hard the situation must have been for her to have inherited the absolute wreck that I was, I am awed by her love for me. [At the time] of course, my seventeen-year-old mind was too preoccupied by the rejection of my mother to realize what I had. I changed schools and lost most of my "old friends."
>
> After three months, I went to live with my grandmother. She had been my primary caregiver most of my life and I have never felt such unconditional love and support. I could have stayed there forever, except that my mother had bailed out my abuser and he was back in her home. Together they were dividing my family. Two sides emerged: those who believed me and those who didn't.
>
> My uncle was one of the latter. He was also a raging alcoholic. He lived with my grandmother and paid most of her bills. After a night of drinking, he and another uncle decided to confront me and force me to recant. . . . My grandmother eventually [told] both of them to leave her home. They did and I stayed, until she had the heat cut off the next week. She was afraid she wouldn't be able to pay the electric bill without my uncle. The guilt from that overwhelmed me. How could I let her suffer for loving me? Hadn't my miserable existence caused enough harm? So I packed and left. I stayed wherever I could, bouncing between places, trying to keep going to school. Somehow in my mind, I thought that if I just managed to make it through graduation, I would be okay.

In April 1997, Crystal could not find a haven. She "called number after number" and felt like she had "worn out [her] welcome everywhere." Finally, she was able to move in with her best friend Dean and a number of other kids, "some were from bad home situations and others were just there because it was a roof over their heads." Crystal soon felt relieved to learn that her uncle had moved back in with her grandmother and was again paying the bills.

After only three days in her new "crazy" house, one of her housemates invited her to join a road trip to New Orleans during Crystal's spring break.

> Not far into the trip, it became apparent that the car we were traveling in was never going to make the trip. We stopped at a fast food chain, and there was talk of stealing a car. I listened to this plan halfheartedly. These people were notoriously big talkers. I didn't believe for a minute that anyone in the group knew how to hot-wire a toaster, much less a car. In Virginia, we stopped at a closed car lot and one of them tried his skills—no luck. We kept driving, and the car we were in seemed to be okay.
>
> In Tennessee, we stopped . . . at a rest area . . . and stretched our legs. Dean and I got something to drink. I saw our group talking with some people I didn't know, but I didn't pay much attention to them. Dean and I went back to the car and were talking and smoking, and Jeff came over to us. He said they were going to go talk to these people awhile. Dean and I shrugged and watched them walk out of sight over a small hill. A while later Jeff again came back to the car, this time with John in tow. The two of them said they were going to take a ride with the people and probably steal their van. They got two guns from the car and left again.
>
> I no more thought they were going to steal the van than I thought they knew how to hot-wire. A few minutes later, things got a bit more real as the family and our group came back over the hill and got into the van. They told us to follow them. I asked Dean what was going on, and he seemed as confused as I was. He kept telling me they weren't really going to do anything. We followed them, and shortly after, the family lay dying.
>
> I didn't know what to do; I have never been more scared in my life. Dean kept trying to tell me that it was going to be okay. [But] nothing was going to be okay after that. I was told to run, so I did. We ran all the way to Mexico before we were finally arrested.

Crystal and her five friends all received three consecutive life sentences without parole, plus twenty-five years. Since the day of that family's terrible death, Crystal has "struggled with forgiveness on just about every level" as she realized she not only had to receive forgiveness but to offer it as well: "I had to forgive my mother, my abuser, my family who turned their backs on me. I had to forgive myself, and even the other perpetrators of my crime."

Forgiveness for Crystal has been a daily journey, a choice she must remake each morning.

> Forgiveness is not instant; it is something that for me doesn't happen just one time. Almost every day I struggle to forgive. That doesn't mean that I have forgotten what was done. It simply means that I choose not to live in the pain and the bitterness of the past. I suffer from PTSD; [some] days . . . I struggle especially. Sometimes I am so wrapped up in the pain and hurt that I can't find forgiveness. The truth is it never really comes from me. I have to pray and hope God will change my heart and my mind. I pray for healing, for myself and for everyone involved. Some days I feel healed, others I am as raw as I was on the day it happened. I have studied about reconciliation, and I am reconciled to my family. This came at great cost. I didn't speak to my uncles for years. It took the death of my grandmother to change our relationship. My alcoholic uncle even got saved and hasn't had a drink now for several years. His life is changed, and I see God in him.
>
> I have often thought of what I would say to those I harmed, to the family who I didn't help, to the child who survived and is now an adult. "I'm sorry" isn't enough. I don't know if I'll ever be contacted by the survivor, but if that happens, I will be open. [But] the debt I owe cannot be paid by my eternal incarceration. I hope that by making something of my life, even where I am, I give those who lost their [lives] honor. I want to live in a way that remembers them *and* gives glory to God for lifting me out of the nightmare I knew before. I am not always sure how to do that, but I pray for guidance. I try to forgive myself for what happened that day; sometimes I can and others I cannot.

Crystal clings to a deep faith in God and the divine forgiveness she professes to have received.

> Until the day when I can come face-to-face with the victims of my crime and be truly reconciled in the love of Christ, my story is not complete. When that day comes, my prayers for healing will finally be answered and the struggle will be over. While I wait, I will continue to pray and have faith that I will get through each day as he [God] sees fit.

5

CHRIS CALDWELL

Age: 40
Current Time Imprisoned: 19 years

"Forgiveness means understanding without requiring the person
to understand themselves."

SITTING ON A WOODEN chapel pew, Chris spoke of life in Goodlettsville, Tennessee.[1] He grew up in a well-respected and financially stable family. His mother worked in cosmetology and his father in the packing plants. But family life was difficult. Chris told me they had no concept of constructive communication.

> My dad was a secret drug addict. My parents only interacted with me when punishing me. I constantly heard what I'm *"supposed to do"* without being instructed on how to do it! They just yelled and belittled: "What's wrong with you, Chris?"

Around fourteen, he began spiraling out of control.

> I started smoking weed during the eighth grade due to peer pressure. I started smoking with adults, even my uncle. Just wanted

1. The name Chris Caldwell is a pseudonym, used at his request.

to experiment, you know. But I got hooked after only a couple of uses. I never really made the emotional transition to high school. I just shifted to the party scene. I was into cocaine and all over drugs. I got addicted to partying. I found sexuality at a young age when I had sex at fourteen. My world consisted of just partying and sex. Education made no sense, so I just skipped school. My lifestyle wreaked havoc in the family. My parents would punish me, and then revoke it, punish, then revoke—like a roller coaster. I think they finally just gave up. They'd cuss me out during commercial breaks while watching TV, and then ignore me when the show came back on.

Chris continued to rebel, staying out all night, sometimes even three to four days at a time.

I just thought I'd "face the trouble tomorrow." At eighteen, I was still acting like fourteen. I was stealing little things to fund drugs. I had dropped out of school at sixteen and begun convincing myself that my parents wouldn't let me come home. I stole a vehicle to go on spring break in Florida one year, was constantly in and out of jail, and even went to drug rehab.

At nineteen, he met seventeen-year-old Kim, and they stole a truck to run away from a house arrest violation. They were caught in Nebraska, and the authorities flew Kim, who was then pregnant, home. Released at the Colorado state line, Chris walked for miles before finally calling home. He returned to Tennessee, whereupon police arrested him and sent him to a halfway house.

The probation officers there didn't care about anything. I got put back on house arrest, but that probation officer said he didn't care if I was there. Told me he'd sign his name either way. Time and again, I had no impetus to straighten out my life. Pretty soon, I was back on the run.

At twenty, Chris stole another car and drove around Nashville for three months.

I was smoking crack and anything else I could get. Felt like an outlaw. I was getting shot at and everything. A gang even put a hit on me. This kid comes out of a car at an intersection with a sawed off shotgun. But an MTA bus came over the hill, so he didn't shoot. I thought, "The devil don't wanna kill me yet. He wants to keep using me."

While Chris was visiting friends in Mississippi one day, his father told him over the phone to "get back up to Nashville, clean out the stolen car for fingerprints, and call [him]." Chris said he thought this was his chance to go home, something he desperately wanted. But when he called his father from Nashville, Chris was told he could walk home, eat, and shower, but he could not stay. Chris rejected this offer.

> I walked toward my grandmother's house. When I got to her street, I could see a lot of family cars in the driveway. I couldn't keep going. I felt like the black sheep already, ruining the family's reputation and stuff. So I walked away.

Continuing through the neighborhood, Chris saw a woman sitting on her porch. His recounting slowed as he paused longer between sentences:

> She waved to me. I waved back. I was wantin' to call my mother to see if she would let me come home, since Dad wouldn't. So I went up and asked the lady if I could use her phone. Standing in her living room, I picked up the phone to call. . . . But then I put it back down 'cause I realized I couldn't call Mom either. She'd be just like Dad. I froze . . . just stared at the phone forever. I think I just had a complete mental break. I was hungry as hell and completely alone. Then the woman comes in, pretty assertive, and says, "You need to leave." She's walking me out, and before we get to the door, I turn to look at her.

Chris paused and adjusted in his seat, his voice heavy as he continued:

> She looked like she saw a monster, Mike. She was terrified. It's like she saw what was going to happen before I realized what I was going to do. Suddenly, I'm pushing her into the bedroom. She's screaming and crying out, and—I attempted to rape her. For whatever reason, though, it wasn't working. I couldn't penetrate. So I just masturbated on a sheet, and then threw it in her drawer. I could hear her calling out for help as I ran out of the house and headed to a friend's nearby.

Chris was arrested a week later, drunk, and attempting a robbery with a fake pistol. He was charged with two counts of rape and offered twenty-five years at 85 percent served, or he could face a trial that could result in a fifty-year sentence. Chris accepted the plea deal and thereupon had to accept the attorneys' version of the event. "According to them, I raped her, left, returned, and raped her again. But that's not really what happened."

Though emphasizing that the precise details of the attorneys' narrative were not factual, Chris quickly owned responsibility for the harm committed.

"I'm guilty," he said firmly. "I raped her, in every way but physically. I violated her in her private space. I deserve to serve time."

When I asked if she had contacted him since, he told me that her family had reached out to his family, offering forgiveness. "I never heard from her, though." He stopped and looked away. "She has since died of natural causes . . . I feel like I contributed to her death."

I asked Chris what it meant to him that he could not receive forgiveness from the woman.

> I would feel guilty to receive forgiveness from her. I feel so sorry that she made herself vulnerable to me and then I took that vulnerability. I think if she had forgiven me, I would feel bolder, and would have more language for the unforgiving society I'll be reentering. I guess I'd be more confident.

When I asked him what it would take for him to have felt forgiven by her, he replied:

> She would have had to see my remorse and acknowledge it, and then we could break free from the victim/offender label. But that didn't happen, so now I'm trying to accept surface forgiveness and live it for both of us. My attorney said since they didn't kill me, they are saying I have the right to live. So I just try to walk and live in forgiveness without constant guilt. I do feel forgiven spiritually, though—enough not to be defined by what I did. But it's a fight, 'cause society won't ever forgive me.

For Chris, forgiveness is other oriented:

> We forgive to help heal the other person. Why else would we do it? I don't think forgiveness requires repentance, though it's pretty hard without it. God forgives me without requiring repentance, and I think we are called to try to get there. But if I forgive out of love, I would want to see the fruits of that. I would want to see some kind of transformation.

Chris said forgiveness is a constant journey for him, speaking of needing to forgive his father "over and over" for the double life he led. Chris felt he would not be incarcerated if his father had parented more responsibly. I ended our conversation by asking Chris to address self-forgiveness.

I have forgiven myself now. It started with understanding victimization. I was being constantly victimized in the county jail for
years. I had to suppress the reality of what I did so I could survive.
Self-forgiveness requires vulnerability; it's really hard to be vulnerable in prison.

Chris spoke of one particular tormenter in prison, a man called "T," who
perpetually harassed and attacked Chris, one day choking him until he
almost passed out. This incident caused a recurring medical condition to
resurface, which eventually led to a mental breakdown. After Chris spent
time in the infirmary, his cell became his own infirmary for the next nine
months.

I nearly died, man. I had to claw to resurrection. Recovering from
that breakdown started a process of self-discovery that enabled me
to start forgiving myself. How could I forgive myself before when
I didn't know who I was? I also realized I had to forgive "T" before
I could deal honestly with myself. That's the challenge of forgiveness: trying to forgive those without remorse, and trying to forgive
"seventy times seven." But I need to do it if I want society to treat
me the way I treat others.

Chris told me that he forgave "T" and involved himself in prison ministry.
One day, Chris received a visit from "T." Full of remorse, "T" asked if he
could work under Chris on the ministry team. They are good friends to
this day.

6

VICTORIA DENNIS

Age: 35
Current Time Imprisoned: 14 years

"I've discovered that forgiveness is less about an 'okay' than it is about closure. There's an open chapter to my life, and I can't move on."

VICTORIA APPROACHED ME ONE Wednesday evening in the "Old School" building of the Tennessee Prison for Women, her voice soft and her demeanor seemingly nervous. She told me she was interested in offering her story for consideration for this book. I asked her to tell me a little about her life. She began her reply by saying, "I don't know how to forgive myself. If I had been a better mother, my son would still be alive."

> I was born July 2, 1980. While I was being born on one floor [of the hospital], my dad was being checked in for pneumonia on another. This was an indication of how my life would play out. I can only recall one time where both my parents were in the same room, and it was years later at my first wedding.
>
> I bounced around growing up. We lived here, then there; with these relatives, and then those. Sometimes my mom went one way, and I went another. I visited my dad often, and as every girl

should, I thought the sun rose and set on him. He exposed me to the world and everything in it. Daddy taught me to be free-spirited and encouraged my intelligence. He gave me half-siblings and friends to play with and introduced me to his friend Uncle Rick ... an amazing man [who] raised three boys by himself and I don't ever remember him having a job. We spent a lot of time hanging out in the basement or garage of whatever rundown place they lived in. Uncle Rick was actually who I ran to whenever something went wrong in my life.

At thirteen, Victoria first encountered Christianity and launched into a search for right religion that provided no lasting sense of sanctuary.

When I was about thirteen, I experienced my first personal loss. Like always I wanted to run to Uncle but couldn't, so in searching for that [comfort and belonging] I'd always gotten around Uncle, I went to church. It was a disaster. It was a small fire-and-brimstone church that made a young girl run as far and fast as she could away from Christianity. Over the next few years, I checked out a handful of religions. They each brought me something and were lacking something else. Buddhism, Catholicism, Wicca, Judaism, atheism, and agnosticism were all tried for a time until, like a pair of shoes, I decided they didn't fit me.

During this time, Victoria says she was "learning the 'rules' of [her] maternal family," a line dominated by powerful women.

My mom's side is a matriarchal line. The women rule it, and the strongest of each generation lead. Growing up, it was my great grandma and then my grandma. In five generations, there were only five boys. . . . There are over twenty women in those generations. All of us were raised together. We lived together at times. Aunts were secondary moms, and cousins were siblings. We took care of each other through it all. [But] being a family that praised strengths, weakness wasn't tolerated. Depression was laziness, abuse was hidden, and rape wasn't spoken of. Keep the family happy—that was the "golden rule."

Victoria did her best to keep her family rules, even marrying at eighteen to "make the family happy." She "had feelings for him, but not the marrying kind," and so the marriage was doomed from the start. Four days after the wedding, Victoria's husband left for one year to South Korea with the Army. Within three months, Victoria had an affair; within a year, she had a baby.

I'd never done the babysitting thing and was always hanging around adults [growing up]. I had no idea what to expect or how to take care of a child. Add to that, I wasn't able to get a divorce for a year due to some obscure military laws. I was living with my baby's dad [Kevin] and we invited my stepsister to move in and help me with our son. I knew something was wrong with me then, but family rules said it had to be hidden. I tried to pretend I was okay, but I was afraid something was going to happen. Within a month, I wouldn't hold my son, bathe him, dress him, or speak to him. My stepsister and boyfriend took turns caring for him. One night in late June, the dread built until I woke from a nightmare and fled at 2 AM to the nearest Greyhound station. I jumped on the first bus headed for Uncle Rick. He told me that it was just nerves and that I needed to go home and take care of my responsibilities like he had. I went back to my hotel room, and on July 2nd, I attempted suicide.

Two weeks later, Victoria returned home where the dynamics remained unaltered until their move to Missouri. They lived with Kevin's parents, from whom Victoria felt much disdain and disapproval. After a while, her son entered the hospital, malnourished and suffering from upper gastro reflux and formula allergy.

When my son was hospitalized . . . the nurses noticed my odd interactions with him and scheduled home visits suspecting postpartum depression. My boyfriend's parents decided they should therefore raise my son as theirs since I was, as they put it, "unfit." In fear, I secretly contacted my aunt who paid for a plane ticket for me and my son. I moved to Oregon, and she began helping me overcome "whatever" was going on between my son and me. My boyfriend joined us after a Missouri sheriff told me it was a felony in that state to remove a child without both parents' permission. During this time, my divorce [from my first husband] was granted.

That Christmas, having moved to Nebraska to live with Kevin's sister for financial reasons, Victoria discovered she was pregnant again. They considered adoption, but instead chose marriage and the Army. In April 2001, Kevin received a posting at Fort Campbell, Tennessee, and the family moved again. In July, her youngest son was born and the cloud which consumed her mind after her first child's birth returned; this one, though, was "ten times worse." Her memories now of those initial months are as hazy as her lucidity was then.

I don't recall [what all actually happened over the next month or so] and there was no one around to help put the pieces together. My husband was [deployed] in Kosovo and the closest family was in Texas. It was two months before I had a name for what had gone wrong with me and another seven months before my close-knit, everyone-together, all-for-one family left me. See, I'd broken every rule, including the all-important "golden" one: the family wasn't happy. At the time of my arrest, little was known or understood about postpartum illnesses and even less about postpartum psychosis. Although not currently proven, it's believed that I suffered from this more severe form after the birth of my youngest son. Things were even worse because of a recent, well-publicized incident in which a mother had drowned her children.

During the time of my break with reality, bills were unpaid, money was spent on blatantly unneeded items, the apartment became unkempt, lice and maggots infested everything, I lost seventy-two pounds, and my sons became malnourished and dehydrated. It's believed that my youngest son survived only because his crib was next to my bed and his cries stirred an instinct in me. On the day of my arrest, I discovered my eldest son dead in his room.

After trying to wake him and attempting CPR, I called 911 and waited on the porch with my youngest until someone got there. I remember this part because it replays in my dreams even now. Most everything is foggy [over the next three years] until about 2004. That's when I was sentenced to fifteen years for Aggravated Child Neglect in the case of my youngest son, to be followed by twenty-five years for Second Degree Murder in my eldest son's case. I took a plea bargain for this sentence after my, by then, ex-husband begged me not to put him and our families through a trial. Had I gone to trial, I could have received anything [from] three years in a mental hospital to a fifty-year [prison] sentence. I have since had [the] opportunity to have my case reopened; I chose not to. I also have the option of filing for a commuted sentence or clemency; I choose not to.

When I asked her why, she told me there are many likely reasons, but the clearest is guilt.

I feel I belong in jail. I panic around young children so just imagine how I wouldn't be able to go to stores or live in neighborhoods around kids. "Mommy, why's that strange lady crying and staring at me?" No thanks. Prison's safer. I can be the mythical ostrich hiding its head in the sand. Going even deeper, I'd have to admit that

I want to punish myself. Lose my freedom? So did my son. Lose my family? So did he. Lose my life? I'm not courageous enough to kill myself, but I am surrounded by criminals. The only other things I can take from myself are opportunities to live again. It's really just the only gift of remorse I can give my son. I know he's in heaven and that he knows I choose to lose my freedom. It's no longer punishment for an act I couldn't control. Staying in prison is my gift of apology. Maybe after forty years [here], I'll feel he's accepted my apology.

I asked Victoria to describe her understanding of forgiveness.

To me personally, forgiveness is that sense of understanding that, "Hey, I understand that you had a stupid moment and did something you shouldn't have. I get it. It hurt me and affected me in ways I didn't like. I doubt I could ever forget what you've done, but *I understand* that you made a mistake." It's not the words; it's the emotion behind it. Do you remember when you were young and did something and an adult told you to say you were sorry? You'd mumble something unintelligible under your breath and pout. The adult would always tell you to "say it like you mean it." That's what I mean about forgiveness. It's what's meant *by* the words, not what you say, that matters. It's just that sense, that awareness that things can be okay once again. Maybe not where they once were, but better than what they are. That's forgiveness.

I asked Victoria to discuss self-forgiveness, an experience she originally told me she could not have and did not deserve.

I don't believe I'll ever truly forgive myself until I know that I've been forgiven by those I've harmed. The list is huge. There's my youngest son, of course, but I also have to question if he isn't better off without me. He now has a loving dad, a "mom" who's cared for him for years, and two younger siblings. However, he lost knowing his maternal family and he lost his older brother. He doesn't know what he's lost, though, so it doesn't really affect him. The knowledge has been kept from him until he turns eighteen. How it will affect him then, there's no telling. I also feel that I need forgiveness from my family. Sadly, a handful have passed away, and I'll never get that forgiveness. When birthdays, holidays, and anniversaries come around, I have sleepless nights because [sleep brings] nightmares. I think if I could finally receive forgiveness from even just half of those I've harmed, then maybe I could sleep at night. It's been over thirteen years since my ultimate—if potentially uncontrollable—betrayal of motherhood, and . . . I've discovered that forgiveness is less about an "okay" than it is about closure. There's an open chapter to my life, and I can't move on.

Victoria told me she did not feel forgiven by her family. She does not receive visits because her family lives too far away. Even if they could visit, however, Victoria would anticipate receiving judgment. "If they cared for me, they might try to hide [the judgment]," she mused, "but it'd be there all the same. Perhaps it's the little girl still inside me somewhere just wanting her family to love her again—maybe then I'd feel forgiven."

Victoria acknowledged that in some moments she believes she has forgiven herself. But those moments are fleeting. Most often, a "deeply depressing sense of unforgiveness" consumes her as "commercials, magazine articles, calendar days, holidays, friends' photos and stories, memories, and even scents" remind her of what happened and what she has lost.

> After all, you always hear those stories of mothers with broken bones, concussions, and unconquerable odds who lift up entire vehicles to save their children, and here I was with just a broken mind and I couldn't take care of my own children. How can I forgive myself for that? I think I'm harder on myself than others are on me. I guess in the end, I've forgiven myself on the days that end in "why," but I refuse to forgive myself on the days that end in "y."
>
> I feel if I were ever able to forgive myself then those I'm asking forgiveness from would look even worse at me. They may be thinking "obviously she doesn't care since she can so easily let it go." . . . [This] is one of the things holding me back from self-forgiveness. I don't believe that if a miracle happened and I received forgiveness from all those I'd harmed that I'd be more able to forgive myself. My brother actually wrote me a couple years ago and ended up forgiving me. It was huge for me but still didn't help me forgive myself.
>
> I think prison's taught me to forgive quicker and easier but trust less. I've seen the worst of humanity, both in staff and inmates, and after that, I believe it's safer to forgive or you might end up alone in here. . . . I still struggle to forgive my mom for leaving me when I got arrested. It's almost as hard to forgive her as it is to forgive myself. That same lost little girl in me keeps saying, "Why don't you love me anymore?" It's a work in progress.

7

JEREMY JACKSON

Age: 32
Current Time Imprisoned: 13 years

"I need to forgive the system. But I can't forgive something that I have no idea where to go to forgive it. It would have to be specific people."

JEREMY IS QUIET, PERHAPS from the eight years he spent in a single-bed cell on Riverbend's Death Row.[1] A black man born in Memphis in 1983, Jeremy and his eleven siblings were raised by his grandmother until she died in 1996. Jeremy has never met his father. At an early age, he felt the pain of death around him, resulting in a sense of abandonment. Opening his journal, Jeremy showed me a list of close friends and family members who had died. The list numbered more than twenty. He told me he has often "burned bridges" with people so that *he* could "do the leaving" and not feel abandoned again. After Jeremy's grandmother's death, an affluent white family adopted him.

> They let me do whatever I wanted. Go wherever I wanted. They just gave me the credit card and let me take off overseas. Even with

1. Jeremy Jackson's name has been changed upon his request.

all that, I thought a day would come when they didn't want me. You know, people kept disappearing from my life. So I tried to burn the bridge with my parents. I started stealing their company checkbooks and writing checks. They kept trying to work it out through family meetings and such. But it didn't really go nowhere. I wasn't used to *seeing* love, only hearing it.

Jeremy then told me about the event in 2002 that changed everything:

> My friends and I celebrated our birthdays all month. Mine is August 2, so in September, we are still partying. So my friend Ben calls me one night and asked me to pick him up. I said "no" 'cause I wanted to stay and hook up with this girl. Later that night I got a call from Ben's brother, asking me to bring clothes to the hospital 'cause Ben had gotten in a car wreck. He had gotten in a car with two drunk girls. But I didn't get to bring him clothes 'cause he died. I blamed myself 'cause I turned him down so I could be with a girl. I couldn't even go into the funeral. The guilt was too bad. I just stood across the street. I had known him for ten or eleven years. I got heavy into drugs after that. I'm talking acid, weed, cocaine. So then, on September 15, the girl I was on-and-off engaged to, Teresa, told me that she had been raped by a friend of mine, whose name was Khaled. I went to his house with another friend, who waited in the car. When I confronted him about it, he got mad and raised his voice and his hands to me. People raising their hands is a trigger for me. So I snapped and we fought. I ended up caving in part of his skull with my bare hands. I broke both my hands in the fight. He's actually still living, though. While the fight was going on, my friend out in the car shot into the house and killed a guy named Hakim.

Prosecution claimed Jeremy committed premeditated murder, a crime for which Jeremy asserts his innocence. At the trial, his girlfriend Teresa actually testified against him, claiming now that the rape did not happen, and that his son Micah was not actually *Jeremy's* son. Jeremy said very matter-of-factly, "I was hurt. If she wanted out of the relationship, she could have just called it off. She didn't have to do all that. I just gave up then. Thought, 'If you're gonna kill me, then kill me.'" The court gave him the death penalty. His friend received nine years.

When I asked Jeremy to speak about the moment when the death verdict was given, he replied:

Prison and the death penalty weren't on my radar at that point in my life. My world consisted of girls, cars, and traveling. But see, the police and media want you to believe one story about people. But there's always more, like the fact I was diagnosed with PTSD since I was eight. Or that I was completely high when I went to Khaled's house. I wasn't in my right mind. But no, I didn't really give Death Row any thought. Knew I'd die eventually. There was no need to be afraid.

Early in 2013, Jeremy was released off Death Row and his sentence "lessened" to 101 years and then to life with parole. Now living among what insiders call prison "general population," he stays positive about this current life.

As the conversation turned to forgiveness, Jeremy defined the term: "Forgiveness means you can't use someone's past against them. All that we've been through is gone." I asked him about interpersonal forgiveness in his life, whether given or received. He spoke first of his adopted family:

My dad has never really shown forgiveness. He just said it. We still don't talk today. In 2008 and 2009, I wrote twenty or so letters to people asking for forgiveness. Only got three responses. One was from my mom. It had lots of grace. I wish I had known how she felt before all this, though. I probably wouldn't be here. . . . I've forgiven Teresa but I don't want to reconcile with her since I found out who she really was—deceitful and manipulative. I started forgiving her when I found out she was having a hard time. You know, I can't do any more damage to a person than they can do to themselves. I could forgive her because I could empathize with her. But I don't necessarily wish her well. Nor do I wish her ill. It wouldn't matter to me if she was good or bad. I have a good life right now. I don't think about her. It doesn't matter. I've also had to forgive my biological family. They never write me. I wrote them all the time from Death Row. But I've only received about thirty-five dollars from them since I've been in prison. The last letter I wrote was at Christmas [2012] saying I was gonna stop writing since they never respond. I never heard back from that one either [as of July 2013] . . . it is what it is.

I asked Jeremy about Khaled. He told me he wrote Khaled asking for forgiveness, but received no response. He said he "could take a guess" about how Khaled feels about him. Jeremy struggles to know how to begin forgiving the prison system that sentenced him to death for something he claims he did not do.

This system is throwing lives away. The prosecutors want us to face the consequences for our actions. They should face theirs too. I think if they would take responsibility and be accountable for the damage they've done, I could begin forgiving them.

To end our conversation, I asked Jeremy if he had forgiven himself.

I still feel guilty about Ben. I used to think that I had to stop blaming myself and move on. But that made me feel guilty. I felt like I would be giving him up. Guilt was what held us together. But he wouldn't want that. So why do I do that? Like I said, we do more damage to ourselves than anyone else can do to us. . . . But I think I have forgiven myself. Instead of thinking about the night I told him no, I think about how we would go skating all day and have rooftop and mud parties. I remember the fun we had.

8

SARAH (HAROLDSON) RIES

Age: 29
Current Time Imprisoned: 4 years

"I know that giving and receiving forgiveness is important, but sometimes
it's the most difficult task to accomplish."

SARAH, LIKE ME, GREW up in a small town with only a few thousand inhab-
itants. "Everybody knows everybody," she said. In June 2006, a year after
graduation, she married her high school sweetheart, Aaron. Within three
months, she had an affair and became pregnant; three months later, she
and Aaron divorced. Over the next few years, Sarah struggled to end the
ongoing abusive relationship with her son's father Chris. Finally, she moved
to Wyoming to retry her relationship with Aaron, eventually gaining steady
employment in a Walmart pharmacy. But everything changed on February
13, 2010 when she totaled Aaron's truck.

> I was off work for about a month. The only thing I had to occupy
> my time was playing on the Internet. I met John around the end
> of February 2010, and he seemed like a really decent guy. He acted
> like a "Southern gentleman." My first clue that something wasn't
> right about him should have been the fact that my son, who was

WHERE THE RIVER BENDS

almost three, didn't like [him] at all. I wish I would have listened
to him and that little voice that said that John wasn't good for me,
but of course I didn't. John was able to "buy" my son's affection
with toys, sweets, and fast food. John has a daughter who is a few
months younger than my son but he was never allowed to see her.
He told me he wanted to marry me so he could sign his rights and
power of attorney to his daughter over to me because he thought
I would have a better chance of getting custody of his daughter. I
had a full-time job with benefits, transportation, a place to live,
daycare, and I had my own child also. [He] claimed he loved me,
but looking back now, I honestly don't think he really did. I think
he just loved the idea of me. So like an idiot, I married [him in
April 2010] at the county courthouse. Turned out to be one of the
biggest mistakes of my life.

In May 2010, John told Sarah they needed to leave Wyoming to escape the
"drama" he felt surrounded them; in reality, Sarah told me, he was fleeing
felony charges. "So May 5, 2010, we packed up my 2000 Dodge Stratus with
[very few possessions] and headed for Nashville, Tennessee." But then John
started to change.

John turned into a completely different person. It was a slow
change over a few months, but he still changed into a different
man. We moved around [between states] a lot and I couldn't get a
job because of [that]. We were probably considered homeless because we either had to sleep in the car or barely had enough money
to pay for a hotel room. We would have to go to just about every
food bank, even though we had a food stamps card. It was a really
hard time. But it was even harder for my son.

Living in Wyoming, my son was on a schedule. . . . [He] was
a well-behaved boy, and I rarely had to get after him about something. If I ever did have to get after him about something, time-out
and redirecting his behavior worked best for him. I never used
physical punishment. [But] apparently John didn't think my son
behaved well enough. He would get after my son for anything and
everything, even when my son [did nothing] wrong. When we
first moved to Nashville, I would get after John about his getting
after my son for stupid things. At first John would listen to me, and
back off. After a while, he took things into his own hands because,
according to him, I wasn't doing a good enough job at being a
mother. . . .

It first started with him being verbally abusive toward both
my son and me and just got progressively worse from there. He

was very neglectful and extremely physically, verbally, mentally, and emotionally abusive to my son. If I would try to interfere and protect my son, John would get mad at me and tell me I was never doing a good enough job "punishing" him. He became very verbally, mentally, and emotionally abusive to me as well. We were over 2,000 miles away from home and any family and friends that I had. It was like I was stranded in the middle of nowhere, with no help, and no idea where I could go for help. Since I had nowhere to go, I felt my only option was to stay. I thought staying was the best option at the time because it provided food for my son and a roof over his head. I didn't know what else to do. John rarely let me call home, so my parents didn't even really know where I was. This went on for almost nine months.

In early January 2011, Sarah, John, and her son lived in Sevierville. On the night of January 8th, Sarah's son, nearly four years old, had an "accident," and John got angry, demanding Sarah bathe her son in cold water to "teach him a lesson."

Since accidents happen all the time, I still don't know what he was trying to teach my son. My son was scared and started crying when I took him into the bathroom to get him ready for his bath. I had started putting warm water in the tub for his bath when John came in, getting mad at me because my son was crying. So he kicks me out of the bathroom to get my son's pajamas and tells me that he's going to give my son his bath and to not come back until he told me to. While I go and get his pajamas, I hear a lot of noise coming from the bathroom: my son crying, John yelling at him, the water running, things hitting the floor and the bath tub. To this day, I still have no clue what went on in that bathroom while John was in there with my son. About ten minutes after he kicked me out of the bathroom, John yelled for me to come back.

When I walk into the bathroom, I notice it was a complete mess—there's water all over the floor, [and so are] my shampoo bottles. My son is sitting in the bathtub crying and shaking . . . when I go to him, I notice something that isn't right. There was something floating in the water. I had no clue what it was, but there was a big piece of skin hanging off one of my son's feet. When I asked John what happened, he said, "I don't know. Why don't you ask your son?" I drained the water, wrapped my son into a big towel, and took him out into the living room so I could look at his feet better. They were red and so raw that my son couldn't even walk on them. John refused to take us to the hospital that night because he said that they would blame me and take my son away from me if I tried to get him help. I didn't know at the time that that was what was going to end up happening anyway. But [he said] if I still wanted to go in the morning, he would take me then. So I did what basic first aid I could at home to try to help my son feel more comfortable. I put aloe and burn cream on his feet, and I gave him some Ibuprofen and Tylenol to help him with the pain. Then I sat and held him, telling him how much I love him while I rocked him until he fell asleep.

The next morning, before Sarah prepared for work, she checked in on her son. When she removed his socks to inspect the state of his feet, steam emerged. At Sarah's insistence, John dropped her and the child at the hospital, telling her to "lie if they called the police because he [didn't] want them at the house." Then he left.

As the nurses checked her son's vitals, he grew more fearful, clutching her as he cried. After examining the child, the doctor ordered X-rays and a CT scan. Soon a detective arrived to photograph the boy's injuries and question Sarah. At this point, she began to feel a new kind of fear.

Since I honestly didn't know what all happened, I kept telling them it was an accident, since that's all I knew to tell them. By then, they had completely scared my son. He was crying for me—trying to hold me, his blanket, and stuffed monkey all in one hand—and the nurses claimed I was the one disturbing him. The detective decided to handcuff me and take me down to the police station while my son is lying in the bed crying for me.

At the station, the questions continued, but Sarah's story remain unaltered. During Sarah's twelve-hour detention in county jail before John posted bond, medical personnel transported her son to the burn center in Augusta, Georgia. Though the authorities prohibited Sarah from joining him, she later discovered that her son suffered second-degree burns on 5 percent of his body, primarily the feet.

The burn center used cadaver skin over my son's burns so they can try to heal. . . . [On] January 18th, I got arrested a second time and was charged with a Class A felony of Aggravated Child Abuse with a $200,000 bond. While sitting in county jail, I learned that my "husband," John, had written two different statements against me. The first one was only about two pages long and said the same thing I had been telling the police from the beginning. The second one, a copy of which my lawyer gave me, was a forty-eight-page

typed statement where John basically says it was all my fault, accused me of being an escort behind his back, and claimed I was
addicted to pills, something I have never done. The only thing true
in his whole statement was that I suffer from depression. The rest
of his statement was nothing but lie after lie after lie, all of which
the detective on the case believed for some reason. I filed for and
received my divorce in June 2011.

My lawyer had me go through a psychological evaluation
which [took] eight hours on two different days. When I received
a copy of the doctor's fourteen-page assessment, I saw that he basically stated that, in his opinion, that there was no way I could
have been capable of doing what they were trying to accuse me of
doing, and according to him, I was innocent. On August 6, 2012, I
decided to take a plea deal because I felt it was in the best interest
of my son, my family, and myself. I took a plea for six years at 30
percent with a Class C felony of Facilitation to Aggravated Child
Abuse and Neglect. I don't know what John was ever officially
charged with, but I do know that he only got three years . . . he was
released March 2013.

Currently, Sarah's son lives with his biological father, and she at the Tennessee Prison for Women. When she began to address forgiveness, she
confessed that defining the term was difficult.

I guess I would define forgiveness as knowing that someone, or
myself, doesn't hold past mistakes against you. They don't blame
you any longer, or they don't hold a grudge against you any longer.
. . . I know, in my heart, that my son doesn't blame me for what
happened. He has been asking my family and his dad about me,
which gives me hope for the future. It lets me know that if he did
blame me for what happened, then he has forgiven me for any
wrong that I may have caused. I know I need to try to forgive myself to be able to help myself heal.

Curious as to how she would articulate her implied connection between
forgiveness and healing, I asked her to elaborate.

How does forgiveness help me heal? To heal means to make whole
or well; to settle or reconcile. Forgiveness will help me let go of all
the hurt and pain that I feel inside because of what happened to
my son. I don't feel like I am whole right now. I feel like there is
a big hole inside of me. . . . Forgiveness will help me heal that big
hole and slowly put all the pain and hurt behind me, in the past
where it belongs. It will help me move forward so I can slowly start

to make a better life for me and my son. . . . I know it's something
that isn't going to happen overnight. Forgiveness is something that
is going to take time, just like healing is going to take time. Time
does heal some wounds, not all wounds, but it does heal some.

Sarah told me that to feel forgiven, she would need to accept her powerlessness in preventing what happened to her son. The guilt and pain which
accompany the memories would need to disappear. This forgiveness, however, eludes Sarah; she feels undeserving, that she "should have been the
mother [her] son needed [her] to be." She wishes she had kept him safer: "I
should have gotten us out of that situation when things first started to get
bad instead of staying and letting things escalate. The result of the escala-
tion [is] me in prison."

I asked her about the connection between inter- and intrapersonal
forgiveness.

> I believe you can receive forgiveness from others without actually
> forgiving yourself. Because to accept forgiveness from someone
> else doesn't require you to forgive yourself. It is easy to accept
> forgiveness from someone else when you have done something
> wrong against them. It is a completely different thing to accept
> self-forgiveness, especially when you feel you should have done
> something when you didn't. For me to feel like I should be for-
> given, I would need to actually see my son and be able to spend
> time with him . . . I need to be able to see and know for myself
> that he's okay and that he's forgiven me before I can start to forgive
> myself. . . . [T]he mother in me needs to be able to physically see
> him, hold him, and spend time with him for me to allow myself to
> try to start the healing process to forgive myself.

For Sarah, coming to prison has helped her realize the necessity of forgiving herself. But her understanding of the importance of forgiveness does
not apply only to herself; she also believes she should forgive John, though
she finds this difficult.

> I have already forgiven him for what he has done to me because I
> can heal and/or hide my scars and hurt easier than my son. [But]
> I have a hard time forgiving him for what he has done to my son.
> I know I need to . . . [but] the mother in me won't let me. I feel it's
> not my right or place to forgive John for the damage he caused my
> son, especially since I don't know if my son has forgiven John. If I
> were to forgive him right now without seeing my son first, it would
> feel like I've given up fighting. . . . It would make me believe that,

as a mother, I failed my son again somehow. It would mean that all the time I have done in county jail and prison was basically for nothing. It would make me feel worse about the whole situation than I already feel.

Sarah finished by telling me that she does believe people can change themselves, but they have to "want that change for it to do any good." Like forgiveness, "change isn't something that can be done easily or overnight"; it requires "time and patience." But without the willingness to want change and forgiveness, people who leave prison will keep "ending up on the same path that led them to prison in the first place." Sarah, though, knows all too well the enormity of such challenges as she works toward changing and forgiving herself.

As I wrote this chapter, Sarah calculated that with "good days," she should complete her sentence in April 2015. She was right. When I returned to TPW at the end of April just before submitting the final manuscript, I received the good news that Sarah is free.

9

BILL ALLEN

Age: 70
Current Time Imprisoned: 35 years

"I didn't want to kill anyone! I was studying premed. I wanted to repair and save lives, not take them!"

BILL WAS BORN INTO a "semi-middle-class," hard-working Nashville family with strong values and goals. His mother was a Unitarian, "open-minded and free thinking," and as a child, Bill attended church regularly. In the 1960s, he became involved in the Civil Rights Movement and was first arrested for a sit-in in 1962. In 1963, after graduating high school with academic honors, Bill studied biochemistry on a premed track at Tennessee State University (TSU) for three years before moving to Cincinnati, Ohio to work in a grocery dairy for a year and a half. In December 1967, Bill returned to Nashville and re-enrolled at TSU.

> On January 16, 1968, some friends of mine visiting from Cincinnati were headed back to Ohio. Earlier that day, I had bought two rifles for my dad as a belated Christmas gift. He was a hunter, and I got a good deal. My friends and I were riding in a white Plymouth with Ohio tags. Allegedly, there were guys in a red Ford

with Michigan tags who had passed money orders at a liquor store earlier. They were staying in the same apartment complex where I lived. Police saw their Ford there and were watching our complex. When we pulled out to head to Ohio, the police started following us. In the police tape you could hear the cops say, "Let's see who's in the car." So they motion for us to pull into a dead-end street. My friend pulls down by the railroad tracks next to a bright light. He gets out of the car, and one of the officers tells him to put his hands on the building. We are all nervous 'cause a white cop and young black men in a back alley was not good news at that time. Then a second cop car shows up, and we were all ordered out of the car. Two of my friends, who were in the back seat, take off running. But due to the Fleeing Felon Law, which said cops could open fire if someone fled arrest, the police started shooting at us. My friend Lawson beside me suddenly dropped to the ground. I thought he was shot, thought he died. I expected to die too. So I dove in the car and grabbed the rifles I bought for my dad and returned fire. I killed one of the officers on the spot. A [black] man named Darrell. The other officer, [a white man named] Jackson, died a few months later from infection. The whole thing happened in about ten seconds.

A few months later, Bill was arrested in New York and extradited back to Tennessee. After a three-week trial in November 1968, an all-white jury sentenced Bill and two of his friends to ninety-nine years in prison. Giving some context, Bill explained, "This was at the height of the 'white backlash' after the black riots across the US in 1967. The media at the time labeled me and my friends 'black militants.'"

After six years in prison, Bill and two others escaped in May 1974. Bill eventually married, had two sons, ran two businesses, and bought a home. In 1986, he was rearrested and sent to Riverbend.

"Forgiveness," Bill told me, "means being able to overcome perceived wrongs and overcoming the emotions of anger and hate." I asked him whether he had received forgiveness from the officers' families.

I've reached out to both families. I was initially tried for Officer Jackson's death. They tried me for Officer Darrell's in 1989. I was given a seventy-eight-year sentence that was later converted to life. During that trial, I spoke to Darrell's wife and son. I expressed my deep regret and sorrow. His wife seemed receptive and understanding, but his son was somewhat hostile. He did shake my hand, though. I wrote Jackson's family through a major named Waters.

Never heard anything back, but I did see an article later indicating that his daughter wasn't harboring ill will. So, I'm not sure if I've been forgiven by them. I had no malice in my heart when I shot at those two officers. I'm a father, brother, son, and husband myself. I am very sorry that I took two people away from a lot of people's lives. I've regretted it every day of my life. But I have been able to forgive myself. I recognized that it wasn't my intent that night to kill anyone. I really don't feel like I have to have their forgiveness. Ultimately, God's the judge. I need to be right with God.

Since he fired in self-defense, Bill is unsure whether forgiveness is necessary or if firing at the officers was "wrong." He processed aloud:

It's a bad feeling knowing what I did. I can rationalize why I did it, but I still have doubts. Maybe I acted too hastily, since Lawson wasn't actually shot like I thought he was.

Yet, whether or not he feels he *needs* forgiveness, Bill hopes the families can forgive for their own sakes. For him, giving forgiveness is a necessary part of life:

I'm still here in prison because the system says one life is more important than another. So I have had to forgive lots of people: the prosecutors, the system as a whole, the media, Jim Crow. I remember the Qur'an: Why wouldn't you forgive when you want to be forgiven? So I forgive by remembering that there are bad people of all races, and there are good people of all races. I learned not to condemn everyone. You have to reach a point where you have peace and happiness.

10

TABATHA WHITE

Age: 42
Current Time Imprisoned: 14 years

"I know the kind of person I am, and I'm still trying to be better because God is not through with me yet."

WHEN TABATHA FIRST APPROACHED me to offer her story, she stood beside her friend Betty Fuson, who is also imprisoned at TPW.[1] Tabatha and Betty are both incarcerated on Criminal Responsibility charges, which in lay terms might be called "guilty by association." The courts decided that Tabatha and Betty did not commit the murders in their cases, but they were criminally responsible because they took no action to stop them. Tabatha is serving a life sentence; Betty is serving eight years. They received the same conviction but drastically different sentences. I wanted to hear their stories to discover why. At the outset, all I could see was that Tabatha is black and Betty is white. Soon, however, I learned Tabatha's story:

> In August 1999, I lost my cousin Ben at the age of eighteen in a
> car wreck when he was coming back from Kentucky. Ben was wise

1. Betty's story is presented below.

beyond his years. Two weeks prior to his death, he contemplated suicide, but his brother, his girlfriend Kat, and I slowly talked him into putting the gun down. He had been going through a lot prior to that, which involved being incarcerated for the first time ever with other grown men. One week after [we talked him down], on a Friday, I had a barbecue at my apartment with other friends and family and I heard someone screaming my name at the top of their lungs. I went outside and it was Ben with a female that I had not met before. They had an argument at the mall that carried on to my apartment. I calmed Ben down and took him into the apartment. He didn't seem like himself. He went into the kitchen and picked up the top off of the pots of the food and started tasting the food. Before I knew it, I had smacked his face and said, "Now you know Grandmomma told us never go into people's pots and eat out of them." So he got upset and grabbed a cup of water to throw on me, but the water landed on his brother and a friend of mine. That started a water fight, which led to me running in the bathroom and him kicking the door off the hinges, which also led to a screaming match outside my apartment. I called my aunt—his mom—and told her to come and get him before we end up having a bad altercation. We both said things that were out of anger that time. So Ben's brother took him home. Ben called me talking crazy and I told him I never wanted to see or talk to him again. When I hung up the phone, I unplugged it. I did not know that would be my last conversation with Ben.

Tabatha did not hear from Ben during the next week, "which wasn't out of the ordinary." But that Friday, Tabatha received a call from Ben's brother saying Ben was in another car wreck, and the family needed to go to the hospital. "The hospital would not give any information until all the family came," Tabatha remembered. This, she said, scared everyone. When the family arrived, the doctor entered the small room where they all waited, delivering tragic news.

The only thing I heard was, "We tried to do all we could do, but he didn't survive." I was hurt, and I didn't know what to do. All I could remember was our last time together and [the] conversation and how really bad it was. Everything hit me all at once. I cried and cried . . . [and] could not stop. The doctor let everyone except me go see Ben's body. He would only let me see Ben if I could calm down and get myself together. No one could understand that I couldn't. Something really bad had happened between Ben and me, and we would not be able to fix it. I would no longer be able to see him face-to-face to tell him I was sorry, or him tell me. How could I forgive myself for not being the bigger person, knowing I was the oldest? So finally, I got myself together and went to see Ben in the hospital room. He had scratches and bruises everywhere. Grass and dirt under his nails from where he was thrown out of the back window of the car because he was lying on the backseat asleep. So Ben never knew what happened to him. He died sleeping.

Over the coming days, weeks, and months, Tabatha blamed herself. Though she was "a mess," she began making some positive changes, ending an abusive relationship and trying to "get [her] life together." After some months, she met Carl. At first, she "tried to brush him off," but his persistence paid off.

Carl was very different from any other. He wanted to take care of me. He did things for me and, as you will soon learn, it almost seemed like he was very protective over me, especially when there was no need for him to be. Carl was a charmer. Let's say he swept me off my feet when no one before him had done that. After a while of dating, we started living together.

During this time, I would often check on Kat, Ben's girlfriend, to see if she needed anything for her and her son. Our family saw Kat as family and always wanted to be there to comfort her. In February 2000, my grandmother passed away. So I had to deal with a lot. I was still missing Ben and now I'd lost my [maternal] grandmother to cancer, and she died quickly. I mean one day I saw her and the next she was gone.

Tabatha checked in on Kat one day and noticed her empty refrigerator. When questioned, Kat explained she had "three days until she had money on her EBT card." Reaching in her own pocket, Tabatha found forty dollars, most of which she needed to buy an outfit for her grandmother's funeral. Nevertheless, she offered Kat ten dollars, asking how she would get to the corner store since she was wearing a leg cast from a recent accident.

She responded that there was a guy in the neighborhood on drugs that did errands for people. Well, I asked her if she was sure that was a good idea to give someone known to use drugs her money. She said, "Yes, it's okay. He's never taken nothing from me." So when she called out the door for him, she turned out the lights and had the door cracked. I asked why she was doing all of this. She said, "I don't want him to break in my apartment when I'm not here. All my stuff is rental and I can't afford to pay all this stuff back." He came and left.

So I left and told her to call me when he came back with her food. Well, it was getting late and I thought maybe she just forgot to call. So I called her. She told me that he had not come back yet. Now, it had been hours later and the store was just five minutes away. So I told her to just call me whenever he came. Well, it was the day of [Grandmother's] funeral . . . [and] after the funeral, I went back to my parents' house to stay. . . . [Eventually] I left the house and went with Carl and his son to the bowling alley to just relax. While there, Kat called and asked if I could come and pick her up and take her somewhere. So Carl and I headed to Kat's apartment. Before we got there, I tried to call [her], but her son answered the phone and was just jabbering in baby talk, but I could hear a lot of noise and arguing in the background . . . .

[W]hen we got there, there were people everywhere. I saw two men in the middle of the yard arguing and fighting. I had no idea who they were, but I saw Kat, standing on her porch. As I was getting Carl's son out of the car, I heard Carl say, "Get down!" So I got on the ground on top of his son and heard several gun shots. Then I heard him say, "Hurry up and get in [the car]!" So we did and he pulled off real fast. I had no idea what had happened. So I called Kat and asked, "What did we drive up to?" So she told me, it was the guy she gave the money to and her brother fighting, and the guy got shot. So I told her to let me know what happened. She told me later that the guy that took her money was shot and didn't know if he was going to make it. . . . Later I learned it was told that Carl and I came and shot this guy over ten dollars worth of cocaine.

Despite the pain of such accusations, Tabatha said she fully cooperated with the police investigation. Though they insisted she implicate Carl in the shooting, Tabatha refused, continually asserting she "didn't see anything" as she was lying "on the ground." Only Carl knew what happened.

[He] knew I had not done anything wrong. But never did he testify to that in court. He just sat there and said nothing in my defense. All he would say is that the court knows I did nothing, that I would go home, [and] for me not worry. It's like he knew they were going to get him, because he asked if I would be there for him and help out with his kids. I said I would. When the jury came back and convicted both of us, I had no understanding. I was angry with

Carl. All I could think about was that I will never forgive him for this. He could have helped me.

Tabatha received a life sentence. In the coming days and months, she tried to "be there" for Carl. She would often write him letters but rarely received replies. After a couple of years of incarceration, a man named Ike, who learned about Tabatha through his assistance to Carl, offered to help her with her case.

[Ike] read the transcripts of our trial and told Carl, "Hey this girl has not done anything. Y'all need to help her get out." Carl's response to Ike was, "I'm not going to help her get out and go on about her life without me." . . . At this point, all the love I felt for Carl turned to hate.

Tabatha then told me of a strange turn of events, when the Tennessee Department of Corrections released her, only to re-incarcerate her later:

I was convicted of aiding and abetting my co-defender Carl. For eight years, I, along with my lawyers and Ike, fought the state to prove my innocence. When I ran out of my state appeals, I filed a petition for writ of habeas corpus in federal court, challenging my conviction. The District Court for the Middle District of Tennessee granted the petition, finding that there was insufficient evidence to support my conviction and ordered my release. The Attorney General filed a motion for stay, and the District Court denied it, and I went home on July 16, 2008. I was out for [nearly] thirteen months while the state's appeal was pending before the Sixth Circuit Court. On July 28, 2009, I was paid a visit by my lawyer's office with a letter stating that I had to return back to the prison by 2:00 PM on July 31st. So when told to do so, I did, along with my family's support. I drove back to the prison with all the stuff I could have with me.

As Tabatha began to reflect on forgiveness, she told me her guilt for not forgiving Ben compelled her to assist Kat and her son in any way she could. But, she confessed, "When my attempt to help Kat turned into a situation that took me away from my family, I found myself resenting Kat, Carl, and myself." Even today, fourteen years later, she battles these resentments. Some days, she feels she has forgiven all involved, but with reminders of the life she's missing, her anger returns.

For Tabatha, forgiveness entails releasing "any ill will toward someone who has hurt you," or finally being able "to let go and get past what you've done."

> If I had it to do all over again and could fix the situation, I would've stood there and been of some help to the man in my case. Nobody deserves to die like that, nor do I feel somebody has the right to take the life of another. This is not what I would wish on anybody or their family, and I understand the family's anger through all of this. I just want them to know that I'm not that kind of human being. I was young and scared for myself and didn't know the person [I said I loved]. I hope that one day the family will forgive me for not doing more and not taking the time to help their loved one. For that, I am so very sorry. I also wish I could go back and tell Ben that there are no hard feelings toward him and that I'm sorry and I love him very much. We don't always realize that we may never get the chance to tell someone that we forgive them. Tomorrow is not always promised to us.

For Tabatha, receiving forgiveness from others directly connects to her ability to forgive herself. "For me to feel forgiven," she explained, "I would need to know that the family has absolutely forgiven me for not doing more and getting to the truth. That they know all that occurred was never any intent on my part." After all, she reminded me, the day of the murder was the day of her grandmother's funeral. Whether regarding her grandmother or Ben, she knows the pain of burying a loved one "too soon" and would never wish this on anyone else.

> I would love for the victim's family to forgive me for not doing more. I've learned, as years have passed and I've matured, that forgiveness comes from within. In order for me to move forward and help others while helping myself, I had to take responsibility for things I did and did not do . . . [but] I am not that same girl I was back then, scared and naïve. I am a forty-one-year-old woman who understands the pain of a loved one taken by someone else. I fully understand the family wanting justice. If I was in their shoes, I would want the same, but I would want the one and only the one responsible to be punished.

Tabatha told me her journey of self-forgiveness has been "hard" and "took years." In fact, she said, it took over eight.

> Self-forgiveness to me means that you forgive yourself for what you've done or didn't do. . . . I could never imagine that day

between Ben and me—ever, even if it was planned. Never in a million years would I have seen us being that way with one another. I know I loved Ben and I know he *knew* I loved him. It took years to learn how to forgive myself. . . . When I got out on appeal in 2008, I went to Ben's grave and I felt a sigh of peace. It was so much different from when I was there after he was buried. [At the store one day] I ran into the brother-in-law of the guy murdered in my case. I was scared at first, [but] then he talked to me and let me know he knew I had nothing to do with his brother-in-law's murder. I felt so much relief because he knew the person I was, the person I am, and that I don't believe in taking someone's life.

Despite Tabatha's disdain for the justice system and the reality of incarceration in the US, she tries to maintain a positive outlook on her current situation. "Prison can make anything hard if you let it," she explained.

You have to make the best out of any situation. I try not to use prison as a scapegoat to hold grudges with people. Here at the prison you deal with all kinds of people who were raised different ways in life. Some of these women raised themselves. They might not have the morals and values you have. So here, you either accept people for who they are or you don't. So it's really up to me if I want to forgive and get through it, or forgive and let that person go. You still have choices about your life and who you let be a part of that. I realize that there are people I need to forgive—in the past and probably now. I struggle, but I keep trying. I feel everybody is not bad; they just made a bad choice or mistake. I try not to give up on people.

11

JAMIE ROUSE

Age: 37
Current Time Imprisoned: 20 years

"I woke up the next morning with the expectation of dying that day."

WHEN I FIRST SAW Jamie, he was standing in the volunteer chaplain's office with several other insiders, talking and laughing before our shared meal. As I prepared to join, one of my incarcerated friends chuckled, "We sure got a bunch of killers up in there!" I saw many men convicted of murder and rape, men I had come to love over my time volunteering at Riverbend. Of the six in the room, I knew four well. I asked my friend about the other two. One, he told me, was a man I'll call Derek, who was charged with multiple counts of murder and given three life sentences, even though he personally had not actually killed anyone. The other was Jamie. My friend said, "He's one of Tennessee's first school shooters." Curious, I sat down next to him. Over the course of our friendship, I would learn that, as with every man I met in there, "murderer" did not tell the whole story.

> I would say it started with my father. Growing up, my father was an alcoholic. He was prone to fits of rage that not only caused fear in me but resentment as well. I would see the harm done to my mom

and the dishonesty alcohol would cause my father to commit. My mom would receive phone calls that my father wouldn't be able to make it home due to work only find out that "work" turned out to be a bar. There would also be the phone call to bail him out of jail.

Not all Jamie's memories of his father are painful, however. "My father wasn't a bad guy," he admitted. "He taught me many things throughout my childhood: how to hunt, to work hard, how to drive and work on cars. I also have many fond memories of family vacations." But as Jamie's dad consumed alcohol, the family was forced to consume his wrath. The resentment built in Jamie over the years, producing a hate that "caused me to choose that terrible action that hurt so many innocent people."

As a child, Jamie was "always quiet," "shy," and "short in stature." In school, bullies looking to assert their dominance preyed on kids with such qualities. Jamie was one of their perpetual victims.

> I felt helpless and shamed. Most of all, I was angry, and I felt there was nothing I could do about it. By the time I reached high school, I was searching for my identity. It was this point in my life that I was introduced to heavy metal music. It made me feel angry. When I listened to it, I no longer felt powerless. It . . . inspire[d] me to rebel against God. I hated God. I didn't realize it at the time, but I projected my feelings of hate of my father onto God. I needed someone to blame for the misery in my life. Unfortunately, this attitude would lead me to make bad choices that would affect my whole high school experience.

As Jamie's sense of alienation and anger increased, so did his hatred of school. He felt forced to endure a reality he experienced as oppressive.

> I was told I had to be eighteen to quit school, so quitting wasn't an option. I had no plans to go to college and did not find meaning in an education. By the time I was in high school, I was no longer bullied because people were afraid of me. I had declared myself a devil worshipper, put an upside-down cross on my forehead, and though I regretted it, there was no taking it back. The day I did it I knew I had made a mistake . . . I would regret and hate myself for it.

For Jamie, school felt like prison, and thus he saw the teachers as prison guards:

> They were part of the system that forced me to endure this torment. In truth, they had done nothing to me personally. They treated me

with more respect than I deserved. They did not deserve what I did to them [but] I was too messed up mentally to see that.

By the time he was a senior, he was consumed with anger and hatred, obsessed with violent movies and music. "I felt I was capable of violence," he confessed. "At home, I would have violent outbursts. I didn't know how to control my emotions and would just explode. One incident caused me to destroy my $400 stereo system and beat the crap out of my car with a lug wrench. I was a ticking time bomb."

Jamie then began to recount the specific events that led to the day he knows he will regret for the rest of his life.

The Sunday before that tragic day, I had driven my dad's truck to a local gas station. My car was in the shop after having engine problems [again]. I was also driving with a restricted driving license because of a speeding ticket. I was only allowed to drive to school and work. So, I was already in violation of that when I drove to the gas station to meet some friends. We rode around in their car for a while and returned to the gas station. I got in my dad's truck and was backing up and felt that sickening thud of hitting another car behind me. I got out and looked but saw no one in the car. I went inside the gas station and asked the owner of the gas station about the car. He replied that they didn't have permission to park there anyway. I wrote a false phone number and put it on the window and fled.

The day before the shooting, I was discussing the incident with my cousin and a girl overheard our conversation. Apparently, it was her boyfriend's car. I refused to give her my real phone number. Tempers flared and threats were made. We parted ways, and I was left in a panic. I couldn't lose my license again. I'd rather die than lose my freedom. But I was filled with so much hate that I wouldn't die alone.

I woke up the next morning with the expectation of dying that day. I had given up on life. I wanted my miserable life to end and I wanted someone to hurt. I hated school and wanted to strike against this "institution." I quit seeing school authorities and teachers as people; I saw them as part of the system. I grabbed my .22 Remington Viper rifle and left for school. I first picked up a friend, and I told him what I intended. When it came down to it, he had hoped I wouldn't go through with it. We reached the school and pulled into a parking space. My only intention was to shoot teachers and the girl I got into an argument with. There were no specific people [other than her]. I walked into school and shot the first two teachers I saw. I shot at another and then was tackled by a teacher and a student. I was arrested and taken to jail.

Jamie says he did not realize the gravity of his actions until hours later. He was lying in his cell, "dazed and resigned," when he heard on a TV in the background the news report of his shooting. He says he began to weep.

> I ended up killing a teacher I had never known. The other teacher was always kind to me, and thankfully she survived, but she has been plagued with the living nightmare I had caused, even after all these years. I ended up killing a student while trying to shoot at another teacher. The student turned out to be the sister of one of my friends. These people were innocent and didn't deserve what I did to them.

Shortly after his seventeenth birthday, the court charged Jamie with two counts of murder and gave him two sentences of life in prison without the possibility of parole. He says two years of incarceration passed before he felt he had truly forgiven himself, a process he attributes to his Christian faith:

> I hated myself and didn't feel like I deserved to live. It wasn't until after I had been sentenced that I decided to fully embrace God's forgiveness and give up the self-hate. I surrendered hate toward God and dedicated my life to serving him. If God forgives me, who was I to say I wasn't worthy to forgive myself? I also felt that my own forgiveness from God was tied in with forgiving myself. Once I was able to, the depression and suicidal thoughts disappeared. I was finally able to live with myself. It came down to making a choice. I was tired of the misery. If I wasn't going to make the choice to end my life, I *had* to forgive myself. I wanted peace and it took forgiving myself to do it. I forgave my father as well, and he forgave me for the pain I caused him and my mom . . . I could now be reconciled to God and my earthly father. I finally have the relationship with my parents I had always wanted.

I asked Jamie about his definition of forgiveness: "Forgiveness to me is letting go. It means giving up harboring anger and hate. It means giving up the need for retaliation. It means choosing peace and healing over hate and misery. Forgiveness reconciles and unforgiveness separates."

I asked him to speak about forgiveness as it relates to his victims.

> I hope my victims can forgive me some day, not just for my sake but for theirs as well. I know how hate destroys. Even though I can't imagine the hurt they feel, I do know the peace that forgiveness

brings. [For me] if the victims chose to forgive, I would have more peace of mind. I cannot express the sorrow I feel over what I have done, and even though their forgiveness would not relieve my guilt, I would feel better that they are more at peace. As of yet, only one of my intended victims has forgiven me, but I have forgiven myself. I do not think self-forgiveness is dependent on interpersonal forgiveness. However, it would have been easier for me to do had my victims forgiven me.

Jamie explained that those who have been wronged should try to pursue forgiveness even if their offenders have not asked for it: "As long as someone refuses to forgive, they cannot heal."

Before I was incarcerated, forgiveness was not even a consideration . . . I always blamed others and never considered how my actions affected others. [But after that fateful day] I was consumed by so much guilt that I didn't think I could be forgiven. Yet, after meeting a kind elderly woman who loved Jesus, I was given a glimmer of hope. I accepted the forgiveness offered by God . . . but it didn't erase the pain and harm I caused.

I have learned that forgiveness is a process and the person who has caused the harm cannot demand to be forgiven. I've learned not to add an additional burden [by] asking something so difficult from someone I have already hurt so much. All I can do is express my regret and remorse. It's up to my victims to forgive when they are ready. . . . So far, only one has: the girl who I got into that argument with.

Fortunately, I did not see her [at school that day]. Still, she later learned what I had intended and that knowledge alone caused her to have nightmares about me. She was devastated by anger and depression. It ruled her life. . . . After years of anger and depression, she reached out to me on the advice of her therapist. She wanted to know what she had done to deserve what I intended to do to her. She wrote out of desperation and expected a response from a monster. [Instead] I pleaded for forgiveness and explained that she had done nothing [wrong]. I was the one to blame, and she had only been in the wrong place at the wrong time . . . I told her I was a troubled teen, a ticking time bomb. It [the target] could have been anyone. . . . She indeed did forgive me, and as a result, her anger disappeared, along with the nightmares, and she is no longer held prisoner by the harm I caused and intended. I also was given peace of mind [regarding] her, and I've gained a wonderful friend.

"I guess forgiveness will always be an issue in my life," Jamie concluded, "whether it's continual self-forgiveness or seeking forgiveness from others. I don't have all the answers, but I do know that true peace and reconciliation won't happen until forgiveness is achieved."

12

BETTY FUSON

Age: 40
Current Time Imprisoned: 6 years

*"I don't have a clue how anyone can do the things I have done
and still find a way to be at peace with it."*

"THE EARLIEST MEMORIES OF my childhood revolve around the fear of my mother being killed." This was the first sentence Betty told me of her story. Household violence and abuse frequent the stories of incarcerated persons. Hers was no different.

> See, my father was abusive. He would get drunk and begin to beat my mother. I remember being afraid to go to sleep at night because I thought I had to protect her. Often I sat outside their bedroom door to listen for any signs that my mommy was in trouble. I don't know what I thought a three-year-old little girl could do with an enraged drunk man, but I was determined to try. In the mornings, Mom would find me sleeping by her door. I would always say I got scared and wanted to be near her. I was telling the truth. Mom just didn't know it wasn't monsters I was afraid of; it was my father. . . .
>
> Every time my father beat my mother up, she would leave him. We would go to my grandmother's. But Dad would follow

us there. He would plead with Mom to "forgive" him. He would promise never to hurt her again. Mom would forgive him every time, and then we would go back home. He was usually on good behavior for about two weeks, but then the process would begin all over again. I can't even begin to count how many times my mom "forgave" my dad. She forgave him for countless affairs, for the abuse he continued to hand out, or anything else he did to hurt her. Looking back, I believe I understand why she did. She loved him and knew his behavior came from his mental illness—because when my father was sober, he was a wonderful man.

Time and again, Betty begged her mother not to go back to the awaiting abuse. But her mother wasn't thinking about herself: "'I have to go back because I can't support you and your brother if I don't,' she always responded." Betty felt she and her brother were to blame for their mother's suffering. "I thought if she had not gotten pregnant with me when she was only seventeen, she would not have had to marry my father. I live with that guilt to this day." She promised herself to never depend on a man; she yearned for her mother's approval and pride.

I worked extra hard in school to get good grades and I always tried to do what she asked of me. I guess I felt that if I excelled in school and behaved well she would see that all she went through was not in vain. I also hoped that if my dad was proud of me he would perhaps not act the way he did. But regardless of how well I did, my dad continued his behavior. And my mother continued to "forgive him." As you might imagine, my childhood caused me to have a very undesirable outlook on forgiveness. Although I loved my father dearly and never really felt as if I held a grudge against him, I vowed I would never let any man treat me that way. I would never forgive anyone. What I didn't count on was "falling in love."

In 1992, at sixteen, Betty fell "madly in love" with a boy named Tom. Dedicated to self-sufficiency, Betty graduated high school with honors and enrolled in community college, compromising on her goal of going to a university so she could stay close to Tom. During her freshman year, a high-risk pregnancy forced her withdrawal from school.

Tom and I had been together for two years and I thought we would be together forever. Nobody could have convinced me otherwise. But during my pregnancy, I found out he was cheating on me. Suddenly, I found myself facing similar circumstances that my mom had faced for years. Although I had vowed never to let a man treat me this way, I found myself accepting his behavior and staying with him. I won't say I *forgave* him because I never again trusted him and I never let him forget what he had done. I constantly threw it up at him. Needless to say, his cheating was not an isolated incident. Just like Dad had done to my mom, Tom cheated on me and mentally abused me repeatedly. And just like Mom, I stayed.

In 1998, I discovered he was once again cheating on me with a woman he worked with. . . . I could not continue to live in [that] environment . . . I could not allow this man to cheat on me, call me names, and accuse me of cheating while I pretended everything was okay. Tom had a problem with the weight I gained while I was pregnant, so I felt his cheating was somehow my fault. I was becoming my mom, making excuses for why Tom did the things he did. So I decided to move back to Kentucky where my mom was. Tom and I had never got married. I always felt as if marriage was a joke [since] people did not really keep their vows. When I finally got the courage to leave him, I thought that it would be for good. But I was wrong about that too.

Soon after separating, Betty met John, whose attention brought her affirmation and comfort, and once again, an unplanned pregnancy complicated her plans. With a child already and no college education, Betty's fear increased when she discovered she was pregnant with twins. John's marriage proposal, therefore, seemed like her salvation. "Although I did not love him the way I had Tom," she explained. "I felt I had no choice. How could I support three children working a minimum-wage job? I had really become my mom."

Betty and John married, and she gave birth to the twins. John's mother, Cary, soon asked Betty to allow her to adopt one of Betty's children in order to receive Social Security benefits to compensate for her husband's inability to work. Betty refused her for some time, but once her in-laws assured her it would only be on paper—her children would never be removed from her—she acquiesced out of a sense of familial duty and compassion. Her son Derek was legally, yet secretly, adopted by his grandparents.

I should have known [we] would not stay married. John was a wonderful man . . . [but] I was not "in love" with him. I loved him for the man he was but I did not want to be with him. I was still "in love" with Tom. John offered to help me through nursing school. And I agreed. In my mind, as soon as I was self-sufficient I could leave him. I even told him [that]. Soon after I finished nursing school, Tom came to my job to see me . . . I was an educated woman with a good job, and I wasn't looking too shabby either. Suddenly, he was interested in me again. And I was excited to death. Within a week, I had left John and took [all] my children and moved in with my aunt. . . . Within two weeks, Tom had left his other girlfriend and we were living together. Suddenly, John and his family had a problem with me having Derek. They took me to court and forced me to turn over my son. I was devastated. John wanted me to come back home. He said if I would, everything would be just fine, but if I didn't, I would lose my children. He was using what I had done for his parents against me. I hated him, his mother, and his father. They had all lied to me. I refused to go back to him.

I got a lawyer, told him the whole story, and he assured me I would get my children back. I knew if the judge would grant me custody of Mark—our other son—John would let me have Derek. Nobody wanted to separate the twins. But we were from a small town, and John's family had connections within the justice system. I ended up getting joint custody of Mark. John was named primary custodian. The judge said I could not get custody of Derek because he was neither John's nor my legal child. His reason for giving John primary custody of Mark was to keep from separating the twins. This made no sense to me. John supposedly did not have custody of Derek either. When my lawyer pointed this out the judge said he knows his ruling was not the best case, but his hands were tied. He felt that the twins would have a better chance of staying together if he gave John primary custody. I was devastated. In my mind, I had done something nice for someone and that had caused me to lose my children. I would never forgive those people.

Every time Betty went to get her children for visitation, "John would cause a scene." Her hatred for him grew as he "bullied" and tried to "force [her] to stay with him if [she] wanted to see [her] children." Eventually, her relationship with Tom deteriorated as he went back to "his old ways" and she "made him leave." This apparently raised John's hopes of reuniting with Betty but her animosity had welded that door shut. Instead, Betty turned to "clubs, drinking, and smoking marijuana." Soon, she met Demarcus.

I was in love again. However, Demarcus was more like my father than Tom ever thought about being. He would get drunk and beat me up, [and] he cheated on me constantly. I stayed with him for about three years. I can't even count how many times I forgave him before I got the courage to walk away. . . . When Demarcus and I split up, I started dating one of the drug dealers I met through him. This guy treated me like a queen. So when he went to jail and asked me to sell drugs to help him pay for his lawyer, I didn't think twice about it. Because of the dangerous lifestyle I was now living, I sent [my oldest son] to live with Tom . . . I was robbed several times. I returned to my old ways of thinking. Forgiveness was not something I was going to hand out. I lived by the principle that if you did something wrong to me or someone I cared about, you were going to pay. That attitude is what led me to prison.

In 2008, I went to jail for failure to appear in court on a minor traffic violation. My bond was only $350. My friend and partner in the drug business, Eric, refused to come bond me out. Since we had over $10,000, I had no understanding of why he refused to come get me. When I did get out of jail the next day, I wanted nothing further to do with him [so] I went to see him one last time to get my share of our money. . . . [He] did not accept that I would no longer supply him with cocaine to sell. This was how he made money. He would threaten to rob me, he would flatten my tires, or anything else to try to scare me, but I refused to give in.

But when a man named Ben stole what little drug money Eric had left, I felt sorry for him. He had planned to use that money to leave town. Again, I forgave someone I cared about. I tried to help him, but he wanted his money back, and he wanted revenge. In retaliation, Eric kidnapped Ben's grandfather, Mr. Hogue, and held him for ransom. Eric had a key to my house [and] knew I rarely stayed home. He took Mr. Hogue [there]. When I got home, I found Eric in my house with Mr. Hogue tied to a chair. I left without notifying anyone of what I had seen. I did not feel that it was my business to get involved. After all, Ben had done something wrong to Eric so I thought he was just taking care of his business. I thought when Eric gets his money back, he'll release Mr. Hogue. I never thought any real harm would be done. But as a result of the kidnapping, the man died.

Betty was eventually charged with aggravated kidnapping and first degree murder. "I had so much anger at Eric for putting me in this situation," she told me. "How could he do this to me?" In the end, Betty took a plea bargain for eight years at 100 percent on a criminal responsibility charge.[1] However, a police investigation began to pursue Betty's association with the "drug dealing community" and discovered she "had been selling cocaine heavily for the past two years."

---

1. "Eight years at 100 percent" means she was sentenced to eight years with no possibility of early release; she has to serve 100 percent of her sentence.

> They turned their investigation over to the feds [who] charged me with conspiracy and distribution of five kilograms in the eastern district of Tennessee. For this charge, I received eleven years at 100 percent. By the time I get to go home my children will be grown. While I have been incarcerated, they have experienced lots of loss. As of now, I feel I can never forgive myself for abandoning my children.

Betty told me that because of her story, she has always regarded forgiveness as "a pass one receives to repeat behaviors with no consequences." Her whole life she was taught that she should forgive because God forgives her: "However, I would see these same people, who had claimed to be forgiven, repeat their erroneous behaviors." This disturbed Betty and prejudiced her against forgiveness. Currently, though, she tries to see forgiveness differently.

> I know the true meaning of forgiveness is to be able to look past a person's behavior and trust that he or she will not hurt you again. And you no longer hold him or her accountable for the pain he or she has caused you.

Seeing forgiveness this way, Betty struggles to feel forgiven by her family: "For me to feel forgiven by my family I would need them to stop bringing up all my mistakes every time I talk to them." She says that while they deny any lingering anger toward her, "they constantly say things like, 'If you hadn't got yourself in this mess, you would be home where you should be.'" Betty acknowledges, though, that her mother is different: "She continues to forgive and love me unconditionally."

In the end, forgiveness eludes Betty. She struggles to know how to experience it, often wondering if she even could.

> As of right now, I don't believe I can forgive myself. I don't have a clue how anyone can do the things I have done and still find a way to be at peace with it. The things I have done have caused so much pain to so many people. And oddly enough, the ones I've hurt most are the ones I love the most. Self-forgiveness to me would mean I could live my life without feeling constant guilt. I'm not sure how to forgive myself. I constantly think of how I have damaged my victim's families, my children, my mother, and my other family members. I've missed out on so much that can never be relived. At times, the pain from the guilt is unbearable. I wish I could forgive myself and move forward with my life. I think the main reason I can't forgive myself is I continue to see how my

past actions continue to hurt my family. [Recently] I found out my nineteen-year-old son had lost his right arm in an accident at work. If I had been home, he would have been in college, not working in some factory.

Betty did not try to conclude with any kind of resolution. She spoke honestly of her struggle to grasp forgiveness. For now, it remains too slippery to hold.

Betty's TDOC sentence is set to expire November 15, 2015. Her incarceration will continue in federal prison.

13

RAHIM BUFORD

Age: 44
Current Time Imprisoned: 26 years

"I never thought life was sacred. But I know now we are representatives of the divine. Jesus taught about a chosen *people. I was taught I was a nigger."*

RAISED IN NASHVILLE, RAHIM grew up in a dysfunctional family.[1] In his world, "survival was the only law. There were no fathers, but daddies would come and go." His mother had her first child at eleven after being raped. Of his thirteen brothers and five sisters, Rahim's mother bore seven. In 1977, six years after Rahim's birth, she married Leroy.

> My biological father had promised to marry her. He had four children with her, but then didn't show up at the wedding. So instead she married a monster. After two years of marriage, that became clear. He was a drunk, used cocaine and marijuana, and brought strange women over when my mother wasn't around. I had to tell her about that, then she and Leroy would fight, and he'd get

---

1. Like Tony, Roger graciously gave me several reflections and correspondences for review. His nine-page memoir is entitled "Wounds and Healing."

violent. I'd hear noises and see the aftereffects. She'd stand in the kitchen with a black eye, looking stunned.

Rahim "hated and feared" Leroy, a man who showed favoritism to his two biological children, who made Rahim and his siblings live in the basement and keep the wood-burning stove alight by gathering and chopping kindling late at night. Leroy even beat them:

> My mother had given my stepdad a license to rob and murder: we were robbed of a normal childhood and our spirits were killed. . . . There are areas on my body where hair does not grow. . . . Naturally I loved my mother but I hated her for the abuse and for marrying a monster.

Rahim's family did not have the financial resources some of his neighbors and classmates had, so it was "either crime, endure shame, or learn how to use jokes to protect our fragile egos." Rahim's brothers exposed him to crime when he was seven. He had his first sexual encounter at eleven and owned his first pistol at twelve. He told me that all his male siblings—as well as his father and one sister—have been incarcerated. He even shared a cell with three of his brothers.

At seventeen, after his mother kicked him out for failure to meet curfew, Rahim moved in with Ted, a man he respected for "manhandling" Leroy once. Ted filed for bankruptcy, however, and asked Rahim to help pay bills by robbing restaurants and stores. Rahim would enter the facility, shoot a gun in the air or at the floor, and then take the cash.

In April 1989, eighteen-year-old Rahim approached a man outside the back of a restaurant, one bullet in the chamber.

> I put a gun in the guy's back, and we moved inside. I felt like he wasn't taking me seriously, so I shot at the floor. But the bullet hit a guy in the abdomen.

Brent, the victim, died that night. When the police arrested Rahim, he pled guilty and was given life plus twenty years with the possibility of parole.

In 2000, Rahim's beloved sister Jessica was murdered by a man named Malone, who received a six-year sentence but walked in three. The family held the funeral at prison so that Rahim could attend.

> I walked in that room chained and shackled, like a slave. I couldn't even hug my mother. I remember saying, "It's a shame that we only come together when someone dies." There we were having a family reunion in prison. My family all talked of wanting to kill Malone.

Then it hit me that this is what I did to another family. I suddenly looked at Malone as myself. I didn't want to harm him. I told my family that whatever they felt about him they had to feel about me. It was then that I forgave some parts of me.

Rahim lived in six different prisons before coming to Riverbend in 2002. Realizing he "couldn't evolve spiritually" with forgiveness absent from his life, he began participating in various transformative programs, learning meditation techniques, and practicing an intentional spirituality. Eventually he wrote a letter to the Victim Offender Reconciliation Program (VORP) asking for mediation with the family of his victim so he could express remorse. VORP ultimately declined since the offender cannot initiate such a process.

In 2007, Rahim began using MySpace to advocate for clemency, believing himself to be a "changed man." Rahim declined an interview for *The Tennessean*, but an article was published on April 17 with the title, "Killer Angers Dad on MySpace." The reporter had shown Rahim's page to Brent's father, who became furious and demanded that MySpace remove it.

> I felt really bad. I experienced the remorse all over again. I felt everything, felt like I had revictimized the family, that I had reopened wounds that might have been healing. The next day, another article appeared in the paper saying that Brent's sister Rachel and the rest of her family would be protesting my parole.

Rahim's attempts to contact the family to explain were fruitless until 2012, when he received a letter from Rachel. Rahim graciously allowed me to see the correspondences between them, letters which seemed to provide some healing on both sides. "When I think of Jessica, I think of Brent," he told me. "I can't be mad at them [Brent's family]."

At this point in the conversation, Rahim began to speak more directly about forgiveness, saying, "Forgiveness isn't about God. It's about people. I didn't hurt God. I hurt flesh-and-blood human beings. I made victims. Forgiveness has to come from them." When asked his understanding of forgiveness, Rahim offered:

> If I've allowed myself to be offended, forgiveness entails me not harboring resentment toward the person but entering back into a state of peace as it relates to the previous relationship. I don't regard the person in the light of the offense. Forgiveness is the expression of acknowledging the equality of the other's humanity. It has to be from the heart, not for religion.

Rahim described forgiveness as a "condition of the inner being," occurring when one is no longer reminded of the wrong. But, as he wrote in a personal reflection:

> Forgiveness does not mean that responsibility is erased. The hurts we perpetrate on each other do not disappear; damage has been done, and the scars remain. Forgiveness means that we can move on, not bound by hatred or apathy or denial.... Forgiveness means a new way of experiencing life.

Turning to self-forgiveness, Rahim commented:

> I had to forgive myself. I couldn't go on harboring guilt. The "me" before the crime was a good person who cared about others and was loved. To forgive myself, I remembered the good deeds of my life. I put *all* the pieces together. The event that put me in prison was *ten minutes* of my entire life. If those ten minutes define me, then what occurred before and in the twenty-four years after has no meaning.

For Rahim, self-forgiveness came after experiencing forgiveness for those wrongs he himself had suffered. While in prison, he realized he had much to forgive. As he wrote in the reflection referenced above:

> I must forgive my mother for being too strong in her pride and for not seeking the help she needed . . . I must forgive my dad for not being a father. I must forgive my older brother for introducing me to crime. I must forgive America for perpetuating a system that did not offer me the benefits it offered to children of a different race or class. I must forgive organized religion for promising to visit people in prison and then ignoring us.

Rahim also spoke of having to forgive the woman he married while incarcerated, for the money she consistently took from him. He said, "I couldn't look at her negatively because then I'd have to see myself that way. So I kept forgiving her."

As our conversation ended, Rahim spoke of responsibility and vented his frustration regarding unforgiving Christians:

> If you can't forgive, don't claim Jesus Christ. Even on the cross, it was people like me beside him, and at least one of them was forgiven! Or take Paul. Is there no forgiveness for modern Sauls? I'm not the worst thing America has produced. Nearly 5,000 black men were lynched in this country, and not one [white person]

served time. . . . As a human, I failed to meet expectations. Consequences follow from that . . . I know that the conditions of my
childhood directly contributed to my criminal actions, but I accept full responsibility for the choices that I have made and for the
pain I have caused. By accepting responsibility, I have been able to
break the cycle of crime that plagues my family.

In April 2014, Rahim went before the Tennessee parole board. At the end of
his hearing, which I attended, the parole board chairman confessed to Rahim that he had never seen a more impressive incarceration record. "You've
done everything we asked of you," he said. Then after a few moments de-
liberation, the chairman made his decision: "I'm voting to put you off for
another year due to seriousness of the offense."

Despite Rahim's impeccable prison behavior, engaging in all encouraged and numerous self-initiated "rehabilitative" activities, despite a
guaranteed full-ride education at American Baptist College and a job with
the Children's Defense Fund awaiting him on the outside, his parole was
postponed for "seriousness of the offense," a reality that will never change.[2]

2. In June 2015, after submission of this manuscript, Rahim was released from prison
on parole and now lives, active and well, in Nashville.

14

SHELLY BREEDEN

Age: 40
Current Time Imprisoned: 18 years

"It was a beautiful, clear day when the apocalypse began. The sun shone like nothing would ever be wrong again. I never saw it coming."

WHEN SHELLY HANDED ME the papers containing the first draft of her story and the thoughts of forgiveness which emerge from it, she avoided specifics about her past. Her opening words, though, devastated me:

> I am nobody; I had always been nobody. The only thing that was special about me was that I was a pretty child. Unfortunately, the very thing that makes you special often is the thing that makes you a target.

As I continued reading, standing against a whitewashed hallway wall at TPW, my body slowly slid to the floor as I encountered references to a lifetime of sexual abuse. Then came the following paragraph:

> It was the last [abuse] that truly broke me. I had never heard of PTSD and didn't really know what Stockholm Syndrome was until I was diagnosed with them after the crime. It has been a little over

seventeen years now, and I still have night terrors, crushing anxiety, and more than anything else, the weighty guilt. If I had been a stronger person, if I would have taken the abuse in silence like I was supposed to, my best friend Abby would still be alive.

I went to find Shelly and asked her if she would be willing to tell me that story. What happened to Abby? Why did she blame herself? The acuteness of the pain made it difficult to tell, she confessed. Additionally, she explained "it would take an entire novel series for me to tell you the whole story of why I am here." I gently encouraged her to try, if she was willing. A week later, she handed me the following letter, included here in full:

My story is very difficult for me to tell. I am still terrified every day and talking about it only seems to make it worse; the pain, the memories, are sharper and more vivid, and therefore, more real and fresh.

You asked me about the truth, my truth, compared to what was reported about me. The story you may have heard would be that I am the evil mastermind of my best friend's murder. You would have heard me called a monster. What you didn't hear was the real story.

From the time I was five years old until my incarceration at age twenty-one, there was someone in my life to abuse me—sexually, mentally, and physically. Each person got their own stretch of time to work toward destroying me. It never mattered if they were a loyal family friend, a devoted grandfather, or a loving boyfriend; they lined up to take me down. I had a brief stint of what I believed was my sexual liberation when I was nineteen, but I was quickly discovered by a new tormentor and made to renew my submission to my chains.

I was twenty years old and five months pregnant with my third child. I had dropped out of high school at seventeen when I was pregnant with my first. I had no job, no money, and lived very much in the middle of nowhere. I was not very concerned with myself; all I wanted was for my children to be healthy and happy. Besides having a boyfriend who was cheating on me, never loved me, and was only with me because he was the father of my two youngest, I was content. I didn't think I deserved any better, and he wasn't hitting me or the children, so things must be okay.

A strange car came rolling down my driveway [one day]. I went out to see who it was. Abby, my dearest friend since I was sixteen, bounded out of the car. She always made me feel so happy just to be around her. She had no idea that she was a passenger in a demon's chariot. She never would have brought him to my house had she known her boyfriend was secretly evil.

[At] the first meeting, he was nice—normal even. After that, he came to my house alone, after he had dropped her off at work and knew that my boyfriend was also at work. He said he had a fetish for pregnant women. He made me perform sexual acts with him and do exactly what he said. He threatened the lives of my children and my loved ones. He said if I told anyone, or was disobedient, he would kill them and I would live with their deaths on my hands for the rest of my life. I had no idea how true it really was.

I took the abuse as long as I could. I wish God had made me stronger. After three months of the rapes, of pretending I was okay, of acting how he wanted me to act, of suffering, of unanswered prayers, of hearing the gory details of the others he had killed, I was falling apart.

Despite him drugging me regularly to keep me quiet and compliant, I was a wreck. I was so nervous and constantly in terror. I couldn't sleep. I tried to eat for the baby I was carrying. [Abby's boyfriend] followed me everywhere, even to the bathroom. I was counting down the days to my baby being born. Then he would either lose interest or kill me, I hoped.

Then I was invaded by a terrible thought: "What if he kills me before my baby is born?" So, I desperately and tearfully ruined my friend's life. Abby and I were washing dishes and her boyfriend went outside. I whispered it, so low I almost thought she hadn't heard me at all. I just told her he had been raping me for months and we needed to get the children and get away, without him knowing I told. I had never, and still haven't, driven a car. I had no idea how to run from this on my own. I needed her to save me, and it got her killed.

A few days later, her boyfriend, his friend, and Abby went outside. Only the men came back in. It was the middle of the night. He had drugged me heavier [that day] than he usually did. It took me a minute to figure out she would not return.

I don't really know the details of what happened to her. His abuse was particularly rough that night. It was his victory and my punishment. I had to go to the hospital after a couple of hours. Premature labor. I was eight months pregnant [with a baby girl] at the time.

He was no longer Abby's boyfriend; he was now my tormentor. When my boyfriend asked if he should come to the hospital, my tormenter made me tell him no. He said he'd finish my boyfriend off too if I said yes. I tried asking the nurses to help me, but I knew he'd kill my children, and the nurses wouldn't have been able to save [them] from him.

I was a good girl. I was more obedient than ever. It was my fault Abby was dead. I wouldn't make a mistake again. I couldn't live with it. I couldn't live with the one I had made already.

My tormentor was a master at manipulation. People believed whatever he told them to believe—especially me. One day, he went to get some money from my boyfriend. I can't remember what it was for. His buddy watched me while he was gone. I barely breathed. When he returned, he said he was taking me and my children to my grandfather's house (the one who molested me through childhood) or he would go back and kill my boyfriend. Of course, we left.

I don't know how he knew about my grandfather. I was more scared than ever for my children. I was certain if we left Tennessee that my children and I would all be dead or worse in a matter of hours, maybe days. We were halfway through the trip when I pretended to call my grandfather. This was long before cell phones, so when I hung up, I said that my grandparents' answering machine said they would be out of the state for several weeks. He then made us go to my mother's. I was steeled in my resolve to never disobey him again. I did anything he said, spoke what he instructed. I was perfect.

Even when the police came, I told the story he made me tell. I tried to tell it right every time they asked. As days passed between interviews and the TBI [Tennessee Bureau of Investigation] agent had said my tormentor would be out soon, fear broke into the story I was supposed to tell. A vengeful tormentor—who said if I wouldn't be with him he'd make sure I could be with no one—not having the money to afford real justice, and the crushing weight of my own feelings of guilt, made short work of me.

Since the drugs had blacked out days of my torture, I started getting high in the jail to ease my suffering. I don't even remember my plea bargain hearing except that my court-appointed attorney said for me to say "yes" when he nodded and "no" when he shook his head, and that the sheriff gave me candy. I found out I was sentenced when I saw it on the news in my cell that night. That's when my dad found out too. He had to have quadruple bypass surgery—something else that is my fault [due to the stress I caused].

Now here I am, seventeen years later, and I can't forgive myself for any of it. He may have been killing me for months, but I've been doing it for years. Sometimes I dream that Abby is still alive, still my children's godmother. Things are so wonderful in those fleeting moments; then I lose her again. All the pain, suffering, and grief return like a tidal wave crushing and drowning me. And it all begins again.

Abby's murder haunts Shelly, as her sense of responsibility prevents her self-forgiveness. Shelly has tended to see forgiveness as "self-centered," an "individual's choice" undertaken for that particular "individual's benefit."

> For example, if I went to my victim's [Abby's] family and they all miraculously forgave me, their wounds might begin to heal because they have dropped the burden. But my wounds remain because I cannot forgive myself. I hope her family does forgive me. It won't resolve my grief or theirs, but I don't want to be a burden that they carry. I don't want their unforgiveness to continuously renew their pain. The Bible talks a lot about forgiving because we are forgiven. For me, that is much easier to give than to receive. Unless it is about giving to myself, then it is impossible because I would also have to receive the forgiveness.

Shelly sees forgiveness as "trusting G-d to take care of the things that hurt [her], and to heal [her] wounds—physical, emotional, and spiritual."[1] Daily, she offers prayers for divine grace and strives to better herself and be a "vessel of G-d's will," but her grief is too overwhelming. "Maybe I have too much grief to ever feel forgiven," she wondered.

I asked Shelly why she could not forgive herself for Abby's death. "If I forgave myself," she answered, "I worry that I'd lose Abby and my memories of her."

> When we grieve a loss, it seems we "get over it" and move on. We go about our lives without them. I am terrified of losing her: the sound of her laugh, how she looked, her scent. What would I have of her if I lost those things? I am afraid I would stop missing her. Even one minute would be too much.

Though Shelly has not forgiven herself for seeking Abby's help, she has forgiven her own family and friends.

> All my loved ones abandoned me when I was incarcerated . . . I am out of sight and therefore out of mind. I have no idea if any of them think they need my forgiveness, but I forgave them. [But] how could that have any effect on them, being forgiven but not

1. Out of respect for Shelly's Jewish faith, I have not written the name of God in her story.

knowing it? They go about their lives without missing a beat—or me.

Shelly turned next to her relationship with her sister, observing that while they forgive each other for harms done, their inability to forgive themselves recycles old conflicts.

> We have had our difficulties, but we talked them out. If she forgives me and I forgive her but we don't forgive ourselves, there is no relief to the misery. Our own lack of self-forgiveness makes us over-analyze each other's every word and action. Then we fight again about the same things we already forgave each other for. She'll say she's going to send me money, and I go on the defensive because I think she is saying I can't take care of myself. No matter how much I need the money, I refuse it, [and] so she thinks I am refusing to take her love. Why? Because she thinks if we had been closer she could have saved me and taken care of me, and I think if I had been stronger and took care of myself, I wouldn't be a burden to her now. Unforgiveness makes us crazy.

When asked how prison has affected her life, Shelly told me that prison offered her survival. Despite the trauma of incarceration, it is better than the life she previously endured.

> I miss my children and I have missed out on all the big events of their lives, but it would have been worse if I were dead right now. If I had stayed in that life, I might have lived another three or four months before someone killed me or pushed me too far and I took my own life.

Shelly endeavors to make the most of her imprisonment, focusing on self-growth and "getting closer to G-d." These pursuits have led her to believe she "should love everyone completely and that you can't love someone the way G-d wants you to if you hold unforgiveness for them in your heart." And though this is a work in progress—as sometimes it can be difficult to "remember that forgiveness does not negate [her] pain, nor does it validate the transgressions against [her]"—she strives "to forgive everyone for all real and perceived transgressions."

> I say "real or perceived" because the things that may feel very real to me may be no big deal to the next person. Like cutting in line. This is nothing to many, but to some of us, it is the rudest thing you can do in prison. The cold food you are getting served is no better if you are first in line or fiftieth. You may just want to get in

the line with your friends, but to the sixty-three women you just walked around, you are saying that you are better than them and deserve to be first. That's what I mean by perceived transgressions. It doesn't have to be on G-d's top ten for someone to become offended and need to forgive you for it. Perceived transgressions feel just as real as any other. [But] for all the people of my past, they truly are forgiven. Holding on to the pain only hurts me.

In prison, it is often and heavily preached about the need to forgive in every aspect of our lives. It is not widely taught how to receive forgiveness, though. Sometimes this makes it hard to forgive because the preachers and teachers are from the outside world, a world that has discarded and forgotten us, a world that does not understand us. Then you have a whole domain of people who don't care about anyone but themselves. Running over you is no big deal to them. Their friendship is fake, but the betrayals and pain you feel are real. If I can forgive and walk away *in here*, it really means I don't have to be a person I don't want to be, no matter where in the world I am. . . . It sets me free from a suffering I don't have to endure. Forgiveness opens a door between me and G-d. Forgiveness is really me saying, "Hey G-d, I trust you to heal my heart and bring *your* justice to this situation. I am not afraid to trust you, and I know giving these things to you is not taking anything away from me."

At the advice of counsel in 1998, Shelly accepted a plea bargain and received twenty-five years for second degree murder and twelve years for conspiracy to commit second degree murder, to be served concurrently. With "good-time credits," she is scheduled to complete her sentence in February 2019 after twenty-one years in confinement.

15

JACOB DAVIS

Age: 36
Current Time Imprisoned: 17 years

"I think nature is helpful when thinking about forgiveness. I think of that silver maple tree I gashed as a kid. It didn't die; it kept growing, but it will always have a scar. Or I think of an animal in a trap: It may live, but it will limp forever."

IN 1985, JACOB'S FAMILY moved to a rural setting outside Fayetteville, Tennessee, the type of place where "everybody had a dog and fishing pole," as Jacob put it. His family was poor, Christian, and working class. Growing up, Jacob was an average kid. He wanted to be a fighter pilot or a computer programmer. He loved nature and Boy Scouts, eventually completing all the requirements for the prestigious Eagle Scout ranking. He played sports until high school and then worked as a waiter to save money for college. During his teenage years, though, the family dynamics changed. Internal conflicts increased, and they stopped attending church. With family life "unstable and splintering," Jacob escaped through drugs, alcohol, and sex.

During his third year of high school, he felt extreme "burnout." He was overwhelmed with work and school, hooking up with random girls, and binge drinking. Then a girl named Becky became employed at his work, and Jacob was intrigued. Though initially hesitant to get involved with her due to her long relationship with a schoolmate named Nate, Jacob and Becky eventually dated for six months.

> Come Christmas of '97, I was really in love with her. I was experiencing complete tunnel vision. I began questioning my entire life direction. So much was expected of me. I was supposed go to college, be successful, do everything society says a man is supposed to do. Everybody expected me to be the most successful person in the family. But I started asking myself, "Is this really what I want? Do I really want to walk this path laid out for me?"

In 1998, Jacob's relationship with Becky "got rocky" when he publicly learned from a schoolteacher that Becky had been cheating on him with Nate for a couple of months. Jacob felt humiliated as he learned that everyone at his school knew except him. He described Nate as very belligerent toward him, but Jacob felt he could not risk expulsion for fighting, as graduation was fast approaching. Thus, the suppressed anger began to build more and more.

Jacob told me he tried breaking up with Becky and fell into a deep depression, even becoming suicidal. But Becky clung to him in what Jacob called a "functional dysfunction." By May of 1998, Jacob was not sleeping and began deteriorating mentally, even to the point of hallucinations. Shaking his head, he said:

> I was having random breakdowns. I could barely function. I was a prisoner to those emotions and events. I couldn't break free of the anger. My parents tried helping, but I wouldn't let them. I blocked everyone out. I felt so ashamed and marginalized. Didn't think people accepted me. We didn't live in the same reality. This was a complete existential crisis. But through it all, Becky was there.

On May 18, while shopping for a pregnancy test, Becky told Jacob about getting a pregnancy test with Nate during their affair. The news knocked Jacob to the floor, shaking in a fit of psychosis. The next day, while Jacob and Becky walked down the school hallway, a friend of Nate's threw a coin at their backs. Jacob said he turned to see Nate staring him down. Mustering all possible restraint, he walked away. During his next class, though, Jacob broke.

Something snapped. My mind blanked out. My actions felt righteous, and I was certain people would agree with me if they knew my story. This was a quest of liberation, a rite of passage. In my mind at the time, it was not only justified but *required*.

Leaving school, Jacob acquired a gun, returned to campus, shot Nate three times in the parking lot, and collapsed. Nate died on the way to the hospital.

Jacob was arrested and spent one and half years awaiting trial. Immediately following his arrest, he slept for days, overwhelmed with exhaustion and a sense of relief that it was all over. Attempting to describe how he felt at the time, Jacob told me, "Killing my victim was like an animal chewing off its own leg to get out of a trap."

He then began to describe his own journey of forgiveness:

> In the first six to eight months of imprisonment while awaiting trial, once I had gained enough sleep and recovered a normal state of mind, the first stage of repentance began. I was locked in solitude most of the day. Teachers and friends donated books and paper, so I began reading and writing a lot. I read stuff like Dickens, Toni Morrison, and *1984*. I spent a ton of time praying and crying, trying to work through all the feelings of guilt. I couldn't sleep much at all. I wanted forgiveness from God but wasn't sure I could ever forgive myself.

Describing watershed moments in his forgiveness process, Jacob told me about his friendship with an elderly Christian couple in 2005–2006, and the knowledge that changed his thinking.

> I learned they had chosen to visit prison because their daughter was murdered. She was killed by a jealous rival . . . it devastated me. I saw the pain of good people and realized I had given that same pain to others. I also learned we are all part of the same tapestry. We're not isolated. If I wanted forgiveness, I had to forgive others too. Today, I've lost all ill will toward anyone involved in that period of my life.

I asked Jacob what forgiveness meant to him. After a few minutes of quiet, he responded:

> Forgiveness is something we do for our own sake when we've been wronged, in order to regain peace. When we don't forgive, we hold on to pain. Through forgiveness, we release bitterness, vengeance, and hate. I think we all have innate internal demands to repress and get retribution. I mean, I wasn't raised to forgive really. I was

raised to protect those I saw as good and resist those I saw as bad. But forgiveness affects this "us" versus "them" dynamic.

Turning his comments to the nature of the prison system, he continued:

> You know, I fully understand society's perspective that they can't just let people victimize loved ones . . . but I have to call for a *reform* of the system. Whatever forgiveness I have found, it is in *spite* of the system. The system doesn't facilitate any kind of forgiveness. It is focused like a laser on vengeance, motivated out of fear. It uses suffering and pain to punish suffering and pain. It chains me to my past. Forgiveness in Christian theology tries to offer new garments, but this system just chains you to the mud in them. It really makes it impossible to fully forgive yourself.

After I asked Jacob to elaborate on attempts to forgive himself, he spoke with passion and eloquence:

> None of the people involved in the event are the same now. Most don't know me anymore, and I don't know them. We have no effect on each other. But the system is determined to take us back to the event.

Sitting forward in his chair, he then proclaimed:

> The man I am now didn't do it! The person who did do it wasn't in a normal state. So if I forgive myself, I forgive my *old* self. Identity is quite slippery. . . . It was like the butterfly effect: a billion coincidences had to happen that day for that event to occur, and nobody can change what happened. There's such futility in chaining yourself to an event and bringing it into the future. We have to recognize we are destroying ourselves. I wish they [his direct and indirect victims] could forgive for their own sake and live as much as they can with what they have left. We all have to face down the specter of suffering and appreciate that it's wonderful to be alive. I can live here at Riverbend forever, but I can't be chained to that event. It can't define me.

As our conversation neared its end, Jacob spoke of his home and the sense of responsibility he still feels. He was looking away, clearly immersed in memories:

> I have a great deal of fondness for my home. But I couldn't ever live there again. People couldn't be at peace with me there. I've heard that Nate's brother gets drunk a lot and threatens to kill me if I ever get out. And my family is still suffering. . . . I'm not there

to go fishing with them. I feel responsible for that. And no one will allow me to fix it.

I've had to forgive myself many times [but] memory itself makes it really difficult. Sometimes I'll remember with great anger the choices I made, that I didn't seek help. I remember that I am not allowed to heal certain things. But then I have to remind myself that I've been down this road. I've done everything I could. I don't believe that suffering makes up for mistakes.

Jacob concluded by eloquently turning to metaphor, as he so often does:

Just as the course of every river changes with time, so does the flow of painful memory through our souls. If we allow them, the sands of grace accumulate day by day until slowly a bend in the river appears, and our hearts travel a new path across an old landscape to sink in to the rich soil of hope and renewal previously out of reach. That bend in the river that leads to life is forgiveness. It is the moment of breakthrough, the moment of release, the moment when we choose to live and grow again even though our world will never be the same, because that is what we needed, what we had to have. It is understandably human to resist, but the waters of our hearts will either move forward, charting a new course with time, or cease to flow, stagnate, and die.

Jacob is serving a life sentence with the possibility of parole, which in Tennessee is a mandatory minimum of fifty-one years. He is eligible for release in 2049. He will be seventy years old.

16

MOVEMENT AND LOCATION

THE ABOVE FOURTEEN STORIES from men and women in Tennessee prisons are filled with insight, born from struggle, defeat, triumph, loss, and discovery. Though the knowledge and wisdom in these stories stretch beyond the realm of forgiveness, I will only address their relevance to forgiveness in this chapter, showing succinctly how the men and women's perspectives mix with each other, as well as how they move and locate within the "map" created in chapter one. To begin, I will incorporate their perspectives into an analysis of the forgiveness perhaps most pertinent and difficult for these men and women, or for any of us: self-forgiveness.

Self-Forgiveness

Self-forgiveness is a divisive issue in the literature. Some antagonistic toward self-forgiveness claim it is dangerous and immoral: dangerous because self-forgiveness gives offenders a way to alleviate guilt and shame without a requirement to turn from harmful practices, and thus violations will likely reoccur; immoral because it is a "hollow and self-serving" way of abandoning one's moral responsibility to the victim.[1] Some in favor claim it is a way of "welcoming ourselves back into the human community," of both judging and healing ourselves.[2] Is self-forgiveness moral, then? What exactly does it mean? Should it only follow interpersonal forgiveness? To

1. Gordon Marino, quoted in Schimmel, *Wounds Not Healed by Time*, 121.
2. Robert Enright, quoted in ibid., 124; Smedes, *Forgive and Forget*, 77.

explore these questions, I will follow arguments put forth in Smedes's, Schimmel's, Murphy's, and the Tutus' chapters on self-forgiveness, creating a philosophical framework through which to encounter self-forgiveness in the stories presented above.[3]

The Process of Self-Forgiveness

Essentially, the strands of self-forgiveness are the same as in interpersonal forgiveness. One renounces claims for reciprocal suffering, one overcomes feelings of animosity, and seeks to practice goodwill toward oneself. As evident in several of the above stories, often those who claim the inability or unwillingness to forgive themselves neglect their personal health, denying themselves pleasures, or even necessities, as punishment or self-inflicted suffering. To forgive oneself entails caring for oneself, looking out for one's own well-being. Regarding absolution, self-forgiveness means refusing to define oneself forever by the harm committed or the worst thing one has done, which was a common theme in the stories above.

Finally, self-forgiveness is not a "free pass."[4] It does not mean one "*never* feels bad or wrong [about a certain wrongdoing], but [rather] that these feelings do not pervade the entire fabric of one's life."[5] Like interpersonal forgiveness, self-forgiveness is about coming to reinterpret oneself in light of the wrongdoing, acknowledging both the good and the evil within, and turning from such harmful practices to every extent possible. Contrary to various critiques, self-forgiveness does not exempt the wrongdoer from making amends to the individual harmed. Rather, self-forgiveness addresses one's relationship to oneself. Halling writes that self-forgiveness is the transitioning process from believing "something is fundamentally wrong about one's life, and a feeling of estrangement from self and others" to a place of an "embracing who one is."[6]

3. Smedes, "Forgiving Ourselves," in *Forgive and Forget*, 71–77; Schimmel, "Forgiving Ourselves and Forgiving God," in *Wounds Not Healed by Time*, 121–40; Murphy, "Self-Forgiveness," in *Getting Even*, 57–72; Tutu and Tutu, "Forgiving Yourself," in *Book of Forgiving*, 195–214.

4. Tutu and Tutu, *Book of Forgiving*, 196.

5. Steen Halling, quoted in Schimmel, *Wounds Not Healed by Time*, 130.

6. Quoted in ibid., 129. Brené Brown calls this moving out of *shame*, simply summarized as "I am bad" versus guilt's "I did something bad." Shame produces isolation and disconnection. Self-forgiveness is one way to combat shame's toxicity. See Brown, *Daring Greatly*, 71–74.

This is affirmed in the above stories. Those who acknowledged forgiving themselves still felt great sorrow when reflecting on the wake of suffering their actions produced. But, in keeping with Halling's observation above, these feelings of shame and debilitating guilt no longer consume them. For these individuals, genuine self-forgiveness did not excuse their actions, void them of responsibility for apologizing or making amends, or remove contrition. Rather, self-forgiveness seemed to *increase* their understanding of both their responsibility as well as the wrongdoing's significance. Self-forgiveness required facing the truth of what they had done and coming to terms with the impact of their choices. They could not forgive themselves without either condemning the wrongdoing or acknowledging the harm it caused. In this way, *true* self-forgiveness can never be "moral shallowness."

Self-Forgiveness and Repentance

As noted above, a consistent critique of self-forgiveness claims it is simply a way for offenders to alleviate unpleasant feelings of *deserved* guilt and shame; a way of getting out of responsibility. Schimmel criticizes the immorality of forgiving oneself without also changing one's behavior or trying to make amends to whatever extent possible.[7] Likewise, Murphy writes:

> Self-forgiveness strikes me as an unambiguous good only in cases where the wrongdoer has inflicted an injury for which repentance and atonement are appropriate and where that wrongdoer has in fact sincerely repented and atoned. Absent the requisite change of heart, self-forgiveness is probably hasty and is a sign of nothing more than moral shallowness.[8]

To this, I suggest that *without* a renewal of spirit and will, one has not truly forgiven oneself, and thus such acts as would constitute "moral shallowness" should not be termed *self-forgiveness*. Self-forgiveness is impossible without contrition and repentance. Just like interpersonal forgiveness, self-forgiveness entails full acknowledgement of wrongdoing and thereupon condemnation of said wrong, or—as in the case of Bill—a realization of and deep regret for harm caused. The distinction here is that self-forgiveness can have relevance even in such cases where one does not consider an action

7. Schimmel, *Wounds Not Healed by Time*, 129
8. Murphy, *Getting Even*, 69.

"wrong" per se. Murphy notes the example of a submarine captain who is forced by an imminent air attack to dive his vessel, saving all the men inside but drowning the few on deck. Certainly from a utilitarian perspective of ethics, the captain made the right decision, or even the *only responsible* decision he could make in such circumstances, yet the captain experiences deep guilt and self-loathing because his decision cost men their lives. Thus, the captain needs self-forgiveness even though his action was not necessarily "wrong."[9] Likewise, even though Bill was unsure whether he did *wrong* by reciprocating gunfire, he spoke of needing to forgive himself because of the harm and pain his actions caused the officers' families.

Thus, when facing one's mistake, naming it, and acknowledging the harm done to another, contrition, apology, and changed behavior will follow. Without this, self-forgiveness has not occurred. In the stories above, the men and women's processes of self-forgiveness have produced, or transpired simultaneously with, personal transformation—save perhaps Bill, who was not engaged in destructive behavior leading up to the killing of the officers, but rather was "guilty" of being black in a white-dominated Jim Crow South. Talking with each person, I saw clearly the sincerity of the remorse, the deep desire to make healing amends, and the genuineness of their transformations. Thus, in following Murphy's argument, because it exists in harmony with self-transformation, the self-forgiveness of these men and women can be said to be an "unambiguous good."

The Nature of Self-Hatred

In *Getting Even*, Murphy engages Jean Hampton's assessment that self-forgiveness addresses a "moral hatred" of the self, or a type of self-loathing, relating to the argument put forward in *forgiveness as transcendence* that forgiveness emerges from feelings of hatred or similar emotions.[10] Hampton saw moral hatred of self or other stemming from a defiance of a categorical moral imperative, and thus one comes to hate the self when one rebels against such an imperative. Murphy, however, argues that this does

9. Murphy, *Getting Even*, 67.

10. Hampton defines "moral hatred" as follows: "an aversion to someone who has identified himself with an immoral cause or practice, prompted by moral indignation and accompanied by the wish to triumph over him and his cause or practice in the name of some fundamental moral principle or objective, most notably justice." Quoted in Murphy, *Getting Even*, 59.

not resonate with personal experience. Self-hatred, he argues, is "*shame placed atop guilt*" that makes life "less bearable."[11] This shame develops from the inflicting of *harm* on another individual—particularly one with whom a person shares an intimate relationship—rather than from a willed resistance to some moral law. For example, if an intoxicated driver speeds through a sidewalk and kills someone, the driver will likely feel a much greater sense of self-hatred than will another intoxicated driver who speeds through a sidewalk and injures no one. The latter may in fact feel no self-hatred at all, even though both violated the imperative "don't drink and drive."[12] This self-loathing, in Murphy's words, "come[s] with specific names and specific faces attached." In other words, people do not generally hate themselves because of a violation of an abstract moral code, but rather because their actions brought harm to another human being.[13]

Murphy's view here resonates strongly with the experiences of the men and women I interviewed. Not one suggested needing forgiveness for breaking the law or violating any codes of conduct. Rather, self-forgiveness spoke to the terrible irreversibility of having harmed *others*. Jamie spoke of his "victims" rather than of breaking the state's laws. Tony still weeps with remorse when remembering what he "put those families through." Tonya spoke of the "pain and struggle" she has caused her family. Jacob grieved the devastation of seeing the "pain of good people and [realizing he] had given that same pain to others." Chris regretted violating a woman "in her private space." Victoria spoke of not being able to "take care of my own children." Shelly struggles to forgive herself for the role she thinks she played in the death of her best friend. Their hatred has an object—i.e., themselves—because their harmful actions had objects—i.e., other people. As Smedes writes: "*The pain we cause other people becomes the hate we feel for ourselves. For having done them wrong.*"[14] For Sarah and Betty, self-forgiveness is obstructed by witnessing the continuation of harm to others. Sarah said, "For

11. Ibid., 60, emphasis original.

12. Ibid., 60–61, 64.

13. Ibid., 62. Of course, there are circumstances where failure to abide by rules or an inability to meet expectations can produce self-hatred. For example, having lived my life in the abstinence culture of the Bible Belt, I too have often witnessed shame and self-loathing emerge in people who found themselves unable or unwilling to save sex for marriage. Yet, due to the religious wrappings of much of that abstinence culture, it is hard to discern whether the self-hatred stems from violating the cultural imperative to stay abstinent, or from a belief that premarital sex harms and betrays God.

14. Smedes, *Forgive and Forget*, 72, emphasis original.

me to feel like I should be forgiven, I would need to actually see my son . . . and know for myself that he's okay." Betty reflected that "the main reason I can't forgive myself is I continue to see how my past actions continue to hurt my family." When one can see one's direct or indirect victim(s) still suffering, forgiving oneself becomes far more difficult, if not impossible.

For Hampton, self-hatred can lead people to believe "there is nothing good or decent" within them, that they are "cloaked in evil," or "infected with moral rot."[15] In such beliefs, though, the first task of self-forgiveness is to rehumanize one's self-perception. As Smedes writes, when an individual is declared by self or other to be "*absolutely* evil," he or she essentially moves "beyond the pale of forgiveness . . . [being] excused from judgment by the fact that he or she is beyond humanity."[16] Self-forgiveness has relevance and attainability when one *knows* there is something good or decent within, and thus experiences the guilt and shame of acting in ways that are *inconsistent* with that good. Self-hatred emerges from a sense of betrayal of self, which by definition implies an expectation of otherness. This is evident in the language of regret: "I *shouldn't* have done that." If one could be fully evil, then one would expect oneself to act consistently with that evil, and thus self-hatred and self-forgiveness are unlikely. Thus, when people experience self-hatred as "moral rot," the forgiveness process must include rehumanizing their self-perception.[17] Self-forgiveness addresses a hatred of the self—and all subsets of hatred, such as resentment, anger, contempt, etc.—by learning to "differentiate between the specific offense(s) he [or she] committed and [the] overall estimate of his [or her] worth as a human being."[18]

The stories above reflect the necessity of humanizing self-perceptions. For example, Tony had to accept first his identity as a gay man, and that such an identity did not make him inherently unforgivable, before he could forgive himself for murdering his wives. Self-acceptance led to self-forgiveness. Chris too spoke of the connection between his processes of self-discovery and self-forgiveness. To forgive himself, he had to "deal honestly"

15. Quoted in Murphy, *Getting Even*, 59.

16. Smedes, *Forgive and Forget*, 80.

17. Ibid., 77; McRay, *Letters from "Apartheid Street,"* 114.

18. Schimmel, *Wounds Not Healed by Time*, 123. Schimmel likens this to interpersonal forgiveness, where the victim overcomes hostility through an "appreciation of the intrinsic human worth of the offender." This resembles McCullough's observation that people are more likely to forgive if they "perceive their relationship with the transgressor to be a valuable one" and thus are aware of the value of the individual. See McCullough, *Beyond Revenge*, 149–53.

with his humanity. Rahim engaged self-forgiveness by remembering the "good deeds" of his life, putting "*all* the pieces together." Self-forgiveness for each came through acknowledging his complex humanity and personal evolution, recognizing that his worth as an individual was not confined to the nature of his offense(s). This recognition speaks to the plurality of individual identity.

Self-Forgiveness and the Plurality of Self

As noted in chapter one, Hannah Arendt argues that "nobody can forgive himself" because forgiveness is "an eminently personal . . . affair in which *what* was done is forgiven for the sake of *who* did it."[19] This *who* can only be understood, she argues, in a relational context and can only be perceived by another who can observe one's "distinctness" in relation to himself or herself. Forgiveness depends on "plurality," and thus cannot be given to the self by the self.[20] Interestingly enough, while Arendt's analysis resonates with the findings herein, her conclusion—self-forgiveness is impossible—is problematic.

I agree with Arendt that forgiveness is a personal affair, focused on the *who* involved, and requiring plurality. However, while she dismisses self-forgiveness for these reasons, I promote it. Naturally, understanding forgiveness as a personal affair would not exclude the notion of self-forgiveness, as that is an intimately personal process. Arendt's argument of plurality and an "other" to observe one's distinctness presents the more complicated opposition. Here, Jacob's reflections prove most helpful.

He spoke of the fluidity of personal identity, arguing that the person he is today did not, or would not, murder Nate. Self-forgiveness for Jacob addressed his "*old* self." Thus, thirty-six-year-old Jacob sees in *himself* a plurality, a distinctness from his eighteen-year-old self. Listening to Jacob called to mind a caterpillar's metamorphosis into a butterfly. The butterfly emerging from the cocoon is both the caterpillar that entered as well as a new being. Thus, as Jacob experiences transformation, he is able to reflect on his old self, seeing that "identity is slippery" and kinetic, and thus offers forgiveness to a self *distinct* from his current self. Tabatha expressed

19. Similarly, Gobodo-Madikizela writes, "I doubt that when forgiveness is offered, the gaze is cast on the specifics of the deed. Forgiveness, while not disregarding the act, begins not with it but with the person." *Human Being Died*, 95.

20. Arendt, *Human Condition*, 237–43, emphasis original.

a similar transformation: "I am not that same girl I was back then, scared and naïve. I am a forty-one-year-old woman who understands the pain of a loved one taken by someone else." Therefore, while Arendt's analysis of forgiveness's plurality can be accepted, her conclusion must be rejected, as it does not account for the plurality of self.

Connecting Intra- and Interpersonal Forgiveness

Finally, the following questions emerge: What is the appropriate relationship between self-forgiveness and interpersonal forgiveness? Should self-forgiveness only follow interpersonal forgiveness? To begin, there are two directions of interpersonal forgiveness: outward (forgiving others) and inward (being forgiven by others). Enright elaborates on the multi-directional nature of forgiveness in what he calls "the forgiveness triad," which consists of self-forgiveness, seeking forgiveness, and giving forgiveness.[21] With this triadic relationship in mind, consider the reflections of Tony, Jacob, Chris, Jamie, and Tonya.

While both Tonya and Jamie acknowledged that receiving forgiveness would certainly make it "easier" to forgive themselves, they did not believe the latter should be conditioned on the former. As Tonya and Tony point out, interpersonal forgiveness may never come, thus to wait for that forgiveness "to get right with God and ourselves" is "psychologically destructive," locking them into a lifetime of "pain and hate." Thus, if the earlier argument that self-forgiveness counters some form of self-loathing is correct, then the absence of self-forgiveness entails the perpetuation of self-loathing. Self-hatred, left uncontested by efforts of positive self-acceptance, can lead to self-destruction, as in the suicidal thoughts of Jamie, Tonya, Tony, and others. In such cases where the direct and indirect victims cannot—e.g., due to death—or will not forgive, rejecting self-forgiveness would lock the "offender" permanently into that label. As Chris acknowledged, forgiveness—particularly *as absolution*—erodes the victim-offender distinctions. Entirely conditional views of forgiveness can cement the victim and offender in their respective roles. It bears repeating that *especially* when self-forgiveness exists apart from received forgiveness, it *must* be coupled with repentance.

Both Jacob and Chris, however, stated that for self-forgiveness to be possible, they had to forgive others. Such comments should highlight the

21. See Enright, "Counseling within the Forgiveness Triad," 107–26.

often blurred lines between "victim" and "offender," roles that are often interchangeable.[22] Though imprisoned for being offenders, each man and woman above suffered great injustices before and after the act(s) for which they are now incarcerated. Chris and Jacob's experiences also prompt the question: *Why* would one need to forgive others in order to forgive oneself? Just as I advocate unconditional interpersonal forgiveness for the sake of the forgiver's freedom, on principle I also promote an unconditional self-forgiveness, given to oneself for liberation and transformation. Some, though, may find experientially that self-forgiveness is impossible without receiving or giving forgiveness to others. I propose two possible reasons for this.

First, one may feel unjustified in forgiving oneself if one has not forgiven those one deems as personal offenders. What moral ground would one have in showing grace for one's own faults if one cannot offer that same grace to others? Second, because no action happens in a vacuum, when forgiving oneself, one takes responsibility for the harm dealt but also acknowledges the contributing events. In such cases where "self-loathing" is truly accurate, the individual has often suffered prior abuse or trauma which she or he thereupon recycles: e.g., Chris was neglected by his drug-addicted father; Tony was condemned for his homosexuality; Jamie was scarred by school bullying and his father's alcoholism; Jeremy experienced abandonment from an early age; Tonya, Shelly, Crystal, and Betty all spoke of suffering physical, emotional, and/or sexual abuse as children, etc.[23] The harms we perpetrate are connected to the harms we receive. Thus, because—as Jacob recognized—people do not exist in isolation, transcending animosity toward self also means transcending external animosities and thereupon finding some liberation as one moves beyond the paralysis of harmful events. Thus, Jacob's and Chris's connection between self-forgiveness and

22. See Bloomfield et al., eds., *Reconciliation After Violent Conflict*, 64–65. Late historian Howard Zinn, in writing about the Spanish invasion of the Americas, instructed: "My point is not to grieve for the victims and denounce the executioners . . . [as] the lines are not always clear. In the long run, the oppressor is also a victim. In the short run . . . victims, themselves desperate and tainted with the culture that oppresses them, often turn on other victims." See Zinn, *People's History*, 11.

23. Gobodo-Madikizela addresses this reality in her chapter "The Evolution of Evil" where she describes the personal development of Eugene de Kock, an apartheid perpetrator known as "Prime Evil," who suffered from paternal abuse. See Gobodo-Madikizela, *Human Being Died*, 48–78, esp. 55–59.

interpersonal forgiveness may be found both in moral necessity and in gaining a holistic liberation from potentially destructive hatred.[24]

It is helpful to view this interplay of Enright's triad as a triangle with the connecting lines containing arrows pointing both ways, demonstrating the multi-directional relationship at work. Experientially, no formula exists for chronologically organizing these triadic components. They take place at different times and in different ways for different people. Morally, however, one might argue against self-forgiveness preempting the receipt of forgiveness, protesting—as previously noted—that such an exercise releases the wrongdoer from responsibility by prematurely appeasing the conscience. However, if it is indeed *self-forgiveness*—as described above—and not a hasty attempt to alleviate unpleasant guilt, then that self-forgiveness *will* result in seeking forgiveness. If the moral right lies in repentance and making amends, then I cannot see how it matters whether self-forgiveness precipitates interpersonal forgiveness if the result—i.e., transformation and reparations—is the same.

Seeking Forgiveness and Apology

I have claimed that self-forgiveness necessitates seeking forgiveness, but what of the nature of that seeking? How is it done? Should the one who committed the harm ask for forgiveness? Here, as regarding most aspects of forgiveness, perspectives vary. The Tutus believe requesting forgiveness is essential, claiming it as "the highest form of accountability," since "there is no asking for forgiveness without admitting the wrong and witnessing the anguish."[25] Jamie, though, has come to believe that asking for forgiveness may not be appropriate:

> I've learned not to add an additional burden [by] asking something so difficult from someone I have already hurt so much. All I can do is express my regret and remorse. It's up to my victims to forgive when they are ready.

24. It is possible that a similar reciprocal relationship exists between self-forgiveness and interpersonal forgiveness: i.e., one may need to forgive oneself *before* one can forgive others. To paraphrase Vanier's quote from earlier, we often cannot accept the weaknesses of others because we have not come to accept our own weaknesses. Thus, sometimes before forgiveness can be given to others, one must first forgive oneself by accepting one's own weaknesses.

25. Tutu and Tutu, *Book of Forgiving*, 180–81.

Jamie's insight is important, as it is crucial to distinguish apology from explicitly asking for forgiveness: apology offers something *to* the other; requesting forgiveness asks something *from* the other.

When I harm another, I breach her boundaries; I invade and violate his identity. We may have been on different life-tracks before, but now our trains have collided. To ask that same person to extend forgiveness risks recreating the same dynamic: moving from my tracks onto hers. For some, "will you forgive me?" may help repair the damaged landscape caused by the collision, but for others, it may increase damage if the person I have harmed is not yet ready to forgive. Perhaps my request fuels feelings of inadequacy and insufficiency in the other; perhaps it produces anger as the other thinks I am requesting a "get out of jail free" card. Asking for forgiveness is to prompt a response from someone who may not be prepared to offer one.

Expressing regret and remorse, however—i.e., genuine apology—acknowledges the other's suffering, owns the wrong, and stays off the other's tracks. The Tutus go on to write that asking for forgiveness encompasses more than those four words we are taught to ask as children; it includes expressing remorse and apologizing, "acknowledg[ing] the harm and explain[ing] why and how we will not hurt the victim again." If my hope for forgiveness is genuine, I "will do whatever it takes to make things right."[26] Thus, the components of authentic forgiveness-seeking are these: feeling regret, expressing remorse, offering apology, and a willingness and readiness to make things right. Through this, the other may extend forgiveness, but explicitly requesting forgiveness is to step out of the realm of personal responsibility and into the journey of the other's recovery. Assuming they are genuine, remorse and apology are *noninvasive* self-judgments that many harmed persons need to hear, especially if reconciliation is a hope. The explicit, verbal request for forgiveness—more so than an apology—lends itself to misunderstanding and thus perpetuated conflict and pain. I must stay on my tracks until the other invites me onto hers or sends me on my way.

Placing Pins

I was homeschooled for several years before high school, and we had two large maps on the paneled schoolroom wall, one of the US and one of the

26. Ibid., 181.

world. On it, we charted our family travels, domestic and international, with tacks and pins placed in various cities and colored lines tracing the interconnecting routes. In this final short section, I will do this same exercise with the stories above, placing them like pins on the map created in chapter one.

The Necessity of Forgiveness

In one way or another, each person addressed or demonstrated the undeniable necessity of forgiveness. Tonya believes if she had been able to forgive the man who raped her and not been "bound so tightly to [her] negative emotions," she would not currently be in prison. As she concluded, "I'm in prison today because I grew up as a broken individual who was traumatized emotionally . . . and never healed from it. I was fueled by hate . . . and carried it through to adulthood." During her days of unforgiveness for the man who abused her sister, she felt "sick and violent . . . [and] would hit anyone or anything." For Jamie, his unforgiveness of his father "caused me to choose that terrible action that hurt so many innocent people." Then, his unforgiveness toward himself produced "depression and suicidal thoughts," until he finally "tired of the misery." When he forgave, all those thoughts "disappeared." But as Rahim claimed, "the hurts . . . do not disappear. . . . The scars remain." "Nobody can change what happened," Jacob said. "There's such futility in chaining yourself to an event and bringing it into the future." This irreversibility shackles both the victim and contrite offender to the event as neither can travel back in time to alter the past. Forgiveness offers the possibility of liberation that perpetual vindictiveness and revenge do not. As Tonya said, it offers "emotional freedom." Without forgiveness, each person would be consumed with paralyzing guilt, incapable of functioning productively outside their shame. And indeed, some still live in this prison.

Shelly told how her and her sister's lack of self-forgiveness continue to perpetuate conflicts between them: "There is no relief to the misery. . . . [We] over-analyze each other's every word and action. . . . Unforgiveness makes us crazy." She confessed that this unforgiveness has been "killing" her "for years." Victoria believes that if she could "receive forgiveness from even just half of those I've harmed," including herself, she might be able to "sleep at night." Unforgiveness damages emotional, physical, and mental health. Forgiveness is not only necessary for the liberation of identity, the transformation of relationships, and the melting of moments of frozen time; it is also for the diagnosable health and well-being of the body and spirit.

What Forgiveness Is Not

Forgiveness addresses wrongdoing through judgment and grace, facilitated by empathy and understanding, as both Chris and Jeremy noted. Among those who actually committed harms, no one tried to excuse his or her actions, and only Bill hinted at justification through self-defense and thus questioned the relevance of forgiveness. Tony, Crystal, and Tonya stated that forgiving does not mean forgetting, though a few worried that forgiveness would lead to forgetting. (I will explore this in "Forgiveness as Reinterpretation" below.) As stated in the first chapter, forgiveness and reconciliation are clearly connected, though certainly distinguishable. Forgiveness, while naturally oriented toward the possibility of reconciliation, does not require it. Jeremy spoke to this when he told of forgiving Teresa without wanting to reconcile, and Tonya admitted that forgiving the man who abused her sister did not need to lead to reconciliation: "There's nothing to mend between us," no ongoing relationship that needs healing and restructuring. Yet, as Jamie saw with his father, to experience full reconciliation, forgiveness is necessary. Tonya too acknowledged this when she said, "I do believe that our relationships' healing and growth are dependent on forgiveness." We can forgive and not reconcile, but we cannot reconcile without forgiving.

Forgiveness as Release

To paraphrase Jacob, reciprocal suffering does not right wrongs. These individuals see that forgiveness entails ending the spiral of suffering—or as Jamie said, "giving up the need for retaliation"—even if some cannot yet break free of the self-inflicted suffering of unforgiveness toward themselves. Forgiveness must mean refusing to inflict further damage. As Tonya said regarding self-forgiveness, it means "choosing not to do harm to myself … I am not allowed to torment myself with an all-consuming hate and shame."

Regarding the notion of punishment and incarceration, nearly all acknowledged the justification for some length of social separation. But, as Crystal observed, her "debt" will not be paid by "eternal incarceration." Several addressed the tension between the retributive focus of the prison system and the concept of forgiveness, emphasizing the system's unforgiving nature and the difficulty of pursuing forgiveness in such a context. In Jacob's words:

> Whatever forgiveness I have found, it is in *spite* of the system. The system doesn't facilitate any kind of forgiveness. It is focused like a laser on vengeance, motivated out of fear. It uses suffering and pain to punish suffering and pain. It chains me to my past. . . . It really makes it impossible to fully forgive yourself.

As Chris noted, forgiveness requires vulnerability, which the system does not facilitate. It is "continual emotional punishment," Tonya claimed, "a constant reminder" of those negative choices that continue to plague her and her family. "This hinders the self-forgiveness process," she said. The consensus among these men and women in prison was clear: retributive punishment, whether external or internal, does not lend itself toward forgiveness.

Forgiveness as Transcendence and Goodwill

Almost everyone directly defined forgiveness as the overcoming of vindictive emotions, supporting my earlier claim that *forgiveness as transcendence* is the "indispensable core" of forgiveness. "[Losing] ill will" (Tony and Tabatha) and "overcoming" or "giving up" the emotions of "anger and hate" (Bill and Jamie) are central to forgiveness. The forgiver must choose "not to live in the . . . bitterness of the past," as Crystal put it. In overcoming this bitterness, empathy is essential. Rahim's experience is illustrative:

> My family all talked of wanting to kill Malone [the man who killed Rahim's sister]. Then it hit me that this is what I did to another family. I suddenly looked at Malone as myself. I didn't want to harm him. I told my family that whatever they felt about him they had to feel about me. It was then that I forgave some parts of me.

In connecting the pain of his victim's family to his own pain, Rahim began to be able to forgive himself as well as the man who killed his sister.

Yet, as one transcends this animosity, one may or may not pursue goodwill. Jeremy forgave Teresa (*transcendence*) but now experiences relative indifference toward her well-being. He exists in the middle space between these two strands, neither actively wishing her ill nor actively wishing her well. Likewise, when Tonya forgave her sister's boyfriend, she did not develop well-wishes for him but rather "no longer want[ed] him to pay for what he did, at least not by my hands." Instead, forgiveness let her be "completely free of him." Others, like Chris and Jamie, experienced positive fellow feeling through forgiveness: Chris *toward* "T" and Jamie *from* the woman he intended to kill in high school.

Forgiveness as Absolution

While Tony spoke explicitly of absolution, others only referenced its components. For Sarah, forgiveness means not "hold[ing] past mistakes against" the other, and for Betty, it means "no longer hold[ing] him or her accountable for the pain he or she has caused." Jeremy said, "Forgiveness means you can't use someone's past against them. All that we've been through is gone." Clearly, if he meant that the event itself is "gone," as in forgotten or the pain erased, then he speaks unrealistically. However, if he means that the event is "as if not" in the context of the relationship, then I agree. Neither the memory nor the pain has magically vanished, but rather, the memory cannot be stored away for future ammunition. Its relational relevance is silenced.

Forgiveness as Reinterpretation

In the original articulation of *forgiveness as reinterpretation* in the first chapter, I noted how forgiveness requires memory. After an event's occurrence, it survives through memory, and with each re-membering, the familiar intersection returns: perpetual bitterness or re-given grace? Since Crystal cannot forget what happened years ago, she struggles "every day" to forgive herself and those who have harmed her. For Jamie, "forgiveness is a process" that will "always be an issue." Whenever Tabatha encounters reminders of the life she is missing on the outside, her anger returns and she must re-forgive. Tonya spoke of her "daily decision" to forgive since the "anger, guilt, and shame [don't] just go away"; she is reminded of the pain "every single day I wake up in prison." Jacob told me that "memory itself makes it really difficult" to forgive. With the memories comes "great anger," both at his choices and that he is "not allowed to heal certain things."

The perpetuity of these memories tends to carry negative identity markers that fuel resentment, or even hatred, of the self. Forgiveness, though, reinterprets that negative identity. The memories are not erased, but rather the message conveyed by those memories changes. Rahim spoke of this, saying that forgiveness is "a new way of experiencing life," refusing to define himself by those fateful ten minutes in 1989. Forgiveness entails reframing and renaming oneself and one's experiences—past, present, and future. As Rahim noted, the scars remain—much like the imprint of the palimpsest—but a new story can be written, one not dictated by victimization or shame. When Jacob is overwhelmed by the memories of that fateful day at the end of high school, he says he has to re-forgive himself, reminding himself he has "done everything" within his power to make things right. In this re-forgiving, he is reinterpreting his identity, away from one of murderer and toward one of aspiring healer. His forgiveness reminds him that he can no longer be defined as that disturbed boy who killed his classmate Nate; he is a grown man who wants more than anything to repair and restore what he took. Likewise, I believe if Victoria and Sarah could genuinely forgive themselves, they would cease categorizing themselves as neglectful, inadequate mothers who could not protect their children. Forgiveness would not mean they forget what happened to their children, nor would they forgo responsibility for any harm they caused. Instead, forgiveness opens the cell doors from the prison of those destructive identities and gives the opportunity to imagine a new story for their futures.

Forgiveness as reinterpretation allows the immediacy of the memories to fade so they no longer consume. Shelly, it seems, recognizes and fears this, worrying that she'd "lose Abby" by losing her memories of her:

> When we grieve a loss, it seems we "get over it" and move on . . . I am terrified of losing her: the sound of her laugh, how she looked, her scent. What would I have of her if I lost those things? I am afraid I would stop missing her. Even one minute would be too much.

Shelly's memories of Abby are all she has left; she naturally resists anything that might take those memories away. Yet, forgiveness is not interested in— nor perhaps capable of—erasing memories; again, it is about reinterpreting them. Jeremy referenced this when he said: "But I think I have forgiven myself. Instead of thinking about the night I told Ben no . . . I remember the fun we had." Jeremy is observing the fruits of forgiveness as the immediacy of the negative memory fades, and he begins to reinterpret himself and his lingering connection to his friend.

Though I am no psychologist, I suspect that if Shelly forgave herself for any real or perceived wrongs toward Abby, her attachment to Abby would not disappear but rather change. The focus would transform from guilt and self-hatred to nostalgia and fondness. She would not *lose* the memories, but rather remember them *differently*. Even her perception of the *facts* may change. Instead of telling the story as someone responsible for Abby's murder—"If I had been a stronger person, if I would have taken the abuse in silence like I was supposed to, my best friend Abby would still be alive"—she might come to see herself as another *victim*, not a perpetrator, of Abby's murder, abandoning all notions of "supposed to" as she realizes that asking for help in the midst of brutal and monstrous abuse does not make her responsible for the actions taken by her abusers against Abby. Forgiveness may show her she is a survivor without fault in the death of her closest friend.

In the end, positing a multi-stranded understanding of forgiveness proved helpful as it allowed for experiential variety and theoretical multiplicity. The first chapter's exercise in cartography exposed the complex topography one must navigate and made it possible to move and locate the voices from exile within that terrain. These stories demonstrated that forgiveness does not excuse or condone harms committed. Forgiveness names the harm *as* harm and takes responsibility for it. Forgiveness does not forget the damage done but rather provides the opportunity to free ourselves from being consumed by the memories and the negative identifiers associated with those memories. Forgiveness is antithetical to vengeance and retribution, whether toward another or ourselves. Forgiveness means letting go of ill will and offers us the possibility of cultivating goodwill. Through forgiveness, debts can be cancelled, and relationships released or reconciled. Finally, forgiveness is storytelling; it is about daring to tell a new story about ourselves or our *other*. It is about believing, hoping, imagining that new life can grow from the damaged and decaying soil of our pain. To borrow theological language, forgiveness is in the business of resurrection.

17

THE TOP OF THE PYRAMID

Toward Forgiving the Prodigals

MY COLLEGE PROFESSOR RICHARD Goode often used a three-tiered pyramid in his history class presentations. The bottom level read *Data and Information*, the middle level *Knowledge*, and the top *Wisdom*: data and information build to knowledge, which, given the right questions, leads to wisdom. Richard was never content simply to teach the "facts" of history; he cared much more for the "so what?" questions: "Why should we care about any of this? How does it help us live well?" In this final short chapter, I am interested in the top of that pyramid, the "so what?" questions. What wisdom regarding forgiveness and prison might be discerned from the data, information, and knowledge explored herein? Here are some possibilities.

Forgiveness is "as mysterious as love"; it is a complex, courageous endeavor in human life.[1] People continually perpetrate harms on each other that create corpses, permanent scarring, and disfigurement, both physically and emotionally. Damaging events can neither be reversed nor often avoided, and some impact us so profoundly that full recovery is impossible. Thus, the enthusiastic "boosterism" surrounding forgiveness can create a pressure to forgive that may *increase* trauma and spark feelings of guilt for those who cannot forgive, especially when forgiveness is defined with singularity and simplification. Forgiveness is complicated and confrontational—if not relationally then morally, as it often counters one's intuition regarding just course following a violation. Though much effort is rightly

1. Quoted in Cantacuzino, *Forgiveness Project*, 7.

exerted to render forgiveness attainable for most people, forgiveness cannot become simple or easy. It is—to a degree—scandalous, as it offers grace when both instincts and a retributive culture demand otherwise. Essentially, forgiveness faces down "the specter of suffering," as Jacob put it, and interrupts the destructive spiral of reciprocity, offering a way to address pain and loss by reinterpreting life in the context of one's altered reality.

While the men and women featured above hope for forgiveness *from* their victims and *for* their own offenders, the struggle to forgive themselves remains constant—in no small part due to their confinement. The prison system is adversarial, deliberately denying possibilities for expressing forgiveness and pursuing reconciliation. It imprisons bodies and, without deliberate resistance, identities. As Jacob passionately acknowledged, "The man I am today didn't do it!" The logic of retribution, though, aims to hold him captive in that tragic moment his senior year of high school. For the prison, Jacob's identity—as well as all those above—is *offender*. There is no complexity; only simple categories. Forgiveness, though, recognizes and embraces complexity, releasing so as to transform and move forward. This is antithetical to the mission of the prison system that seeks daily to remind its captives that they are defined by a moment, by a set of harmful actions, by the things they have done wrong. Seeking forgiveness in such a context is immensely challenging, as the imposed identity of "forever an offender" and the impossibility of reaching out to those one has harmed causes frequent setbacks. To quote Jacob yet again, "Forgiveness ... tries to offer new garments, but this system just chains you to the mud in them. It really makes it impossible to fully forgive yourself."

In writing and researching for this book and in previous volunteer work, I witnessed prison conditions firsthand, conversed with insiders and staff, and surveyed the relevant literature. All this revealed the deeply disturbing nature of a racist, classist, arbitrary, retributive system oriented toward profit rather than rehabilitation.[2] Richard Goode and Will Campbell's edited work *And the Criminals With Him* opens with striking essays from such writers as Preston Shipp, Alex Friedmann, and Andrew Krinks show-

2. Michelle Alexander's *The New Jim Crow* exposes in well-documented detail how the "racial caste" system of the United States—clearly evident in slavery and the Jim Crow laws of the South—has "not ended . . . [but been] merely redesigned." Alexander, *New Jim Crow*, 2. Attorney Preston Shipp's essay "What Has Happened Since 1973" also shows how the severest criminal convictions both target and are disproportionally imposed on the nonwhite population. See Campbell and Goode, eds., *And the Criminals With Him*, 33–42.

ing how the birth of privately owned prisons has restructured the criminal justice system so that "justice literally is for sale and crime does in fact pay—for private prison companies and their shareholders."[3] Rehabilitation is not only less important but actually counterproductive in such a system because high recidivism means "repeat customers"—that is, guaranteed income. Certainly for those interested in forgiveness, such realities of profit and retribution should be alarming.

More than 95 percent of all those in prison will be released back to society, and thus, while we are wise to care about the security of our communities, we are confused about the ideal methods for ensuring that security. Gilligan exposes the problem:

> [W]hen one tests against empirical data the assumption that punishment will prevent violence, by examining how people who are punished actually behave, one finds that far from preventing violence, *punishment is the most powerful stimulus to violent behavior that we have yet discovered ...*"[4]

Gilligan shows through statistical research and professional experience that punishment does not deter violence as much as provoke it. Given the retributive obsession of the current American system, it is little wonder that US recidivism rates hover steadily between 50 and 70 percent. Such unacceptable and dangerous rates are unnecessary and preventable through reimagining the purpose and practice of prisons. Articulating a holistic re-visioning and restructuring of the US prison system is certainly not the task of this last chapter, but fortunately, we will not need to reinvent the wheel, so to speak, but rather take lessons from the "radical humaneness" of prisons like that in Norway, which play a significant role in the sub-20-percent recidivism rate that country boasts.[5] If forgiveness can lead to healthy personal transformation, and transformation facilitates rehabilitation, and rehabilitation is conducive to societal safety, we should demand a system that facilitates forgiveness rather than discourages it.

The stories above, as well as countless others not included, confess the terrible struggle of seeking, finding, and sustaining forgiveness in a context expressly dedicated to the opposite, one fueled by categorical condemnation. Poet-farmer and American prophet Wendell Berry writes:

3. Alex Friedmann, "Societal Impact of the Prison," in ibid., 53. See also Andrew Krinks, "Why It Pays to Imprison," in ibid., 54–69.

4. Gilligan, *Preventing Violence*, 18, emphasis original.

5. Benko, "Radical Humaneness."

> Condemnation by category is the lowest form of hatred, for it is
> cold-hearted and abstract, lacking the heat and even the courage
> of a personal hatred. Categorical condemnation is the hatred of
> the mob. . . . This mob violence can happen only after we have
> made a categorical refusal of kindness to heretics, foreigners, en-
> emies, or any other group different from ourselves.[6]

It was Richard Goode, to whom this book is dedicated, who first exposed
for me the categorical condemnation we as a society project on prisoners.

When I studied "Religion and American Culture" with Richard my
sophomore year, everything changed, and I took him every opportunity
I could during the next couple years. After graduation, the relationship of
professor/student turned into friendship. That relationship has altered the
direction of my life. Most of my current pursuits are linked to Richard,
including my proximity to prison. He told me once that famous quote,
"an enemy is someone whose story we've not yet heard," and invited me
to come with him to Riverbend prison one Saturday night and hear some
different stories: "Shorten the distance," he said. I had no idea how that first
visit would change the course of my life.

In the years since, I have learned a profound lesson: proximity affects
everything. Whether with people experiencing homelessness, developmen-
tal and intellectual disabilities, oppression, state execution, deportation,
poverty, incarceration, or any other embodiment of life "from below," our
proximity to people changes our relationship to them and the issues they
represent. While on opposite sides of the walls—whether prison walls in
Nashville, "peace walls" in Belfast, separation walls in Palestine, or border
walls in Texas—we believe we have something to fear on the other side. The
walls become self-fulfilling prophecies: their existence fuels fear and the desire for security, thereupon justifying the need for the wall. Often, though,
when we get close—physically and relationally—to those behind the walls,
we learn our fears were misplaced. We hear new stories, and people we once
saw as enemies are enemies no longer. I echo Tony's words: "When I got
[inside prison], I realized that these are normal people with value. I started
hearing stories and realized it's not as easy as we all like to think. There are
more veins than just one. The men in here are not the product of the worst
thing they ever did."

Proximity changes us. Shortening the distance between me and people
in prison dismantled whatever categorical condemnation I had constructed

6. Berry, "Caught in the Middle."

of those inside. Though before entering prison I paid little attention to is-sues of criminal justice and incarceration, my proximity to the men and women directly affected by these issues encouraged me to reevaluate my judgments, and I began wondering how it was we could condemn people to live and die in suffering and exile. While there likely are people who, for various reasons, are unable to live well in community with others and must remain perpetually separated, no one should ever be *sentenced* to that. For Tennessee to decide that an eighteen-year-old Jacob Davis will be dangerous, useless, and irredeemable until he is seventy is an unimaginable travesty. In our society, categorical condemnation of criminals seems to last forever. We tend to reserve our "forgiveness" for the wealthy kid suffering from "affluenza" rather than the homeless veteran with PTSD.

I also started wondering what would happen to my new friends when they returned to the free world. How would they be received? Though we speak of incarceration as "paying one's debt to society," we clearly do not mean it, since upon return, many freed men and women cannot vote or sit on juries and can legally suffer housing, education, and employment discrimination due to felony records.[7] Their punishment continues long after release from prison.

But I am interested in social forgiveness for prisoners. If unforgiveness corrodes our health and sanity at the individual level, it stands to reason it also poisons us socially. To function as cultures of violence, retribution, vengeance, and shame is to compromise our social health. To begin this journey toward social and personal forgiveness and cultivating a healthier society, we must get proximate to those we have categorically condemned and listen to their stories. If we tell and hear different stories—ones of re-morse and redemption, transformation and broken humanity, forgiveness and reconciliation—we may come to imagine a different world, where even the prisoners are forgiven and set free.

To close, I present these words from Jacob Davis. It seems fitting for the final words to belong to someone on the inside. Writing as "Moses" for the Tennessee prisoners' blog "Prodigal Sons," Jacob questions the purpose of retribution and longs for reconnection:

> We are living question marks. What is the point of all this? Are we still human? Is there any value in our lives? Is there any forgive-ness, any redemption for those who have truly repented? If not, what does that say about us all?

7. For more on this, see Alexander, *New Jim Crow*, esp. 93–96, 140–200.

We are human like you and we want to show that. We are your brothers and fathers and cousins and uncles and sons. . . . We need help in order to construct a positive future in community with all peaceful people. Why in the name of all human good and the future of our society would you refuse to help us in such an endeavor? . . .

We are the prodigal sons. We have been told it doesn't matter if we repent, that we shall not have a chance to give anything back, and there is no return no matter what. We come back to the gates anyway in the name of peace and hope and love. Where else will we go? For human beings, life means forever seeking a home and the love of family and community. No other home exists for us but the one from which we were exiled. We know some of you will kick us and spit on us no matter how true our words or how pure our hearts. We know you are not evil, only afraid and asleep. Wake up. Wake up. We are not monsters. Hear us knocking. We will come back to you again and again.

Where else could we go?[8]

8. Davis, "Who We Are and What We Want."

APPENDIX

From Behind the Walls

When I returned to Nashville from Belfast in May 2013 and began my conversations with the men at Riverbend prison, the institutional chaplain—Jeannie Alexander—soon invited me to volunteer as a chaplain in her department. "I think you would be good in Unit 4," she told me. "I think you could handle it." At that time, Unit 4 housed Riverbend's "mental health" prisoners in maximum security, which means they experienced incarceration locked in single cells for twenty-three hours per day, seven days per week. Insiders call this "twenty-three, one." Jeannie confessed that, the week before, one of the men in Unit 4 cut his throat in front of her. "Unit 4 is a place of devastation," she said. "It crushes the spirit and breeds death."

Despite my four years of prison experience up to that point, the truth of her words did not fully resonate with me. My weekly contemplative prayer and discussion visits with minimum-security men from Unit 6 had opened my eyes significantly to the brokenness of the prison system, but it had not prepared me for the brutality of Unit 4's inferno. After a few weeks of my chaplaincy work on Unit 4, Jacob Davis—one of the chaplain's clerks—cautioned, "The light is disappearing from your eyes, Mike. Your spirit seems far heavier than it was before." He was right. Unit 4 changed me—theologically, politically, psychologically. It turned me into a prison abolitionist.[1] It traumatized me in ways similar to and yet different than my experiences confronting the Israeli occupation of Palestine with Christian Peacemaker Teams (CPT). But like my time with CPT, I had no choice but

1. For more on my meaning of "prison abolition," see the home page and "Core Values" section of the No Exceptions Prison Collective website: www.noexceptions.net.

155

to write. I needed to tell the stories of what I saw. These stories are this appendix.[2]

The five stories herein are of chaplaincy, but they are not stories of evangelism. My work as a volunteer prison chaplain on Unit 4 had less to do with explicitly discussing religion or Jesus and more to do with violence de-escalation. Jeannie saw my graduate studies in Belfast and my experiences with CPT in Palestine as sufficient preparation for the work. The men I encountered were traumatized by destructive systems, both inside and outside the prison walls. They did not need evangelism; they needed listening and presence. Thus, the following narratives are not ones of comfort and salvation, at least not the salvation commonly assumed.[3] These stories are of violence and trauma; they profess the profane, both of language and circumstance.

Each story ends with a prayer, offered as both experiment and exasperated expression. Growing up in East Tennessee, I often heard my father share stories with visiting Vanderbilt students, exposing the challenges and intimacy of practicing rural medicine. He consistently ended these stories with prayerful reflections, influenced by the work of Michel Quoist. I composed these story prayers to imitate my father's writings, as well as to try to live in the question, "How do we pray to a loving God in the midst of violence and suffering?" When at nineteen I stood with my father at the ovens of Auschwitz and he said, "Whatever you believe about God has to make sense here or it can't make sense anywhere," my confident and comfortable prayer language became another casualty of the Nazi's death camp.[4] How do we speak to and of God in such places? Yet, despite my disillusionment

2. The names of all involved in these stories, save for the first and last stories, have been changed.

3. After an honest conversation with friend, author, and theologian/philosopher Peter Rollins about prison, he wrote a powerful blog piece entitled "Getting Thrown Out of Prison." In it, he spoke of the salvation I am referencing here: "prisoners have the potential of offering . . . a type of salvation for the system that holds them. For if we look at those within the system, get to know them and discover the context that contributed to their imprisonment, we can begin to glimpse how the system we participate in is corrupt, violent and full of darkness. This is, of course, a disturbing activity to engage in. For, in doing so, we are no longer able to maintain the fantasy that we are a type of hero helping poor, unfortunate people. Rather we realize that we need to do this work in order to discover how poor and unfortunate we are, and how violent the structure we participate in is for some people."

4. For a video of a live telling of this story at Tenx9 Nashville, see www.tenx9nashville.com/2014/08/25/michael-mcray/i-was-never-the-same-again/.

and confusion about how to pray, I did not know what else to do after writing these stories. I am haunted by God, and in the midst of suffering, I felt compelled to cry out.

When my older brother Jonathan was living in Searcy, Arkansas, he and a small group of friends organized an alternative theological event called *Lost & Found*, creating an inquisitive space for the challenging of often un-critiqued notions of evangelical orthodoxy and orthopraxy. During the evening, my brother's friend noted how churches frequently invite congregants to sing hymns of praise as images of running rivers and majestic mountains project on the screen. John and his friends wondered if such hymns might be more difficult to express if people sang while viewing images of suffering. Those in attendance were then asked to sing "How Great Thou Art" while the faces of starving children, the devastation of war, and the isolation of the homeless slowly transitioned on the screen. The verses echoed timidly. Afterwards, when all were invited to come forward for the Eucharist, everyone accepted.

In that spirit, I invite you into these stories and prayers, each written within a few days of the events they describe. I wanted words that were fresh and raw. I hope you find them honest, yet not overly didactic. Good storytelling, I believe, often leaves the interpretation open to the reader. We do not always need to give a moral to the story. Sometimes we must trust the reader to find what he or she should find at the time he or she should find it, for stories have many purposes. To me, these stories expose, inform, and—I pray—persuade. What they expose and persuade toward is for you to decide.

For the Christian reader, I offer them as Eucharistic moments. If we encounter Jesus in the prisoner (Matt 25:36, 40), then these stories depict interactions with the literal body and blood of Christ.

Take and eat.

Jesus Under Lockdown

That Friday, I saw Jesus in the infirmary.[5]

Encountering Christ in prison was one of the primary purposes for my first visit behind the walls nearly four and a half years ago. I have often struggled in my life to understand how and where God "works" in the world. But I have held tightly to Jesus' claim in Matthew 25 that he is encountered when we encounter the "least of these": the hungry, the naked, the alone, the sick, the imprisoned. German theologian Dietrich Bonhoeffer wrote of learning to the see the world "from below . . . from the perspective of those who suffer."[6] When we see the world "from below," we see where Jesus is hanging out. This particular day, he was in the infirmary, and his name was David Shepherd.

I had known David for awhile. I actually roomed with a relative of his for three years during undergrad, and around late 2011, David joined the Saturday-night contemplative study group I had been a part of since early 2010. David has lived incarcerated for nearly twenty-one of his forty-one years on this earth. When Chaplain Alexander asked me to make rounds at the infirmary, I assumed it would be to visit with one of the men from the maximum security side—like the young man I saw the week before who set fire to the shirt on his back in order to gain attention. But instead, the chaplain asked me to see David. "Mr. Honey died," she said.

I walked out of the chaplain's office and up the sidewalk to the infirmary, a long beige concrete building adjacent to Building 11 where the chaplain's office is located. Inside, I entered the Long Hall, one of two corridors housing inmates who, among other reasons, are placed on suicide watch, mental health seclusion, or have serious medical needs. The halls are cold and lifeless, except for the warm bodies kept in those solitary cells. David was caged at the far end of the Long Hall. As I walked toward his temporary residence, other men on the hall called out to me. "Damn dude!" one greeted, "You look like a rock star." This was undoubtedly in reference to the previous day's haircut, returning to a look that had unfortunately elicited many a "Hey Justin Bieber!" from jeering voices inside Units 3 and 4 on the max side. David heard me enter the hall and was standing at his window waiting for me.

5. A revised version of this story was published at *Red Letter Christians*: http://www.redletterchristians.org/behind-walls-pt-1-jesus-lockdown/. The names in this story are real.

6. Bonhoeffer, *Letters and Papers*, 17.

"Hey Mike," his bass voice welcomed. "Thanks for stopping by." I always loved seeing David. He is a warm soul, kind and compassionate, with an embrace you could get lost in. He is a big man, tall and stout, with long, graying hair, fashioned like a mullet pulled back in a ponytail. His face often shows stubble, sometimes even a goatee, but that day he was clean shaven. His laugh is deep and inviting, and he often tries to lift other's spirits with encouraging words. But when I saw him that Friday, his eyes revealed grief. After all, Mr. Honey had died.

I knew Mr. Honey's health had been declining rapidly for months. His stomach had swollen to the point of seeming pregnancy and required frequent drainage. The prison's private medical provider, however, did little to assist Mr. Honey's healing or even alleviate his excruciating pain. "Time and again," David later told me, "Honey'd say he wished he had a gun so he could just end it already and stop hurtin' so bad." Mr. Honey was only fifty-five, but he appeared to be approaching his late sixties.

His failing health required constant caretaking, an activity the prison did not feel obliged to undertake. But David did. Though he had only met Mr. Honey less than a year before, he requested Mr. Honey become his "celly" (cellmate) back in the summer when Mr. Honey's health began to plummet. I wondered if David realized just how serious a responsibility he had accepted. Regardless, from the moment Mr. Honey moved into David's cell in Unit 6, David rarely left his side. But now, Mr. Honey had left David's, and David was under lockdown.

As I stood outside the massive steel door dividing us, I wondered what to say. For a few moments, we just stood there, looking at each other and the tile floor, as if something more powerful than us was compelling a reverent silence. Finally, I broke the quiet, saying the only appropriate thing I could think of: "I'm sorry, David. How are you feeling?"

He looked away and began nodding. "I'm okay. My emotions are everywhere though. I feel angry, then sad, then relieved, then angry again." He looked back at me, tears brimming. "I'm just real happy he's not suffering no more." David told me Mr. Honey passed peacefully in his cell, surrounded by David, the chaplain, and a couple of other friends. The months leading to his death nearly incapacitated Mr. Honey. His pain was immense, but it was finally gone, and for that, we felt grateful.

I wondered if there was more to David's feeling of relief than simply that Mr. Honey's suffering had ceased. I wondered if he felt relief that his full-time caretaking role had also ended. I suspected that such thoughts produced guilt and were thus unwelcome. I carefully explored this with him, gently encouraging him to release any guilt and allow himself to feel the understandable gratitude of relief from such exhausting service.

"It definitely was a lot of work," he allowed, chuckling to himself in a kind of nostalgic disbelief. "I was with him through it all."

His eyes reddened as he recounted the months of constant attentiveness. Several weeks before, Mr. Honey lost the strength to walk even relatively short distances. Frequently, as I entered the compound for chaplaincy work or to teach, I would see David, leading the evening procession to the chow hall, pushing Mr. Honey's wheelchair in front of him. Anytime Mr. Honey required moving, David's sturdy arms guided his wheelchair to the necessary destination. Back in their cell, David cooked hot meals for Mr. Honey in the microwave and fed him when he lacked the sufficient strength for even such simple actions. In the last couple of weeks, Mr. Honey lost control of nearly all physical faculties.

"He couldn't even go to the bathroom without help," David confessed, shaking his head. "I'd pick him up off his bunk and carry him to the toilet. He couldn't even sit up, so he'd lean his head against my chest. He was bleeding internally so he had blood on him, too. 'Don't worry. I'll clean ya up when you're finished,' I told him." David cared for Mr. Honey like that until the end. He gave completely and unreservedly of himself to preserve whatever dignity he could for his friend, to ease his suffering, and ensure that he would not die alone. Mr. Honey died on a Saturday night, and David was placed on lockdown in the infirmary.

Apparently, this is prison protocol. Because Mr. Honey died in his cell, the cell must be declared a "crime scene." David was present, so he is contained in solitary pending the conclusion of the investigation. Besides the fact that the chaplain herself had also been present, the prison knew for months that Mr. Honey was dying. His death was expected, perhaps even encouraged through the system's apathy. Despite all this, David—the man who exhausted himself for *months* in selfless service to the needs of Mr. Honey—had to mourn in solitary.

When David finished his story, I placed my hand on the thin glass window in the door, pointing at him. "I am inspired by you David. You have done exactly as I suspect Jesus would have."

In retrospect, that statement seems obvious, since it was in fact Christ with whom I spoke, God-in-the-flesh. His hair was grayer than most religious paintings depict, and his skin much lighter than the Middle Eastern Jew of the first century.

Nevertheless, I talked with Jesus in prison that day. His name was David, and the prison had him under lockdown.

Prayer:

Lord Jesus Christ, have mercy on us.

If the system we've created baffles me, it must surely baffle you—for you are just. We humans can astound sometimes with our inhumanity to one another. To punish a man for showing compassion and selflessness, to punish David for love, devotion, and kindness . . . it hurts and angers me. I want to tear down the steel doors and set him free! Christ, the Scriptures say you have come to set the prisoners free. How long must we wait, O Lord, for it to be so?

I struggle with waiting. I am impatient. I know this. When I see something I want, I want it now. I am a child of the culture of instant gratification. I work diligently to change this about myself. But this is an ongoing process, and today, living with serenity in the moment is a true challenge for me.

This is especially true regarding injustice. Witnessing the powerful abuse their power boils my blood. I want to throw tables like you did. I want to drive them out like you did. I want to yell and scream and curse.

God of justice and mercy, grant me the courage to cleanse the temple, grant me the serenity to wait patiently and watch expectantly, and grant me the wisdom to know which is needed.

And please, please, have mercy.

For our inhumanity to each other—Lord, have mercy. Christ, have mercy.

For our condemnation and confinement of broken people to broken systems—Lord, have mercy. Christ, have mercy.

For believing in punishment when restoration is needed—Lord, have mercy. Christ, have mercy.

For abusing our power and creating suffering—Lord, have mercy. Christ, have mercy.

For not always seeing the image of you in each human being—Lord, have mercy. Christ, have mercy.

Amen.

A Human Being (Almost) Died That Night

That particular Friday began as my Fridays usually did: quiet morning of conversation with my grandmother over coffee and muffins, silent meditation, and a thirty-minute drive to the prison.[7] The first couple of hours inside the compound produced great joy and laughter as the chaplain's department held a pizza party for those minimum security prisoners who volunteered their time preparing and distributing Christmas packages to every insider. After making quick work of four pieces, I grabbed a handheld radio and headed to the high side—where I would not be making quick work.

My assignment was Unit 4, a maximum-security unit where two of the four pods were designated as "mental health."[8] Each pod contains twenty-four cells that held both young and old men who received classifications of suffering from more extreme psychological afflictions. This unit is certainly the most violent in the prison as the stress levels of inmates and staff stayed dangerously high. Before I walked across the compound to the unit, a minimum-security prisoner told me that a Unit-4 inmate threw feces in an officer's face the day before, and another inmate bit that same officer's arm. Tensions were high, so I breathed in deeply and walked through the razor wire gate and into the concrete building.[9]

The smell hit me first, as it always did. With so much blood and feces regularly decorating the walls, a vulgar stench remained, no matter how much scrubbing occurred. It was like working inside a dirty toilet. As was protocol, I waited until a correctional officer (CO) was available to accompany me, and then I entered one of the two mental health pods to begin my cell-side rounds.

Before entering, the officer warned me the pod had "been crazy" all day. Acknowledging his caution, I called into the radio unit, "Charlie main, Charlie gate," and within seconds, the thick steel door and iron gate opened, granting me access to the pod. As soon as the gate closed behind me, a cacophony of "Chaplain, chaplain!" sounded from all corners. I shouted

7. A revised version of this story was published at *Red Letter Christians*: http://www.redletterchristians.org/behind-walls-human-almost-died-night/.

8. I have changed some of the verbs here to past tense in recognition of Riverbend's wise abandonment last year of the Unit 4 mental health project. The mental health inmates confined in Unit 4 have since been shipped to other facilities.

9. Regarding Unit 4, I will often use the term *inmate*, as that is how those men consistently referred to themselves.

from the entrance that I would be around to each cell. I started with Mr. Freeman, a man I met just a few weeks earlier in the infirmary after he had set fire to the shirt on his back to get attention. We seem to have connected surprisingly well that day, so I wanted to pay him another visit.

Next was Mr. Waylen, the man who had bit the officer. He claimed the CO had assaulted him through his pie flap, and thus he bit in self-defense. He had red marks on his neck where he claimed the CO choked him, but those could have been self-inflicted. I didn't know what to believe. While hearing his rage-filled claims, I noticed escalating noise coming from a cell a few down from his. Promising to report this alleged assault to the Officer-In-Charge, I moved to the cell of Mr. Saylor, who within two hours would be rushed to the hospital, close to death.

"Howdy, Mr. Saylor," I greeted cordially. Having never met him before, I introduced myself. "I'm Chaplain McRay."

"Okay," he shrugged, smirking. His clean face looked young, and I guessed we must be very close in age. As I did with each man, I made sure to look him in the eyes while we talked. Many of the men's eyes show despair, windows into souls battered by years of punishment; Mr. Saylor's eyes showed something different: fire.

"Are you doing okay?" I asked him, smiling, trying to keep a positive demeanor so as not to provoke any aggression.

Mr. Saylor titled his head as he looked at me through the glass. He was bouncing slightly, almost as if he was excited about something. Then his right hand took a small razor and quickly cut his left forearm. Raking his hand through the blood, he then smeared it down his face, over his nose, mouth, and chin. One glob rested above his eye.

"Do I look okay?" he challenged. His whole demeanor suggested he wanted me to be intimidated, impressed, perhaps even to quiver in awe. So I laughed instead, trying to remain calm and play a different role than the seeming "terrified spectator" part he'd scripted for me.

"No, sir," I chuckled, "you do not." He just kept smiling. "Is there anything I can do for you?" I asked.

"Just get me a straight ticket to the road to hell!" He had a lively country accent, and he swayed back and forth as he spoke. I asked him why he wanted to go to hell. "*Everybody* wants to go hell!" There was an unsettling confidence in his laugh.

Calmly, I countered, "I don't think anyone really wants to go to hell. Why do you?"

"Ah, it'll be fun," he told me, the fire in his eyes intensifying. "All that buurrrnin'!" The way he drew out his words reminded me of Andy Taylor in the early seasons of *The Andy Griffith Show*. He then lifted his left arm; it was spotted with burn marks and blood from various razor cuts that day. Scars ran in between, telling me this was not the first day he had drawn blood from that limb.

"That looks quite painful," I confessed, removing some cheer from my tone.

"Nah, not yet!" he grinned. When I asked him what was wrong, he shouted at me: "Man, I'm just fuckin' tired of it! I'm fuckin' tired of it! Nobody here cares about me!"

I looked him straight in the eyes, and said as genuinely as I could, "*I'm* trying to care, Mr. Saylor. That's why I'm standing here talking to you."

"Ah, you don't give a *shit* about me," he hollered, turning around laughing. He walked back toward his bed, and I knew he had no reason to believe I cared. He had never seen me before in his life.

When he returned to the narrow window, I told him I needed to call medical since he was bleeding. I asked an officer to make the call, but the officer asked me to leave the pod. My immediate protests did not sway him. Apologizing to Mr. Saylor, I turned to walk down the stairs, passing three officers on their way up to his cell.

Before I reached the floor, I heard one shout, "He's squirting! He got an artery!" The corporal shouted through the radio unit, "Get medical in here now!" Then he yelled to me to run find latex gloves in the central staff pod. Searching frantically, I located two pairs and rushed back into the pod and up the stairs. Taking the gloves from me, the corporal instructed me to wait on the lower level. Four officers gathered at his open door, and from where I stood below, I could see it all.

Just as I had walked away from Mr. Saylor's door, he had sliced clean through an artery in the bend of his left arm. Streaks of blood now covered his whitewashed walls, as if he had squeezed a squirt bottle while turning circles in the room. I saw him sitting calmly on his bed at the back of the cell, a laser quivering on his chest from the Taser one CO pointed at him. A large gash stretched across his arm, blood streaming down his forearm, onto his pants. His face, shirt, and bed were red with blood, and he just sat there, still, smiling at the prison staff in his doorway. The COs handcuffed him so he couldn't cut anymore, and the medical team wrapped a bandage around the severed artery. But by that time, he had already lost so much blood that he soon collapsed, unconscious.

Four COs carried him down the stairs, his arms and legs stretched out and his head hanging back over their shoulders. They carried him out of the pod and toward the infirmary. I stood there, perhaps in shock, unaware of any conscious thoughts. It was as if I was in stupor. Suddenly, I regained a sense of awareness as I heard another man calling for me. Hustling up the stairs, I moved toward his cell and peered into the window. I saw Mr. Jackson there, tattoos covering his face, anger in his eyes, and nothing in his cell.

In cries of anguish, he told me what happened. Yesterday, he had lived in the cell next to Mr. Waylen, and when Mr. Waylen reached through his pie flap and threw something into Mr. Jackson's cell, Mr. Jackson responded by throwing feces back at him. But these feces hit an officer instead. Mr. Jackson cried out to me, "I didn't mean to hit the officer! I told him over and over, 'I'm sorry! I'm sorry!' But they won't listen to me! I can't take it anymore! I can't take it!" He dropped to his bed, head in his hands, body shaking in anger.

My eyes scanned his cell. All his possessions had been taken in punishment. Nothing remained but a coarse blanket. The logic of retribution seemed to spread itself plainly before me: punish the wrongdoer, and when he reacts, punish him harder, and then even harder. This system takes angry, broken people and locks them in small rooms, alone, with very few possessions or constructive human contact, and then acts bewildered when these repressed humans snap. Offering no more than one hour of recreation time per day in a metal cage, serving food that could repel even the most famished dogs, and taking all one's earthly possessions with each misdemeanor, our current system shames and provokes these men until they erupt. And when they do erupt, they are punished more.

Mr. Jackson could not take it anymore. His desperation almost broke me on the spot, and it took all I had to keep it together. Numerous times while listening to him, I had to ask him to pause because I could not hear. The pod had descended into chaos after Mr. Saylor was removed. Men were horse-kicking their doors, shouting at each other and at COs. Some were throwing things in fits of rage. I felt consumed in noise. Even with my ear pressed to the door and Mr. Jackson shouting on the other side, I could barely hear him. It was as if everyone had snapped at once. Inmates shouted obscenities at COs; COs shouted back, taunting the inmates to cut themselves. They seemed ready to oblige, as shirts flew off and razors appeared.

Promising Mr. Jackson I would bring him a book to read to keep his mind occupied until the staff returned his property, I moved swiftly around the pod, trying to de-escalate. I felt like I was back in Hebron, running for cover from oncoming tear gas canisters and rubber bullets, or attempting to alter the plans of Israeli soldiers preparing to invade a Palestinian home. It was as if my experience with Christian Peacemaker Teams in occupied Palestine was preparing me for prison chaplaincy. Just like in Palestine, I felt I had no idea what I was supposed to do. I was just making it up as I went. But one by one, the men grew quieter and their razors disappeared.

I headed out of Unit 4 and walked back to the chaplain's office to get books for Mr. Jackson. As I walked into the crisp cold air, the only words I could muster were those that have begun monastic prayers for centuries: "O God, come to our assistance. O Lord, make haste to help us." Over and over, I repeated the mantra as I walked.

Back at the chaplain's office, Chaplain Alexander was rushing out the door to catch the ambulance that was ferrying Mr. Saylor to the hospital. He was fading. She called me from the ambulance to tell me he might die. Grabbing two books from the library, I made haste back to Unit 4. Inside, I slid the books under Mr. Jackson's door. "This gives me some closure," he told me. I sighed gently from relief.

Wanting to be present with Mr. Saylor at the hospital, I rushed out of the prison and drove to Metro, told the receptionist I was there to see the recently arrived prisoner if possible, and then waited in the ER. After fifteen minutes, my phone vibrated with an email from the chaplain telling me that security would not let anyone in the room with Mr. Saylor, not even her, and that I should return to the prison.

When I arrived back at the chapel, the Friday night service had begun. I slipped in quietly to a pew against a side wall. Chaplain Alexander sat just in front of me. When she saw me sit down, she reached back and squeezed my hand, whispering that Mr. Saylor was stable. Just a few minutes later, I slipped back out, crouched in a corner of the hall, and wept.

I had not been prepared for what I saw that day.

Prayer:

O God, come to our assistance. O Lord, make haste to help us.

God, where are you? How come when we call in our hours of great distress, in our moments of deepest need, you do not answer?

Perhaps you too were weeping, crouched in the corner of your hallway, and could not get up. Perhaps you too choked on your tears and could not raise your voice. In some ways, if I knew that was true, I think it would help. To know you also can be so shocked by our horribleness to each other that you cannot speak, to know that you also can be so traumatized by walking in hell that you must stop to weep, would give me some manner of peace.

God, mother and father of a broken people, what we have created today, this so-called "justice system," is not justice. It is hell; it is darkness and flame. It consumes those who get close; it brutalizes souls.

Jesus, you said that when we encountered the least of these in prison, we encountered you. I try to believe that.

But was that really you in there? Was that really you the officers carried out of the unit to the ambulance? I didn't expect you to look like that. I didn't think you would have a razor in your hand. I didn't think you would smear blood on your face while I talked with you. Have the principalities and powers really broken you so brutally that even you can't resist the demons of despair, fury, and self-hatred? I knew you would be in prison, Lord. That's why I came. But I didn't think you would be in hell.

God, you are merciful, slow to anger, and abounding in steadfast love. Help me be the same—because I'm not. Days like that make me angry, even furious. I want to burn the prison to the ground, and some days, I want all those responsible for it to burn too. Some days I wish for desolation.

I know you said to forgive them, for they know not what they do. But sometimes I think they know.

Breathe into me your spirit of loving-kindness, of a justice kissed by mercy, and a truth met by peace. May I be as present as possible with each person I meet behind those and all walls, and may I always remember that whatever I do for them, I do for you.

Amen.

Scars

I had never seen scars like Sam's, and I never want to again.[10]

I have seen scars, of course, and bad ones too. In 2007, a Palestinian physician handed my father and me a photo album, containing nauseating images of young Palestinians scarred, bruised, and hemorrhaging from rubber bullets and tear gas canisters fired from Israeli military weaponry. I have also seen scars on the bodies of other incarcerated men. Some scars were deep and few in number; others were shallow and numerous.

Some, though, are simply in my imagination—like those belonging to a female patient of my father's from his small community medical practice of twenty years in East Tennessee. Growing up, I listened to him read her story to visiting college groups who came to our town of Jellico to understand the dynamics of rural medicine or the plight of the Appalachian poor. His story described a pregnant woman in her late twenties who visited the clinic for the first ultrasound for her fifth child. Before he raised her shirt to apply the ultrasound gel, she spoke: "I have a lot scars." My father writes:

> What I saw, faintly in the darkened room, caused me to pause. Her entire abdomen was covered by a disordered maze of curved and straight lines. "A bad burn," I thought. "The body looks this way after multiple skin grafts. I wonder if she was in an accident several years before." . . . I resumed my preparations, covering her wounds with the ultrasound gel, and tried to obtain a little more information—"Were you in a car accident, or . . ."
>
> She did not let me finish. Very matter-of-factly, without a hint of emotion, she answered much more than I had intended to ask. "My mother set me on fire when I was three."

In my mind, her scars are perhaps the most vivid, though I have only seen them in my dreams. But I saw Sam's with my own eyes.

It was my third encounter with him, having first met him while making rounds in the mental health pod of Unit 4. In our first two visits, tears filled his eyes, attesting to his emotional exhaustion, as he vented his weariness of *years* of twenty-three-hour lockdown seven days a week in solitary confinement. In both visits, I found Sam to be kind, gentle, vulnerable, and emotional. He seemed stressed but collected, frustrated but grateful for my visits. The third time I visited his cell, however, he was different.

10. For a live telling of a version of this story, see http://tenx9nashville.com/2015/04/17/michael-mcray-i-was-in-prison/.

From the opening exchange, I knew Sam was angry. His agitation produced a visible physical tension. More so than before, his body carried a powerful energy which seemed poised on the edge of his skin ready to launch at any provocation. I tried to embrace a positive but concerned demeanor.

"What's going on with you today, Sam?" I inquired.

"I'm about to lose it," he replied with confidence. I detected a hint of worry in his tone, as if Sam himself feared the consequences of his eruption. He then spoke of turmoil in the pod, detailing the destructive dynamics between correctional officers and inmates. Such relationships of asymmetrical power often *begin* tense and then disintegrate with haste. Sam claimed numerous unmet requests and needs, accused the staff of blatant disregard, and indicated the proximity of his impending retaliation. "I'm about ready to start terrorizin' again," he said.

This language disturbed me. *Terrorizing* is such an expressive yet uncommon term for describing one's actions. I asked him to explain.

Sam's descriptions horrified me: "I take control of my pie flap. I tell them get the fuck off my door. If they don't, I might pull their arm through the pie flap and break it. Maybe cut off a finger with a razor. Sometimes I throw homemade pepper water in their eyes. Maybe some shit and piss." He made this list matter-of-factly and without hesitation, but his tone suggested slight apprehension, as if in this vulnerability he feared my rejection. Though I certainly refused to reject *him*, I also did not want to risk indicating tacit approval of such violence. I dug deeper.

"Why do you want to do that? Do you feel it accomplishes your goals?"

"They fear me," Sam said, his eyes widening. "They learn real quick not to mess with me." We conversed back and forth about this, as I questioned whether fighting fire with fire was the best method for dealing with the abysmal situation in which he lived. With each exchange, I realized more fully the violent past and potential of the man on the other side of the steel door—a man who, as a five-year-old, had to help his mother roll up the body of the dead pimp lying on their carpet; a man who had witnessed women sell their young daughters, as well as their own bodies, to drug lords for twenty dollars worth of crack cocaine. Sam simultaneously held in his body an inviting gentleness as well as an alarming aggression. I had not encountered a more complex creature.

I suddenly noticed what I thought was a rash on his lower neck. "What happened to your neck there, Sam?" I asked, trying to lighten the conversation. I had no idea what revelation that question was about to produce. Sam smiled, and without saying a word, removed his shirt. It was then I saw the scars on his chest.

Sam stepped back from the door so I could see his entire torso. His fit upper body was almost fully covered in interwoven scars, documenting a pattern of extensive self-violence. Numerous uninterrupted scars ran parallel from either shoulder to the opposite hip, crisscrossing in the middle. It looked like Wolverine from the X-Men had slashed Sam's body over and over. The scars rose out from his flesh, some as far as an inch. Clearly, he had cut deep and often. Innumerable scars tattooed both arms. Almost no inch of his upper body had escaped his attacks.

I am sure I slurred my words trying to formulate a response. Sam spoke up quickly, still smiling: "See, I've been cuttin' a long time. A lot of these guys, they cut short. They don't go deep. They can't. Can't take the pain. Me—I'm all in. When I cut, I *rip* through," and he demonstrated this ripping, pulling his right hand across his chest with brute force. I shivered imagining a razor attached to such a powerful motion.

"Why do you cut like that?" I asked with soft voice and sapped energy. For whatever reason, I then stated the obvious: "The pain must be unbearable."

"That's the point," Sam explained. "Sometimes the situation here is too much. I can't stand it. I cut like this so I black out. At least in those moments, I don't have to deal with this place." The tears returned to his eyes. Before I could respond, Sam continued, "Some days I just wanna end it all—ya know, black out and not come back." He leaned his head back slightly as a tear slipped down his cheek, and it was then I noticed his neck again.

His other scars were so grotesque they had distracted me from reexamining the very thing I asked about in the beginning. With his shirt off, I could more clearly see the markings on his neck. They were not the result of a rash, as I had previously assumed. They too were razor scars. Sam then told me how he had sliced deep into his neck at least three times in suicide attempts. His flesh was wrinkled and ragged from layers of scar tissue that formed a complete circle around his neck. As my eyes scanned his whole body, I saw far too much mutilation.

It was now uncomfortably clear that Sam had a painful story to tell. His past must be filled with the same sort of violence I saw displayed on his dark skin. We agreed that I should try to have him pulled out of his cell soon so that he could share some of his story in a more private setting. I told him goodbye as the scars disappeared under his white prison shirt.

Before moving on to the next cell, I paused and leaned against the wall. I needed a moment to process. I had never seen a body more marred than his. I wondered how such a place could exist, a place so violent and dehumanizing that someone would prefer to die or black out from self-mutilation than face another moment incarcerated.

I closed my eyes, breathed deeply, and stepped in front of the next cell. Feigning positivity, I greeted, "Hey Mr. Bedford, how are you?"

Prayer:

Lord, open my lips—and my tongue shall keep silent. Sometimes I do not know what to say. But I need to pray words right now. I need to process what I saw.

O Christ, who suffered mutilation at the hands of others, your body must have looked much like his. Your scarred flesh must have horrified others the way his horrified me. I have never seen scars like that. And they were self-inflicted. What kind of demon must one have in order to suffer in such a way? What kind of story? What lack of love? What ache and pain? I want to cry, God. I want to hug him and hold him. When was the last time he felt someone's hug? When was the last time he felt loved? Are his scars a calendar, tally marks carved deep in his flesh counting the months and years of no affection?

O God, I have never seen scars like that. I know everyone has scars. Even I do. But not everyone has scars like that. He told me he mutilates himself to escape, to cause so much pain that he blacks out. What kind of place have we made? What kind of hell have we built with our own hands? I wish you had been there to cast those demons out of him, like in the story of Legion and the pigs.

Mother of a broken humanity, forgive us and be kind to us, for we can be wretched. Father of all, convict and compel us to right our wrongs and build a new world in which we seek healing and reconciliation rather than shame and pain.

Amen.

Razors

He kept his cell dark.[11] In the numerous times I stood talking with him outside his door, the fluorescent light shone rarely. Sometimes the sunlight lit the cell through the narrow window, but he usually dimmed it with a makeshift newspaper curtain. It took me several lengthy conversations to begin to hear some of his story, but after only a couple of visits, one thing seemed clear: Marcus Hammonds preferred the dark.

My first encounter with Marcus jarred me as much as it intrigued me. His scars were the first I saw in Unit 4. I saw many more after. The first day I met him, I strained my eyes to see in his cell. Finally, he turned on the light.

He was young, in his mid-twenties like me, and his face was clean. His brown eyes screamed rage behind his large-rimmed glasses, and his bulky body served him well surviving prison. His attention span was as short as his fuse, and his thick arms displayed dozens of scars, primarily on his left. Most scars were only an inch or two long, but they ran deep. Two were fresh, leaving his raw, pink tissue exposed.

Marcus was one of those the officers referred to as "a cutter." His self-abuse was as habitual as his fury. Few could appease him, or at least few tried. Almost every time I saw him, he ticked like a bomb ready to explode. Often, I found I could temporarily de-escalate by maintaining a calm tone, keeping my body relaxed, and paying attention. When he felt heard and respected, his anger softened. Yet, even in those moments of relative cool, Marcus still spoke of violence.

"I dream of murder," he said to me one day, after he had begun to trust me more.

"While you're sleeping?" I replied, unsure why I even asked the question.

"Yeah, but when I'm awake too." He shuffled back and forth steadily, wringing his hands together as if rinsing them under a running faucet. "Sometimes, I just sit in here with the lights off and obsess about murder." He then described to me in detail his plan for killing the staff members of the prison whenever the Department of Corrections (DOC) released him.

This was a first for me. I had never talked with someone about a desire to kill. Of course, there was the time an Israeli soldier pointed a rifle at my face and said, "I want to shoot you through the head with this bullet," but

---

11. A live reading of a revised version of this story can be seen here: http://tenx9nash-ville.com/2014/09/23/michael-mcray-nashville/.

we didn't really *discuss* it. This exchange with Marcus was different. I tried exploring these feelings with him for a while, and in the process, learned more of his story.

He told me of growing up in poverty, of how even as a child he had to steal sometimes to provide food for his family of three. He told me about witnessing the murders of friends and family members. He told me how his mother used extension cords to beat him and his sister. He told me of his first experience locked up, when he was arrested for throwing a rock at the head of a white girl who had actually thrown the first stone. He was charged; she was not. He told me he was twelve.

Marcus was like a boomerang—every time the DOC threw him out, he eventually came back. The system claimed to be "*re*habilitating," but I wondered what it was "habilitating" him back to. The environment of dysfunction and violence that sent him to prison was the same environment to which he would return. State punishment had not cured the diseases of poverty, neglect, and abuse.

"Have you always obsessed about murder?" I asked him.

He shook his head, peering off behind me as if searching through memories. "It all started after coming here to max." The DOC had been locking Marcus in maximum security for a couple of years at that point. After Marcus had done several months of time in Unit 3, the prison transferred him to one of the mental health pods of Unit 4. While under maximum security, Marcus remains alone in his cell, locked up for twenty-three hours per day, seven days per week. His typical human encounters involved frequent antagonistic interactions with staff. Occasionally, he phones his sister or a cousin. To my knowledge, though, he rarely received visitors.

I saw then that the prison was functioning as a self-fulfilling prophecy. It further broke an already broken man so thoroughly that he was now truly a danger to others and shouldn't be released. Prison had created a need for itself.

One day I walked into Unit 4 and Marcus shouted to me, "Chaplain, come here now!" I climbed the steel stairs to my left and stood in front of his cell, remaining relaxed.

"Hey man, what's going on today?"

He jerked his shirt off, revealing a fresh, deep slice just above his shorts. Bouncing with rage, he then turned and showed me his left arm. Two raw wounds stared back at me. I asked him why.

"Nobody listens to me!" he shouted back, pacing behind his door. "I ask the officers for something, and they just ignore me! My therapist won't come see me! I need to talk to someone about these thoughts in my head, but nobody gives a fuck!"

I suggested he just start talking to me. With seething resentment, Marcus recounted his newest violent fantasies. I listened for some time as he spat his anger out like a poison. I then asked him when he cut himself.

"A few hours ago."

"And has anyone from medical come yet?"

"They gave me some bandages and gauze. I didn't cut deep enough." I asked him if he still had the razors. He reached up on his shelf and then opened his hand. Three small blades, pried from disposable shaving razors, rested in his left palm, with dried blood still visible. He stood there with cupped hands, almost as if he was receiving the Eucharist from a priest.

I knew my next question would likely be met with laughing dismissal, but I had to ask anyway: "Would you be willing to give me those razors?"

Much to my surprise, Marcus did not shoot down my question. He looked at me for what seemed like minutes, considering my request. Then he smiled slightly and said, "I'm sorry, chaplain, I can't. These razors are my voice."

His confession hit me in the gut: Marcus cuts to be heard. This was the fifth reason I discovered for self-mutilation in prison. Once, when Mr. Hayfield came back from medical, I asked him why he had cut himself. "Sometimes I get really bored," he told me. When I asked Mr. Saylor, sometime after our first meeting, why he cut so often, he confessed to raping his five-year old niece: "I hate myself. I deserve to suffer and be in pain forever." Mr. Freeman once explained that sometimes he cuts because he feels relief when he does it. His emotional turmoil is immense, and slicing open his skin provides physical relief. Sam told me he mutilates himself to black out so he can temporarily escape the hell of prison. Similarly, Mr. Freeman also admitted that sometimes he cuts himself severely (or burns himself, or swallows batteries, etc.) so that he will have to be taken to the infirmary: "I can look up at the sky on the way," he said, "and I get to spend a night or two with a little bit of peace and quiet. It's so chaotic in here." And now Marcus told me he cuts to be heard.

I stood there looking at Marcus, feeling nearly traumatized as I realized that in this dystopic system, boredom, punishment, relief, escape, and voice served as justifications for self-mutilation. In this "department of corrections," little correcting seemed to be occurring.

"Do you feel heard when you cut?" I asked him.

"Well," he chuckled, "I tend to get what I need much quicker than when I just ask for it."

As I stood with Marcus, I soon began to realize that he did not *really* prefer the dark. The dark provided him with an excuse. Marcus wanted to be seen, but even in the light, he was ignored. Darkness gave him a concrete reason for his seeming invisibility. But Marcus does not prefer the dark. In fact, Marcus would kill to be seen.

Prayer:

Christ, you said once that those who live by the sword die by the sword. I think you were right.

Amen.

Freedom

He leaned over and whispered to me, "What the hell does prison even mean right now?" It was perhaps the most beautiful thing I had ever heard.[12]

The chapel in Building 11 was full. Incarcerated and free-world brothers and sisters interwove on the wooden pews. Hardly a seat was vacant that Friday night. At the front of the chapel, Tony had spread a spectacular arrangement of cloths, rugs, and papers, ornaments that brought color to an otherwise colorless concrete chamber. Sitting on the decorations were four musicians, each dressed in appropriate attire for a service of Indian Hindu music.

The leader instructed us. "Chant in unison: OM. Sustain this sound. Try to still your whole being. Center yourself. Find your center through that sound and focus on it. Feel the vibrations in your whole body." Over the next half hour, she led us in various Hindu chants and rhythms, but we continued to circle back to "OM."

I closed my eyes and straightened my spine against the hard back of the pew. I rested my feet flat on the floor and could feel the vibrations from the room traveling up my legs. Time seemed to stop. My whole being resonated with tremors of "OM," produced from my lungs and those of fifty others. I had no idea how long we had been chanting; my focus held like a laser point on the all-consuming sound reverberating throughout the chapel.

Thirty minutes into the service, my dear friend Jacob, a man already incarcerated for sixteen years with the rest of his life to go, turned to me and said, "What the hell does prison even mean right now?" I felt I could cry it was so beautiful. It was beautiful because it was true. It was beautiful because *he* said it. It was beautiful because I felt it. For Jacob at that moment, imprisonment was nonsensical. It did not compute. For me, all the weight of my own burdens of fear and shame disappeared, swept up in the swirling sounds of instrument and voice. The music had moved us, in emotion and dimension. We were no longer where we were when the service began. The sounds stirred our being.

What the hell did prison even mean then?

In those moments, prison didn't mean isolation. It didn't mean exile or punishment. It didn't mean suffering. Really, prison didn't mean much of

12. A revised version of this story was published at *Red Letter Christians*: http://www. redletterchristians.org/behind-walls-pt-3-freedom/

anything. The vibrations of the music collapsed the walls and transported us somewhere, anywhere, everywhere. We sang "OM" and we were lost, immersed in serenity. I have heard that "OM" is the central sound of the universe—the sound from which all sound comes, and to which all sound returns. It is the auditory source of everything, the deep container that unites and holds all sonic utterances. That night, it united and held us, and transported us beyond. Jacob's question said everything—what *did* prison mean right then?

In those moments, we were all free.

Prayer:

O God, in you we live, and move, and have our being. I am grateful for the blessing of music, its transporting and transforming power. It liberates us when we are enclosed. It lifts us when we are depressed. It humbles us when we exalt ourselves. It gives us energy when we have none. It heals us when we are broken. It moves us when we are too still. It stills us when we are too active.

I want to believe in your spirit the way I believe in music. Help my unbelief.

Amen.

BIBLIOGRAPHY AND FURTHER READING

Abramsky, Sasha. *American Furies: Crime, Punishment, and Vengeance in the Age of Mass Imprisonment.* Boston: Beacon, 2007.

Abuelaish, Izzeldin. *I Shall Not Hate: A Gaza Doctor's Journey on the Road to Peace and Human Dignity.* New York: Walker & Company, 2010.

Abumrad, Jad, and Robert Krulwich. "Memory and Forgetting." *WYNC's Radio Lab Podcast.* 2007.

Alcoholics Anonymous: The Story of How Many Thousands of Men and Women Have Recovered from Alcoholism. 4th ed. New York City: Alcoholics Anonymous World Services, 2001.

Alexander, Michelle. *The New Jim Crow: Mass Incarceration in the Age of Colorblindness.* 2nd ed. New York: The New Press, 2012.

Arendt, Hannah. *The Human Condition.* 2nd ed. Chicago: University of Chicago Press, 1998.

Arnold, Johann Christoph. *Why Forgive?* Farmington, PA: Plough, 2000.

Ateek, Naim. *A Palestinian Christian Cry for Reconciliation.* Maryknoll, NY: Orbis, 2009.

Augsburger, David. *The New Freedom of Forgiveness.* 3rd ed. Chicago: Moody, 2000.

Benko, Jessica. "The Radical Humaneness of Norway's Halden Prison." *New York Times,* March 26, 2015. http://www.nytimes.com/2015/03/29/magazine/the-radical-humaneness-of-norways-halden-prison.html?_r=0.

Berry, Wendell. "Caught in the Middle: On Abortion and Homosexuality." *The Christian Century,* March 20, 2013. http://www.christiancentury.org/article/2013-03/caught-middle.

The Big Question: A Film About Forgiveness. Directed by Vince Dipersio. 2007.

Biggar, Nigel. "Forgiving Enemies in Ireland." *Journal of Religious Ethics* 36.4 (2008) 559–79.

Biggar, Nigel, ed. *Burying the Past: Making Peace and Doing Justice after Civil Conflict.* Washington, DC: Georgetown University Press, 2003.

Blackard, Kirk. *Restoring Peace: Using Lessons from Prison to Mend Broken Relationships.* Victoria, BC: Trafford, 2004.

Bloomfield, David. *On Good Terms: Clarifying Reconciliation.* Berghof Report 14. Berlin: Berghof Research Centre, 2006.

Bloomfield, David, Teresa Barnes, and Luc Huyse, eds. *Reconciliation After Violent Conflict: A Handbook.* Stockholm, Sweden: IDEA, 2003.

Boesak, Alan Aubrey, and Curtiss Paul DeYoung. *Radical Reconciliation: Beyond Political Pietism and Christian Quietism.* Maryknoll: Orbis, 2012.

Bole, William, Drew Christiansen, SJ, and Robert T. Hennemeyer, eds. *Forgiveness in International Politics: An Alternative Road to Peace.* Washington, DC: United States Conference of Catholic Bishops, 2004.

Bonhoeffer, Dietrich. *The Cost of Discipleship.* New York: Touchstone, 1995.

———. *Letters and Papers from Prison.* New York: Touchstone, 2007.

Bosco, Antoinette. *Radical Forgiveness.* Maryknoll, NY: Orbis, 2009.

Bosworth, Mary. *Explaining U.S. Imprisonment.* Los Angeles: Sage, 2010.

Brooks, Roy L., ed. *When Sorry Isn't Enough: The Controversy over Apologies and Reparations of Human Injustice.* New York: New York University Press, 1999.

Brown, Brené. *Daring Greatly: How the Courage to Be Vulnerable Transforms the Way We Live, Love, Parent and Lead.* New York: Portfolio Penguin, 2012.

Brudholm, Thomas. *Resentment's Virtue: Jean Améry and the Refusal to Forgive.* Philadelphia: Temple University Press, 2008.

Burton-Rose, Daniel, ed. *The Celling of America: An Inside Look at the U.S. Prison Industry.* Monroe, ME: Common Courage, 1998.

Cabral, Michael. "How Solitary Confinement in Pelican Bay Almost Drove Me Mad." *New America Media,* July 30, 2013. http://newamericamedia.org/2013/07/how-solitary-confinement-in-pelican-bay-almost-drove-me-mad.php.

Cahill, Thomas, interview by Bill Moyers. *Thomas Cahill on the People's Pope* (December 27, 2013).

Campbell, Will D., and Richard C. Goode, eds. *And the Criminals With Him: Essays on Behalf of Will D. Campbell and All the Reconciled.* Eugene, OR: Cascade, 2012.

Cantacuzino, Marina. *The Forgiveness Project: Stories for a Vengeful Age.* London: Jessica Kingsley, 2015.

Caputo, John D. *The Weakness of God: A Theology of the Event.* Bloomington, IN: Indiana University Press, 2006.

Casarjian, Robin. *Houses of Healing: A Prisoner's Guide to Inner Power and Freedom.* Boston: Lionheart Foundation, 1995.

Cayley, David. *The Expanding Prison: The Crisis in Crime and Punishment and the Search for Alternatives.* Toronto: Anansi, 1998.

Cose, Ellis. *Bone to Pick: On Forgiveness, Reconciliation, Reparation, and Revenge.* New York: Washington Square, 2004.

Dalai Lama, and Victor Chan. *The Wisdom of Forgiveness: Intimate Conversations and Journeys.* London: Hodder and Stoughton, 2004.

Damelin, Robi, interview by Krista Tippett. "No More Taking Sides." *On Being.* American Public Media. http://www.onbeing.org/program/no-more-taking-sides/134/audio?embed=1.

Davis, Jacob L. "Redemptive Imagination: The Fallacy of Judging Across Borders of Ignorance." *Contemporary Justice Review: Issues in Criminal, Social and Restorative Justice* 17.4 (2014) 455–64.

———. "Who We Are and What We Want." *Prodigal Sons: Voices from the Inside.* June 5, 2014. http://www.prodigalsons1.blogspot.com/2014/06/who-we-are-and-what-we-want.html.

de Gruchy, John W. *Reconciliation: Restoring Justice.* London: SCM, 2002.

Derrida, Jacques. *On Cosmopolitanism and Forgiveness.* London: Routledge, 2001.

DeWolf, L. Harold. *Crime and Justice in America: A Paradox of Conscience.* New York: Harper & Row, 1975.

Digeser, P. E. *Political Forgiveness.* Ithaca, NY: Cornell University Press, 2001.

Eagleman, David. *Incognito: The Secret Lives of the Brain.* Edinburgh: Canongate, 2011.

Enright, Robert D. "Counseling within the Forgiveness Triad: On Forgiving, Receiving Forgiveness, and Self-forgiveness." *Counseling and Values* 40.2 (1996) 107–26.

———. *Forgiveness Is a Choice: A Step-by-Step Process for Resolving Anger and Restoring Hope.* Washington, DC: APA LifeTools, 2001.

Enright, Robert D., and Joanna North, eds. *Exploring Forgiveness.* Madison, WI: University of Wisconsin Press, 1998.

Five Minutes of Heaven. Directed by Oliver Hirschbiegel. Performed by Liam Neeson and James Nesbitt. 2009.

Forgiveness: A Time to Love and a Time to Hate. Directed by Helen Whitney. 2011.

Forgiving Dr. Mengele. Directed by Bob Hercules and Cheri Pugh. 2010.

Foucault, Michel. *Discipline and Punish: The Birth of the Prison.* Translated by Alan Sheridan. New York: Vintage, 1979.

Fricke, Christel, ed. *The Ethics of Forgiveness: A Collection of Essays.* New York: Routledge, 2011.

Friedman, Lawrence M. *Crime and Punishment in American History.* New York: Basic, 1993.

Garrard, Eve, and David McNaughton. *Forgiveness.* Durham, UK: Acumen, 2010.

Gilligan, James. *Preventing Violence.* New York: Thames & Hudson, 2001.

Gobodo-Madikizela, Pumla. *A Human Being Died That Night: A South African Woman Confronts the Legacy of Apartheid.* New York: Mariner, 2003.

Govier, Trudy, and Wilhelm Verwoerd. "Trust and the Problem of National Reconciliation." *Philosophy of the Social Sciences* 32.2 (2002) 178–205.

Griffith, Lee. *The Fall of Prison: Biblical Perspectives on Prison Abolition.* Grand Rapids: Eerdmans, 1993.

Griswold, Charles L. *Forgiveness: A Philosophical Exploration.* Cambridge: Cambridge University Press, 2007.

Haggard, Amanda. "Finding Forgiveness on Death Row." *The Contributor,* March 27, 2015. http://thecontributor.org/2015/03/finding-forgiveness-on-death-row/.

Halpern, Jodi, and Harvey Weinstein. "Rehumanzing the Other: Empathy and Reconciliation." *Human Rights Quarterly* 26 (2004) 561–83.

Hauerwas, Stanley, and Jean Vanier. *Living Gently in a Violent World: The Prophetic Witness of Weakness.* Downers Grove, IL: InterVarsity, 2008.

Helmick, Raymond G, and Rodney L. Petersen, eds. *Forgiveness and Reconciliation: Religion, Public Policy, and Conflict Transformation.* Philadelphia: Templeton Foundation, 2001.

Hemenway, Joanne. *Forget Them Not: A Holistic Guide to Prison Ministry.* Eugene, OR: Wipf and Stock, 2010.

Henderson, Michael. *Forgiveness: Breaking the Chain of Hate.* Newberg, OR: BookPartners, 2002.

Herman, Judith Lewis. *Trauma and Recovery.* London: Pandora, 1992.

Hoffman, Morris B. *The Punisher's Brain: The Evolution of Judge and Jury.* New York: Cambridge University Press, 2014.

Holloway, Richard. *On Forgiveness: How Can We Forgive the Unforgivable?* Edinburgh: Canongate, 2002.

Ilibagiza, Immaculée. *Left To Tell: Discovering God Amidst the Rwandan Holocaust.* New York: Hay House, 2006.

James, Steven. "Life Sentence." *Christianity Today.* http://www.christianitytoday.com/iyf/truelifestories/interestingpeople/3.32.html?start=1.

Jones, L. Gregory. *Embodying Forgiveness: A Theological Analysis.* Grand Rapids: Eerdmans, 1995.

Jones, L. Gregory, and Célestin Musekura. *Forgiving As We've Been Forgiven: Community Practices for Making Peace.* Downers Grove, IL: InterVarsity, 2010.

Jones, W. Paul. *A Different Kind of Cell: The Story of a Murderer Who Became a Monk.* Grand Rapids: Eerdmans, 2011.

Journey Toward Forgiveness. Directed by Mennonite Media Productions. N.d.

Katongole, Emmanuel, and Chris Rice. *Reconciling All Things: A Christian Vision for Justice, Peace and Healing.* Downers Grove, IL: InterVarsity, 2008.

Kravetz, Lee Daniel, and David Feldman. "Holding Grudges Is Bad for Our Health." *Huffington Post,* May 1, 2015. http://www.huffingtonpost.com/lee-daniel-kravetz/forgiveness-health_b_7155694.html.

Kraybill, Donald B., Steven M. Nolt, and David L. Weaver-Zercher. *Amish Grace: How Forgiveness Transcended Tragedy.* San Francisco: Jossey-Bass, 2007.

Kurtz, Ernest, and Katherine Ketcham. *The Spirituality of Imperfection: Storytelling and the Journey to Wholeness.* New York: Bantam, 1992.

Lawson, Catherine Claire. *As We Forgive: Stories of Reconciliation from Rwanda.* Grand Rapids: Zondervan, 2009.

Lederach, John Paul. *Building Peace: Sustainable Reconciliation in Divided Societies.* Washington, DC: United States Institute of Peace, 1997.

———. *The Little Book of Conflict Transformation.* Interocurse, PA: Good Books, 2003.

———. *The Moral Imagination: The Art and Soul of Building Peace.* New York: Oxford University Press, 2005.

———. *Reconcile: Conflict Transformation for Ordinary Christians.* Harrisonburg, VA: Herald, 2014.

Lederach, John Paul, and Angela Jill Lederach. *When Blood and Bones Cry Out: Journeys Through the Soundscape of Healing and Reconciliation.* New York: Oxford University Press, 2010.

Little, Alistair, and Wilhelm Verwoerd. *Journey through Conflict Trail Guide: Introduction.* Victoria, BC: Trafford, 2013.

70x7: The Forgiveness Equation. Directed by Jacqui Lofaro and Victor Teich. 2008.

Lomax, Eric. *The Railway Man.* London: Vintage, 1996.

Magnani, Laura, and Harmon Wray. *Beyond Prisons: A New Interfaith Paradigm for Our Failed Prison System.* Minneapolis: Fortress, 2006.

Marsh, Charles, and John M. Perkins. *Welcoming Justice: God's Movement Toward Beloved Community.* Downers Grove, IL: InterVarsity, 2009.

McCullough, Michael E. *Beyond Revenge: The Evolution of the Forgiveness Instinct.* San Francisco: Jossey-Bass, 2008.

McCullough, Michael E., Kenneth I. Pargament, and Carl E. Thoresen, eds. *Forgiveness: Theory, Research, and Practice.* New York: Guilford, 2000.

McCullough, Michael. Interview by Krista Tippett. "Getting Revenge and Forgiveness." *On Being.* American Public Media. http://www.onbeing.org/program/getting-revenge-and-forgiveness/104/audio?embed=1.

McRay, Jonathan. *You Have Heard It Said: Events of Reconciliation.* Eugene, OR: Resource, 2011.

McRay, Michael T. *Letters from "Apartheid Street": A Christian Peacemaker in Occupied Palestine.* Eugene, OR: Cascade, 2013.

Menninger, Karl A. *The Crime of Punishment.* New York: Viking, 1969.

Minow, Martha. *Between Vengeance and Forgiveness: Facing History after Genocide and Mass Violence.* Boston: Beacon, 1998.

Mitford, Jessica. *Kind and Usual Punishment: The Prison Business.* New York: Alfred A. Knopf, 1973.

Morris, Norval, and David J. Rothman, eds. *The Oxford History of the Prison: The Practice of Punishment in Western Society.* New York: Oxford University Press, 1995.

Müller-Fahrenholz, Geiko. *The Art of Forgiveness: Theological Reflections on Healing and Reconciliation.* Geneva: WCC, 1996.

Murphy, Jeffrie G. *Getting Even: Forgiveness and Its Limits.* New York: Oxford University Press, 2003.

Murphy, Jeffrie G., ed. *Punishment and Rehabilitation.* 2nd ed. Belmont, CA: Wadsworth, 1985.

Murphy, Jeffrie G., and Jean Hampton, eds. *Forgiveness and Mercy.* Cambridge: Cambridge University Press, 1988.

Niehoff, Debra. *The Biology of Violence: How Understanding the Brain, Behavior, and Environment Can Break the Vicious Circle of Aggression.* New York: Free Press, 1999.

Nietzsche, Friedrich. *On the Genealogy of Morals.* Translated by Carol Diethe. Cambridge: Cambridge University Press, 1994.

No Exceptions Prison Collective. "Core Values." *No Exceptions Prison Collective.* http://noexceptions.net/core-values/.

Patchett, Ann. "The Worthless Servant." *Chapter 16.* March 27, 2013. http://www.chapter16.org/content/novelist-ann-patchett-takes-ride-charlie-strobel-nashville-advocate-homeless.

Philomena. Directed by Stephen Frears. 2013.

The Power of Forgiveness. Directed by Martin Doblmeier. 2007.

Prager, Carol A. L., and Trudy Govier, eds. *Dilemmas of Reconciliation: Cases and Concepts.* Waterloo, Ontario: Wilfrid Laurier University Press, 2003.

Ramsbotham, Oliver, Tom Woodhouse, and Hugh Miall. *Contemporary Conflict Resolution.* 3rd ed. Cambridge, UK: Polity, 2011.

Redekop, Vern Neufold. *From Violence to Blessing: How an Understanding of Deep-Rooted Conflict Can Open Paths to Reconciliation.* Ottawa: Novalis, 2002.

Resseguie, James L. "Reader-Reponse Criticism and the Synoptic Gospels." *Journal of the American Academy of Religion* 52.2 (1984) 307–24.

Rollins, Peter. "Getting Thrown Out of Prison: Judge Dredd, the Oppressed, and Salvation." *PeterRollins.net.* September 09, 2014. www.peterrollins.net/2014/09/getting-thrown-out-of-prison-judge-dredd-the-oppressed-and-salvation/.

———. *The Orthodox Heretic: And Other Impossible Tales.* Brewster, MA: Paraclete, 2009.

Schimmel, Solomon. *Wounds Not Healed by Time: The Power of Repentance and Forgiveness.* New York: Oxford University Press, 2002.

Shriver, Donald W., Jr. *An Ethic for Enemies: Forgiveness in Politics.* New York: Oxford University Press, 1995.

Slifer, Stephanie. "Once a Criminal, Always a Criminal?" *CBS News.* April 23, 2014. http://www.cbsnews.com/news/once-a-criminal-always-a-criminal/.

Smedes, Lewis B. *Forgive and Forget: Healing the Hurts We Don't Deserve.* 2nd ed. New York: HarperOne, 1996.

Spencer, Graham, ed. *Forgiving and Remembering in Northern Ireland.* London: Continuum, 2011.

Sternberg, Esther. Interview by Krista Tippett. "Stress and the Balance Within." *On Being.* American Public Media. http://www.onbeing.org/program/stress-and-balance-within/179/audio?embed=1.

Toews, Barb. *The Little Book of Restorative Justice for People in Prison.* Intercourse, PA: Good Books, 2006.

Tombs, David. "Meaning of Reconciliation." Lecture, Belfast: Irish School of Ecumenics (Trinity College Dublin), 2012.

———. "The Offer of Forgiveness." *Journal of Religious Ethics* 36.4 (2008) 587–93.

Tombs, David, and Joseph Liechty, eds. *Explorations in Reconciliation: New Directions in Theology.* Hants: Ashgate, 2006.

TRC of South Africa. *Truth and Reconciliation Commission of South Africa Final Report.* Cape Town: Juta, 1998.

Tulluis, Paul. "Can Forgiveness Play a Role in Criminal Justice?" *New York Times.* January 4, 2013. http://www.nytimes.com/2013/01/06/magazine/can-forgiveness-play-a-role-in-criminal-justice.html?pagewanted=1&_r=3&.

Tutu, Desmond. *No Future Without Forgiveness.* London: Rider, 1999.

Tutu, Desmond, and Mpho Tutu. *The Book of Forgiving: The Fourfold Path for Healing Ourselves and Our World.* London: William Collins, 2014.

Vanier, Jean. *Becoming Human.* 2nd ed. New York: Paulist, 2008.

Vanier, Jean, interview by Krista Tippett. "The Wisdom of Tenderness." *On Being.* American Public Media. http://www.onbeing.org/program/wisdom-tenderness/234/audio?embed=1. December 24, 2009.

Vaughn, Cynthia, interview by Michael McRay. May 31, 2014.

Vick, Tony. "Coming In and Coming Out." Unpublished, n.d.

Volf, Miroslav. *The End of Memory: Remembering Rightly in a Violent World.* Grand Rapids: Eerdmans, 2006.

———. *Exclusion and Embrace: A Theological Exploration of Identity, Otherness, and Reconciliation.* Nashville: Abingdon, 1996.

———. *Free of Charge: Giving and Forgiving in a Culture Stripped of Grace.* Grand Rapids: Zondervan, 2005.

Whitney, Helen. *Forgiveness: A Time to Love and a Time to Hate.* Campbell, CA: FastPencil, 2011.

Wiesenthal, Simon. *The Sunflower: On the Possibilities and Limits of Forgiveness.* New York: Schocken, 1997.

Woolford, Andrew. *The Politics of Restorative Justice: A Critical Introduction.* Winnipeg: Fernwood, 2010.

Worthington, Everett L., Jr. *A Just Forgiveness: Responsible Healing Without Excusing Injustice.* Downers Grove, IL: InterVarsity, 2009.

Wrong Side of the Bus: A Quest for Reconciliation Becomes a Journey to Forgiveness. Directed by Rod Freedman. 2009.

Yancey, Phillip. *What's So Amazing About Grace?* Grand Rapids: Zondervan, 1997.

Yoder, Carolyn. *The Little Book of Trauma Healing: When Violence Strikes and Community Security Is Threatened.* Intercourse, PA: Good Books, 2005.

Zehr, Howard. *Changing Lenses: A New Focus for Crime and Justice.* 3rd ed. Scottdale, PA: Herald, 2005.

———. *Doing Life: Reflections of Men and Women Serving Life Sentences.* Intercourse, PA: Good Books, 1996.

———. *The Little Book of Restorative Justice.* Intercourse, PA: Good Books, 2002.

Zinn, Howard. *A People's History of the United States: Volume 1: American Beginnings to Reconstruction.* New York: The New Press, 2003.

ABOUT THE AUTHOR

Michael T. McRay is a writer, advocate, educator, and speaker. He is the author of *Letters from "Apartheid Street": A Christian Peacemaker in Occupied Palestine* (Cascade Books, 2013) and a featured author at the 2016 Search for Meaning Book Festival at Seattle University. Since 2013, he has taught as an adjunct instructor in restorative justice, forgiveness and reconciliation, storytelling, the Israeli-Palestinian conflict, and international conflict resolution at Lipscomb University in Nashville, and has taught courses inside Riverbend Maximum Security Institution and the Tennessee Prison for Women as part of Lipscomb's LIFE program. In the fall of 2015, hired as a Visiting Scholar at Texas Christian University, Michael spent two months traveling through Israel-Palestine, Northern Ireland, and South Africa, conducting dozens of interviews about the complexities of pursuing reconciliation in divided societies.

He is the co-founder of No Exceptions Prison Collective (noexceptions.net) and founded, organizes, and co-hosts Tenx9 Nashville (www. tenx9nashville.com), a Belfast-originated monthly community storytelling night for the sharing of true-life stories around a theme. He volunteered at Riverbend prison for over four years and served as a volunteer prison chaplain for nearly one year before being banned by the warden in April 2014 for organizing on behalf of the inmates.

Michael holds an MPhil (with *Distinction*) in Conflict Resolution and Reconciliation Studies from Trinity College Dublin at Belfast, as well as a BA in History from Lipscomb University. Having received invitations as a panelist, presenter, and guest speaker regarding nonviolence, Christian Peacemaker Teams, and the Israeli-Palestinian conflict, as well as reconciliation, restorative justice, and incarceration, Michael has spoken at various churches, schools, and universities in the US and Northern Ireland, as well as at Riverbend prison, the Nashville Film Festival, the Scarritt-Bennett Center, and the Thomas H. Olbricht Christian Scholars' Conference. His work has been published, discussed, and reviewed on such websites as *Englewood Review of Books*, *Experimental Theology*, *The Tokens Show Blog*, *Middle East Experience*, *The Examiner*, and *Red Letter Christians*.

Facebook (Michael T. McRay)
Instagram and Twitter (@michaelmcray)
www.michaelmcray.com